Language in Hand

Language in Hand

WHY SIGN CAME BEFORE SPEECH

William C. Stokoe

GALLAUDET UNIVERSITY PRESS
WASHINGTON, D.C.

Gallaudet University Press

Washington, DC 20002

Library of Congress Cataloging-in-Publication Data

Stokoe, William C.
  Language in hand : why sign came before speech / William C. Stokoe.
    p. cm.
  Includes bibliographical references and index.
  ISBN 1-56368-103-X (alk. paper)
    1. Sign language—History. 2. American Sign Language—History.
  I. Title

HV2474 .S69 2001
419—dc21   2001023122

Contents

⁓

	Preface	vii
1.	An Idea That Would Not Go Away	1
2.	Chasing the Language Butterfly	17
3.	Gesture to Language to Speech	31
4.	Signed Languages and Language Essentials	52
5.	Language Signs	67
6.	Descartes Thought Wrong	78
7.	Language Metamorphosis	103
8.	Language in a Chrysalis	119
9.	Emerging from the Cocoon	131
10.	Families of Signed Languages	147
11.	Languages in Parallel	162
12.	Visible Verbs Become Spoken	176
13.	A Difference That Makes a Difference	193
	Notes	203
	Bibliography	215
	Index	223

Preface

WHEN I WAS VERY YOUNG the certainty of the physical sciences appealed to me. Mendeleev's periodic table showed how elegantly the elements repeated a simple pattern as atoms added electrons one at a time. Newton's laws of motion were as exact as the theorems in my first intellectual love, plane geometry. Little did I know.

Of course, my teachers didn't know either. "In 1927," when I was in third grade, "Heisenberg invented his uncertainty relations, which put the cap on the great scientific revolution we call quantum theory," Leon Lederman wrote in his splendid account of particle physics from Democritus and earlier to 1993 (*The God Particle* [Boston: Houghton Mifflin, 1993], 175). Came the revolution, and one thing physicists are certain of now is, in a word, uncertainty.

The macro-universe Isaac Newton described in the seventeenth century, the universe we live in, still works as Newton said it did. But inside an atom's nucleus, it's a whole new ball game, and the ball in that game, the electron, has no mass and a radius measured in 1990 at "*less than* .00000000000000001 inches" (Lederman, 142). In that hard-to-imagine world, physicists find they cannot be certain, only approximate.

Some of this uncertainty seems to leak back into our normal world. Meteorologists know pretty well at what temperature moisture in the air can condense into droplets and fall as rain, but they can't tell us how much rain will fall at what time in any given place. So they resort to averages, statistics, like "The chance of rain on Thursday is 40 percent." Meteorologists keep trying to predict weather more precisely, but physicists know there is much they cannot be precise about. If they can detect the velocity of an electron or other particle they cannot know its location, and vice versa.

Government agencies have been exercised recently over the year 2000 census. They ask: should everyone be counted, or would equally good or better information come from sampling and statistics? No doubt a compromise will be worked out, but in particle physics there can be no exact count.

Suppose a census taker was assigned to a very odd community; its transients are becoming residents and residents becoming transient. Where they come from and where they go they don't tell even if they know. Any one of them may stay a day or two or a week or even less than an hour, or perhaps never leave, and even when they are "in the community," they may or not be in the house when the census taker calls. I don't pretend to understand quantum theory, but it seems to me what goes on in inner space may be something like life in this imagined community.

Leon Lederman's book is so fascinating and readable that I am giving it to my teenage grandson. He may be a little young for it, but he is good at mathematics, and at his age a little mind stretching won't hurt a bit. Lederman focuses attention on each genius who moved physics forward, but amazingly, he keeps coming back to the truth of what Democritus said twenty-four hundred years ago: "Everything existing in the universe is the fruit of chance and necessity" (59).

What about Language?

If Democritus had it right, language, which exists in the universe, also has to be the fruit of chance and necessity. Necessity? Yes—anything anyone says must have some regularity to it. If not, we wouldn't understand a word of it. Not surprisingly, a scholar named Pānini, almost at the same time as Democritus but farther east in India, was finding necessity, or necessary regularity, in the Sanskrit language. He may not have realized it, but in doing that he became the world's first grammarian.

Since Pānini, for two and a half millennia, grammarians have been concentrating on necessity—the necessary regularity of pattern or structure in what people say (usually after it has been written down). Grammarians discover patterns, or rules. And the rules, some of them say, determine the whole structure of language, with the full force of necessity—world without end, amen. And yet, what anyone actually does say or will say is hardly more predictable than the weather or the position and velocity of an electron. Democritus said "chance *and* necessity." We may not have as much to say about chance in language, and there is even less that we can do about it, but necessity is only part of the story.

I'm long out of third grade and high school physics, so I'm not infallible any more, but I think that a great deal of nonsense has been written and believed about language because grammarians get mixed up about necessity. They mistake what is sufficient for what is necessary. The proof of this proposition does not need quantum theory, just basic logic and a fact: speech is sufficient for language, but not necessary.

Granted, 99.9 percent of us use speech for language, and many cannot conceive of language any other way; yet millions of people who cannot hear make up the other 0.1 percent. They use languages of visible, not audible, signs. Because deaf people have and use signed languages, we must conclude that either speech or signing is sufficient for language and that neither by itself is necessary.

Then, just what about language does necessity rule, and where does chance come into it? We cannot go back to physicists for an answer to this one. Or perhaps we can. From physical laws and theories came the basis of the knowledge chemists have gained about the composition of things. Chemists' findings enable biologists to understand anatomy, physiology, and genetics. Biologists guided by Darwin and many after him can tell us a great deal about chance and necessity.

Evolution

About five million years ago, some apes came down out of trees and lived in new ways. Some of them must have differed—by chance, what else?—

from their relatives left up there. Among the new breed too there must have been differences. There always are. These differences, one way or another, resulted in more of the odd ones' offspring surviving. Given long enough, a new species that walked upright and was not as well adapted as the old for living in trees evolved. This origin of a new species happened more than once in those few million years. Fossils show that *Australopithecines* and a few species of genus *Homo* originated and became extinct (or evolved into others) in that long period. At the same time, however, gorillas, chimpanzees, and orangutans continued pretty much unchanged. Apparently they differed or departed less from our remote common ancestor's physical form and way of behaving.

Necessity sees to it that parents' genes largely determine their offspring's physical form. And physical form necessarily influences behavior, what can be done and how. Chance has already entered as variation, as every parent knows who has two or more children (not identical twins). Siblings differ in many ways. Multiply that by the variation within offspring in one generation of a whole population or species and it's clear that chance has ample room to work, generation after generation.

No question then. Necessity and chance, in the form of natural selection, produced the human species. We're here, but so is language. And language is not physiology—or is it? Because language cannot be weighed or measured or even directly tied to the events we suppose it may have caused, some philosophers in every age have thought that language is separate from our bodies and everything else physical. Yet no evidence can be found for the separate existence of mind, spirit, soul, language, thought, concepts, and so on. They belong to us, inhabitants of this physical universe. Evidence keeps turning up that human brains, vision, hearing, and actions not only suffice but must be there for language. Necessity again. Language must have the human species, with all its chance or random variation, to operate in and on.

But note well that none of this had to happen. Chance brought it about. No necessity forced some apes to come out of the trees five million years ago. Necessity did not force some of their descendants to evolve into apemen and humans. Chance, not necessity, determined that some of the population happened to look at the world and each other a little differently and act differently.

But even with differences enough to evolve into various human species, the whole hominid line remains very similar in one way to the ancestral strain. From chimpanzees to the girl next door, we primates communicate, we live *socially.* Good thing, too. The infant anthropoid ape is helpless and needs maternal care for many months. How long does a human infant and child remain dependent? We haven't really determined yet how much and what kind of care for how long one needs to become fully human.

Whether we are communicating as well as we should with our children, communication is as necessary for social life as oxygen is for physical life. And ever since there were social species, chance has had plenty of scope to select the kind of communication that social species need. In some species, chemical signs are produced and interpreted. Scent continues to keep many social mammals identified and connected. Virtually all social animals, including those that may be prey or predator, also interpret sounds and what they see others doing. Above all, literally, are the songs and calls that birds make and hear and interpret.

And then there is language, the uniquely human system—which some will tell you is special and exempt from the necessity and chance governing the rest of life. If you believe that, I have a little invention here I'd like to sell you. A few drops of it in your car's tank and you'll never have to fill up with gas again.

Of course, chance and necessity rule a language. Democritus was speaking of the whole universe and *everything* in it, no exemptions, no exceptions. Let's look again at the evolutionary trail. Our hands and apes' hands are homologues, but ours are differently proportioned; we have more nerves and more freedom in several joints—actually all the way from shoulders to fingertips. We can do many, many different kinds of things with our hands. Some of these things apes have no reason to do, but others they can't possibly do because their anatomy has not evolved as human anatomy has.

So we are like other primates and yet we differ from them. Can we speak of behavioral "homologues" as well? Why not? Just like other primates, humans communicate mainly via sight and hearing. Could it be then that natural selection—chance and necessity—enabled language to evolve from some form of communication that came before?

To go back a bit, we can reexamine our fact-based conclusion: speech and signing are each sufficient for language, and therefore neither by itself is necessary. Careful observation tells us that this is true as things stand at the present time. Humans either speak or sign their languages. And some Australian and Native American tribes still have and use both a signed and a spoken language. But would this always have been so? Or ask the question in another way: Would either speech or signing (gesture-like movements) have sufficed to *begin* language? Try first to imagine who could possibly have told the first speakers what the sounds they produced were supposed to mean.

In many different times and places long ago, leading thinkers must have tried to imagine this; for they have left us great stories. They tell of how a god from heaven or a spirit from the deep in the sea or a sacred animal from the forest or a voice from the whirlwind spoke to the first people, endowing them too with speech, telling them the names of things—sometimes giving them very strict dos and don'ts as well.

Other thinkers have steered away from myth and come up with other suggestions about how language—as speech—might have begun. The "bowwow theory" says the first word for *dog* was an imitation of its bark, and so on and on as far as convenient sound sources like that go. The "yo-heave-ho theory" says the word *heave,* or something like it, might have been unintentionally squeezed out as the first speakers strained at heavy weights. Others make lists of words that show sound symbolism.

All these are valiant attempts to explain only the semantics of speech—how a spoken word might have come to mean what it means in the very first place. But none of them can, nor try to, explain syntax—the way language expresses word meanings *and also the meaning of meanings somehow related and interconnected*. These myths fail to notice that as "the fruit of necessity and chance," language grows singly and in clusters, as words and at the same time as sentences. Simply stated, language includes syntax as well as semantics.

Syntax did not need to be elaborate or complicated to begin with, as a simple thought experiment will make clear. Picture this situation: a third person sees you and a companion together, leaves for a moment, returns, and shows surprise at seeing you alone. You immediately interpret that show of surprise and make a gesture. Little imagination is needed for what you did and what it means. The gesture said, "She went that way." But your gesture literally tells that third person more than this translation does. The gesture shows which way she went; the words of the translation do not really mean anything unless spoken with a pointing gesture (reading the words, you do not know which way she went). In the imagined setting, your hand pointed out the direction of your companion's departure, but your hand also stands for her, the one who departed. The gesture also has or contains syntax because the hand for the person and its movement telling what she did are subject and predicate (or noun phrase [NP] + verb phrase [VP]). Without any speech at all, this experiment demonstrates that gesture is sufficient to *initiate* syntax. Could anything spoken do that? As it has been seventy-two or seventy-three years since I was in third grade, I am afraid I cannot wait until someone can answer that question affirmatively.

The first six chapters of this book will take up these matters in more detail, bringing in evidence when it can be found that evolution proceeded (by chance and necessity) from gesture to language. Chapter 7 continues by showing how gestured language might have led to speech. Once a language had taken hold—a lucky chance for us if there ever was one—handshapes represented people and animals and things (the contents of the visible world) and movements represented actions and changes (observed and reflected on). Together, they did not represent sentences—*they were sentences.* The key to this development is that only gesture use could have initiated syntax, a necessary feature of language.

Eminently useful in the struggle for survival, signs of all kinds have served every kind of animal. But when visible signs easily produced and interpreted contained both word and sentence meanings, the whole potential of language would have been contained in them. The species that began to use gestures in this syntactic-semantic way, whether it was *Homo erectus* or *Homo sapiens,* really began the human story.

Nothing about this early visible language would have prevented its users from making various vocal sounds as they communicated. We are prone to think of language exchanges as spoken. Most are, to be sure; but the fact is gestures accompany most of them, along with other visible changes in the speaker. Few linguists now take any notice of these visible changes, but all of us speakers, when important matters must be discussed, prefer a face-to-face to a telephone discussion. We know that what we can see contains information we do not want to miss. Chapter 8 focuses on the eventual shift from primarily gestural expression of language with vocal accompaniment to primarily vocal production of language with gestural accompaniment.

Spoken language communication, it seems, is usually accompanied by visible behavior. We can easily imagine the converse: when sign language communication dominated, signers would have made and heard vocal sounds, and these would have contained information too. If this was the case, certain sounds would come in time to be used with certain portions of the signed utterances—just as in spoken language communities certain gestures occur regularly with certain spoken expressions (e.g., "I don't know," "no," "maybe"). The incidental sounds would thus carry more information. Then, just as a gesture nowadays can express, without any speech at all, such meanings as those in the example, so the sounds of long ago could have expressed the meanings even if the associated gestures weren't made or seen. This state of affairs—that either the gestural expression or the vocal expression serves for normal conversation—actually exists among some tribal peoples who keep to the old ways (see chapter 9). The relationship of speech to gesture and signed languages in various contemporary cultures is explored in chapter 10.

Chance and necessity, gesture-to-language-to-speech—these do not call for just a new way of looking at language. They suggest that we as a species, and as a literate society, could do better than we now do, both in rearing all our children, educating deaf children, and relating to deaf adults.

⁓

At this point I depart from the custom of making acknowledgments. In the first place, my present opinions and beliefs have been influenced by too many to name, virtually all who have been close to me, as far back as a great-grandmother. I like to think I inherited some of her spirit. She needed more embroidery floss one day when the menfolk were away, but she didn't want to wait. Looking at the Model-T standing in the driveway, she told her daughter-in-law, "If you help me push it out to the hill, Mary, I think I can pedal it down." No thought about driving it into town or getting it back up that hill, that formidable ess-curving hill that even my father's 1925 Dodge coupe sometimes couldn't climb in low gear! Some of the ideas here are similarly outrageous and will annoy many, so it's better to keep the blame to myself. And of course, like Leon Lederman, many another whose words and ideas I lean on heavily will be identified as I do.

Language in Hand

CHAPTER 1

An Idea That Would Not Go Away

T HE IDEA THAT deaf people's signing might be a language aroused bitter opposition in 1960 when I first proposed it, but it wouldn't go away. And when the idea took hold, about a decade later, it began to cause many good things to happen. In its present, developed form, it could be even more beneficial with further research and testing.

The belief that signing can be a language is in some respects new, yet is also a natural extension of an old idea. It grows out of the gestural theory of language origins. When it first came to me, however, the idea was very much my own and bound up in my personal history. My colleagues at Gallaudet College at first wouldn't touch it. Indeed, educators of deaf students across America attacked me, sometimes violently, for thinking and saying in print that in their everyday conversation deaf people might be using a language that was obviously not English but was a language nevertheless.

The intellectual atmosphere has changed in the last forty years, and so has the idea. At first, I had a hunch that the signing I saw deaf people using as they interacted might be a language, but I had no evidence to support my suspicion. Today scholars are studying, describing, and comparing deaf people's sign languages in many parts of the world. Deaf people themselves are signing more openly and being admired for it. And no one thinks it strange to see sign language interpreters at public events and on television.

It pleases me to see this attention given to sign languages. Besides being good for sign language users, it suggests that I was not as crazy as the experts in deaf education thought in 1960, when my first grammar of a sign language was published, and in 1965, when two deaf colleagues and I finished the first dictionary of American Sign Language. My pleasure with the current activity is not unmixed, however. To a certain extent many who study signed languages take that first step over and over again, but one step doesn't get us far. We need the second stage of the original idea to move it forward.

The First Step

It was late August of 1955, and the day was whatever day classes began that fall. The setting was Kendall Hall, a small brick building with a medallion set in its facade, the head of Abraham Lincoln, who signed the charter of the institution that became Gallaudet College and later Gallaudet University. The time was whatever hour the first class I would teach at the college began—morning, I think, but I had many other things to remember. I was worse than unprepared. I was stepping directly into a foreign world. I was facing a class of eight or ten English majors, none of whom could hear and some of whom had speech I could not decipher. I had earned my graduate tuition by teaching English to Cornell University freshmen, and for eight years I had taught composition and literature to Wells College students—and now I was supposed to teach Chaucer in Middle English to deaf students at Gallaudet.

Like other recruits to the faculty of that era, I had been taught the prevailing mode of instruction. We were expected to speak normally, while making some signs with our hands that would represent the English words. When we didn't know a sign for a word, our teacher had told us to "fingerspell it!" To do this we had to form a different handshape for each letter of the word and try to produce them as smoothly linked as the notes of a violin cadenza.

Worse than being unprepared is being misprepared. Some of the old-timers, who considered themselves "dedicated teachers of the deaf," loved to remind us how little we knew. Some of them told me over and over that deaf students could understand only the simplest language. They explained that a deaf person did not really have any language and so could not achieve full mental development. On one occasion, I must have looked sad when I heard this repeated again because the college nurse who said it tried to reassure me. She added that I would still enjoy teaching deaf students because they tried so hard to please a teacher, "just like dogs and nigrahs," she said.

Not all of my orientation was so negative. Richard Phillips, the deaf Dean of Students, supplemented our faculty formal sign classes during those initial two weeks, letting us practice communicating as a relief from striving for the correctness our assigned teacher expected but could not define. And five-year-old Bobby, deaf son of deaf parents Don and Agnes Padden, who waited with me sometimes for a ride home, let me converse in signs with him. That was real communication and excellent practice.

Nevertheless, I felt close to panic that day in August of 1955 when I walked into the classroom. But then I noticed something that gave me hope. I had the full visual attention of all the students in the room. These students were not just looking up momentarily from their normal preoccupations to see what kind of teacher they had been saddled with. They were focusing real curiosity in my direction. Unable to hear, they were poised and eager to see what they could see, what I might be about to tell them. Somehow they seemed to understand me, and we got through that first day.

I learned much that surprised me from that first group of students. One of them, a totally deaf girl from Alabama, spoke with an unmistakable accent; but, of course—unable to hear her own voice, she had had to keep on making sounds until they satisfied her voice teacher's Alabama-bred ear. And I learned more; I discovered more brilliant students in my Gallaudet classes than in classes I had taught elsewhere. Again, the explanation was simple: the brightest among hearing students had many colleges and universities to choose from, but in 1955 only one college openly welcomed deaf students. The top end of the college-age deaf population, domestic and foreign, turned up at Gallaudet. Interacting with

my deaf students and colleagues taught me these and many other positive things, especially the utter falsity of the negative information that
the old hands had been feeding the new faculty.

These personal discoveries fitted well with the cultural and linguistic anthropology I had been reading before coming to Gallaudet. These
studies suggested that people deserved to be recognized on their own
terms, not someone else's. Thus, in this interpretation, deaf people were
not defective hearing people, as the old guard in deaf education had
believed, but simply people to be respected for their unique characteristics. Respect for the intellectual integrity of my deaf students and colleagues, recognition in some measure of the validity of cultural differences,
and my visceral reaction against naysayers needed one more component
to light up the idea that sign could be language.

Reading in Edinburgh libraries about cultural relativism while on a
sabbatical leave also helped develop my thinking about language, as did
living in rural southeastern Scotland in close social contact with gradu-
ates of that country's high schools. I learned as a participant-observer in
a very close-knit society that the way other cultures sort and value the
components of life, including language, can be different, intriguing, and
most interesting.

The Scots dialect, or Lallans, I had attempted to learn in 1953–1954
so that I could interact naturally with East Lothian friends was very different from "Yankee" English. East Lothian members of the Rifle Club
that I joined could carry on a conversation that sounded like a foreign
language to me. I had to learn their dialect if I wanted to find out what
they were saying and enter their conversation; it was up to me to adapt.
A year later at Gallaudet, I must have sensed that what the signing deaf
people were doing was their language too, and it was up to me to find
out about it. It was certainly a language foreign to me.

The signing I saw deaf people using was likewise foreign to the
manual activity mixed with speech that we new hearing teachers were
taught. The official medium of instruction at the college, hearing teachers' signing was a more or less—usually less—complete manual translation of the English sentences we were speaking. Deaf students, by contrast,
put signs together fluently and fast, but the resulting constructions did
not resemble English sentences.

The work of anthropological linguists suggested that differences like those I observed between English and the students' signing do not make one form of language correct and others faulty or defective; the variations reflect social and cultural circumstances. The language any people use is the language they use, *their* language. Thus the idea hatched. Deaf people on the Gallaudet campus were using a different language, not an inferior version of English. But was it real, was it true, or was I deluded?

I could not depend on the old-timers at Gallaudet to answer this question or even give it serious consideration. They, and their clones at schools for the deaf across the country, had already expressed, and put in print, their opinion that the majority of deaf people had no language at all; at best, some had "broken language," that is, poorly acquired spoken English. And they said this despite years of expensive instruction in speaking and lipreading English that they had been paid to give their deaf pupils. In the strictest of the old deaf schools, instruction in reading and writing English was postponed until sufficient success was achieved at producing speech and making some progress in deciphering what people were saying by looking at their faces.

And yet I found that the deaf schools' dropouts ("oral failures," they called them) often performed better in my college courses than students (most likely with some hearing in the speech frequencies) whose speech and lipreading skills were superior. These dropouts were accepted by Gallaudet in those years when their motivation and aptitude showed up on college-entrance tests that did not depend on English fluency. In their late teens, after years of what must have been very unsatisfactory educational experiences, these oral failures were bright and eager to learn.

How could this have happened? How could these students have developed their intellect and their sense of curiosity, when they were not socialized and enculturated? After all, these activities required language understanding and use. The answer was simple: they were socialized and they had learned, not by their classroom experience, which depended on the ability to speak and lipread English, but by their signing peers. Student interaction in dorms, playing fields, dining halls, and so on had to have been carried on in some language, the same one I saw in the halls and when students talked to each other rather than to a hearing teacher. I wanted to know more about that language.

Fortunately, George Detmold, the dean who had invited me to Gallaudet in the first place, welcomed my idea that signing might be language and encouraged me to pursue it. He must have had some such idea himself, but that is a story deserving a chapter of its own. With his backing, suggestions from several interested linguists, and support from the American Council of Learned Societies, I completed the first descriptive grammar of American Sign Language in 1960.[1] Then, with Gallaudet funds that Detmold put at our disposal, two deaf colleagues, Carl Croneberg and Dorothy Sueoka Casterline, and I compiled a dictionary of American Sign Language.[2] A National Science Foundation grant and subsidy made its preparation and 1965 publication possible. So ended the idea's first stage.

The Second Step

At that point my idea was simply that the signing American deaf people do is a language. This grew naturally into a second stage—recognizing that the difference between signing and speaking is highly important. This began to seem self-evident to me. Even though languages are all alike in a very fundamental way—they serve the needs of their users—when the materials of the languages are as different as sounds and visible movements, and when the channels for receiving them are as different as hearing and seeing, the differences cry out to be noted, and they have something to tell us. After all, sameness tells very little; it is differences that make a difference.

It used to be assumed that despite the variations in speech among different people, nothing could separate speech from language. Anything not spoken but gestured had to be "nonverbal"—not language. Most grammarians and linguists and other scholars of language accepted this fallacy. Demographics and cultural oppression facilitated the conceit. The users of spoken languages outnumber the users of signed languages by about one thousand to one. People regularly encounter languages being spoken without expecting them to be just like their own. It is different, however, with deaf signing. Until very recently, the social treatment deaf people and their signing received over centuries had conditioned them to refrain from signing in public, or to make their signs as small and unobtrusive as possible. This cultural oppression made encountering deaf signing an even rarer occurrence than deaf people's small number would merit. Virtually everyone's first impression ("These people are not speaking!") led to the false conclusion that they were not using language. Instead of seeing language in a different channel, the naive observer, hearing no speech, concluded that language was absent.

Unfortunately, much recent scholarship on signed languages has ignored differences and attempted instead to demonstrate that signed language grammars and spoken language grammars are indistinguishable. This must seem strange to nonlinguists and to students who have struggled with the very different grammars of foreign languages they had to study in school or college. But nowadays there are *grammars* and there is *grammar*. That is, there is a school of linguists who believe, despite the differences between specific languages and cases and declensions and conjugations and so on, that all languages are governed by the same rules, the rules of "universal grammar."

The idea that signing can be language, and its corollary that signed languages can differ in important ways from spoken languages, challenges the belief that the rules of grammar are universal. What is universal is that every language does what its users need it to do. Because signed languages are truly and equally languages but differently constructed, they have much to teach us about language that spoken forms cannot.

My doctoral studies were not in sign language or in linguistics. Before 1946 Cornell had no department of linguistics. But during a search back then to fill the vacant English department chair, one of the stimulating candidate-lecturers was Robert A. Hall, who had just written *Leave Your Language Alone* (Ithaca, N.Y.: Linguistica, 1950). Hall's comments about the work of the American school of descriptive, or anthropological, linguists fitted perfectly with what I had learned about language and its users from studies of Old and Middle English, Latin, and Greek. A sabbatical leave in 1953–1954 gave me time to read more linguistics and cultural anthropology.

During that year, I sought out the writings of linguists who looked on each language as part—a central and important part but still a subsystem—of a larger system, a culture. Thus, the original idea that "deaf people's signing *is* language" goes back to understanding a key principle: when members of any community interact among themselves, they use the central interactive system of their culture, its language.

I understood all this much better after I attended the Linguistic Society of America's summer institute in 1957. George L. Trager and Henry Lee Smith Jr., two of the anthropological linguists whose publications had most impressed me earlier, made that institute a high point in my education. Smith's course, Linguistics for Teachers of English, was the best-taught and most informative formal course I ever had. A little later, as a member of the Washington Linguistics Club (WLC), I had the good fortune to interact with linguists, psycholinguists, and psychologists from area universities and with sociolinguists from the Center for Applied Linguistics in Washington, D.C. These experiences and personal interactions, this give and take with leaders from various disciplines, and the absorbing task of editing and publishing some of their presentations as *Proceedings of the WLC,* gave me an interdisciplinary outlook and education.

The WLC also brought me into contact with Thomas A. Sebeok, a world-class scholar and teacher, and through him offered a glimpse into a fascinating branch of philosophy, semiotics, the study of signs of all kinds. Its leading light, Charles Sanders Peirce (1839–1914) identified some sixty-six different kinds of signs and introduced the simple but profound idea that semiosis, the way signs function, is triple not double, as most had thought. More than a sign and what it signifies, sign function is a process with three cardinal points: a sign itself, what the sign denotes, and above all a sign *interpretant,* someone or something to interpret the sign. (By using the word *interpreter,* Peirce would have given the erroneous impression that only human beings interpret signs.)

It was Sebeok too who offered to publish a journal on sign language if I would edit it. Thus *Sign Language Studies* (*SLS*) was born: first as a semiannual jointly published by Mouton and Indiana University (1972–1975), later as a quarterly (1975–1996) by Linstok Press, a corporation that my wife, Ruth, and I formed, and currently by Gallaudet University Press.

Seeing Signs as Language

SLS helped materially to spread and make respectable the idea that there are signed languages. Input from anthropology, archaeology, biology, linguistics, paleontology, philosophy, psychology, sociology, and zoology all helped shape the idea, but I believe that semiotics has had the greatest impact on the original conception that signing can be language. Peirce's discoveries and Sebeok's introduction to semiotics seem to me exactly the right tools for exploring language signs of different kinds.[3]

Not all signs comprise languages, of course. Even one-celled animals may have the ability to respond to a sign of the signal kind: certain bacteria swim toward sugar molecules in solution but tumble about at random when no sugar is present; ants follow a pheromone trail, a chemical secreted by other ants who have gone before. Such sign behaviors are instinctive. Animals with central nervous systems and brain-centered sensory systems also interpret and respond to signs they may see, hear, feel, smell, or taste. Some of the interpretations they make, however, involve more than instinct. In many instances, higher animals choose how and whether to respond and to produce signs themselves.

But I have begun to use the term *sign* with a different meaning. Earlier, in the context of signed languages, I was using the word to refer to the visible movements that signers make with their hands, arms, faces, and more. However, in the more general sense, as semioticians like Sebeok use it, the word *sign* refers to anything that a creature may interpret as standing for something else. Thus, an aromatic chemical is a sign to ants, and usually they interpret it as "follow this trail."

Discussions of signed languages and spoken languages usually make heavy use of the term *symbol*. This term's precise meaning depends on who uses it and in what context. Here it is enough to note that some writers use the term *symbol* to highlight the often striking difference between a language sign—whether heard or seen—and what it means, in other words, to emphasize that the language sign is arbitrary, that it has no necessary relationship to what it means. But many writers use *symbol* in the much more general sense of anything that stands for something else. (All this needs more elucidation and gets it in chapter 5.)

How Signs Function

A sign is either an *icon*, an *index*, or a *symbol*. An *icon* is a sign which would possess the character which renders it significant, even though its object had no existence; such as a lead-pencil streak as representing a geometrical line. An *index* is a sign which would, at once, lose the character which makes it a sign if its object were removed, but would not lose that character if there were no interpretant. Such, for instance, is a piece of mould with a bullet-hole in it as a sign of a shot; for without the shot there would have been no hole; but there is a hole there, whether anybody has the sense to attribute it to a shot or not. A *symbol* is a sign which would lose the character which renders it a sign if there were no interpretant. Such is any utterance of speech which signifies what it does only by virtue of its being understood to have that signification.

Source: *From Justus Buchler, ed.,* Philosophical Writings of Peirce *(New York: Dover Publications, 1955), 104.*

The science of signs has directed my attention to the difference between visible and audible signs and the physiological contrasts involved in interpreting them, especially when they are signs of a language. Visible signs, like pointing to something or miming some action, can signify directly. Thus interpreting such signs may be called natural, although what is natural, the dimensions of nature, changes with the species involved. When members of a grazing herd of wild or domestic animals see one of their number with head raised, ears turned forward, the whole body in a frozen pose, they too, naturally, become poised ready to flee. They appear to interpret the sign they see to mean something like *danger is in the offing.* All this is as natural as the animals themselves.

When a theater audience applauds a stage mime's performance, however, the resemblance of what they see to what it represents may seem natural to them, but neither the mime's art nor the audience's appreciation of it were inborn; they were learned or acquired. Nevertheless, some actions that humans perform do naturally resemble and call to mind something else visible, whether we see the resemblance at first glance or need time to discover it. This too is natural: visible things have an inherent capacity to resemble something else visible.

Some audible signs are natural; for example, thunder or a lion's roar. Such sounds may also be associated with something visible (in this case, lightning or a roaring lion); but they do not and cannot look like a lightning flash or a lion. When audible language signs are patterns of vocal sound forming words and sentences of a spoken language, virtually none of them can resemble what they refer to.* Therefore the connection between sound and meaning is not natural but conventional and arbitrary, *symbolic.*

Visible language movements, by contrast, can stand for things directly. Direct pointing, natural resemblance, and actions that replay other actions are effective in linking language signs to their meanings. This difference between spoken language signs and signed language signs takes the original idea forward—and backward as well. In its present form, the idea visualizes a signed language as the first language ever—in use as much as a million years ago.

Human physiology supplies reasons for thinking that visible signs rather than speech first expressed language. Human vision automatically sorts images and compares them for us. Working with vision and the perceptions it brings, human hands can point to things and imitate them. Furthermore, visible, manually produced signs with obvious meanings provide a context in which vocal sounds can carry meaning, simply by being produced at the same time as the gestural signs. This facet of the idea suggests a way of linking the venerable gestural theory of language origin to all the grammatical and linguistic treatises about spoken languages dating from those made by the first known grammarian, Pānini, in India twenty-four hundred years ago.

---

*Sound symbolism (like sniff, snort, sneer, etc.) and onomatopoeia may seem to contradict this statement, but there are simply not enough sounds of this kind on which to build a spoken language.

Which Came First, Words or Sentences?

Signed languages provide the clues needed to answer this question. A currently popular theory of language and its varieties began by treating sentences as "syntactic structures."[4] These are abstract downward-branching imaginary trees generated, in theory, by a series of rules said to be identical in every human brain. These imaginary trees have highly abstract symbols at the ends of their branches, and according to the theory, these symbols get exchanged for words in "the lexicon," which is the place in our brains where supposedly we store all the words and meanings of our language. I suggest, however, that both words and sentences crystallized out of gestures. The human brain does not assemble together already sorted materials. Instead, it works on wholes, gestalts, undifferentiated complexes. In the words of one brain scientist, the brain "carves or crystallizes" parts out of the whole.[5]

Early humans' eyes and brains would naturally have seen that their hands and their movements pointed directly to other things or reminded them of other things by looking like them. This representation is not the kind of trick that entertains children by making the shadow of a hand look like different animal heads. Rather, this carving up of the whole physical action is something profound. Take for instance a gesture meant by its maker and understood by its watcher to represent "the animal went up that tree." The hand would point at the animal both individuals had seen and move upward as it pointed to the tree. What the brain would have done—a million or two years ago as now—is interpret the hand's pointing first to mean "that animal" and then to mean "that tree," all the while interpreting the hand and arm movement as "climbing."

This deceptively simple interpretation is profound, because it separates nounlike entities (animal, tree) from verblike actions (went up or climbed). Simultaneously with crystallizing out the components, it takes in a complete idea, a sentence. In 1978 researchers Ted Supalla and Elissa Newport pointed out that signers of American Sign Language present a handshape virtually motionlessly, or hold it up with tiny repeated movements, to name something (such as an AIRPLANE); but they move the same handshape more prominently to depict a verb's action (FLY) (see fig. 1).[6]

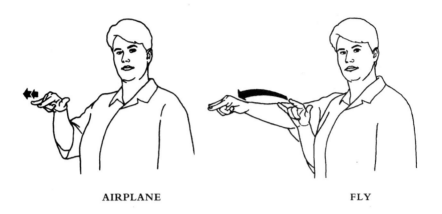

AIRPLANE   FLY

FIGURE 1. *An example of a noun/verb pair differentiated by movement.*

The gesture meaning "it climbed that tree," a simple hand-arm physical action, is an undifferentiated whole. But creatures with brains and bodies like ours long ago grasped the obvious meaning and saw it composed of the animal, the tree, and climbed. (They had both seen that the climbing had happened and was not still going on.) This spontaneous gesture did not require any structured rules to generate it step by step, but seen and interpreted by a hominid or human it was understood—though probably not consciously—to be what we now call a sentence with what we call subject, verb, and object within it.

Looking at sentences and at words—sorted into nouns and verbs—as they crystallized out of meaningful movements resolves the dilemma: Which came first, sentences or words? Neither; they existed together, unsuspected, inside gestures within the capability of humans (and also of chimpanzees and our common ancestor) to decipher. But something special was needed to interpret them in a certain way. Chimpanzees seem to lack the ability to see and separate out the nounlike sign and the verblike sign in the sentence that gestures like *give me food* or *groom me* contain; they don't make sentences spontaneously. Evolution supplied that something special—the body and brain we call human—needed to turn a gesture into sentence-cum-words. The task of human eyes and hands and brains was not to "put two and two (or noun-phrase and verb-phrase) together" but to take one (single gesture) apart and find in it a nounlike sign, a verblike sign, and also keep it together and interpret it whole as a sentence sign.

This constitutes the present state of my thinking about signed language, but of course it implies all kinds of interesting developments that some call grammar and will need more than one chapter to describe.

Languages in Two Channels

Gestures and the sign languages of deaf communities are not alone in suggesting new ways to look at old questions about language. A number of people in both the Eastern and Western hemispheres have cultures that include both the "universal" human attribute of a spoken language and also a signed language—an alternate sign language, as Adam Kendon calls it.[7] Kendon found that the Warlpiri people in Aboriginal Australia treat their sign language and spoken language as equally valid, saying anything in one that they can say in the other; cultural rules indicate when it is appropriate to use each and who should do so.

Brenda Farnell has investigated a sign language of Assiniboines on a reservation in Montana.[8] These people also follow cultural rules in their use of languages. In a formal story recitation that Farnell has transcribed, the storyteller mixes both spoken and signed language. Both must be understood to get the whole meaning. This does not appear to happen with the Australian sign languages, which cultural norms keep carefully separated.

Despite the differences in their use, alternate signed languages like those of the Warlpiri and Assiniboines have features that suggest they may be older than the spoken languages their signers also use. Assiniboine culture includes an orientation to the natural world, its quarters, seasons, winds, and so on that can only come from vision and movement. Assiniboines see the world around them and represent it not in arbitrary terms for abstract features but as a person using eyes and brains and hands and arms takes it in and depicts it. Their languages and mythology also preserve the natural union—not the separation found in different sorts of cultures—of thought and feeling. All this is naturally and transparently

FIGURE 2. *The 3 handshape is used in ASL to represent vehicles.*

expressed by the sign language, and by the gestures used by members of the tribe who may not be fluent in the sign language itself.

Still stronger evidence for the priority of signed languages comes from another Native American tribe and its language, Klamath. The spoken Klamath language, studied by Scott DeLancey and his colleagues at the University of Oregon, has a number of verbs composed of two morphemes.[9] The first of these bound morphemes stands for the agent or patient or instrument (jointly called by linguists "the argument") of the verb, but it is not a specific noun. Instead, it represents any of a class of things that share some physical characteristic. This is exactly what the handshapes of many sign language verbs do. A signer first shapes the hand to look as it would if holding or representing something (see fig. 2).

The second part of these bipartite Klamath verbs stands for the action itself—the action that goes with the kind of thing the handshape represents. This verb construction, unusual in spoken languages but common in sign languages, suggests that spoken two-part Klamath verbs originated as translations into vocal sounds of signed verbs—handshape-movement gestures whether in a complete sign language or not.

These are some of the linguistic, semiotic, cognitive, and paleontological ramifications of a once unthinkable idea about signed languages, and I suspect that all together they could start a scientific revolution as well as effect benefits in everyday life. Virginia Volterra and Jana Iverson have pointed out, for instance, that all children, hearing and deaf, communicate with gestures for months before they use the language (spoken or signed) of their caretakers.[10]

Thus, if it becomes recognized that human language and thought and culture—the mind—must have begun as they continue to begin in the infant, with gesture and vision, we might give all our children, deaf and hearing, a better start in life. Effective gestural communication could begin before hearing infants start to use spoken language. Child care in the first three years of life could become the most effective part of their development. We already know that in these years the brain is growing faster than it ever will again.

Beyond this, the status of deaf people, their education, their opportunities in life, and the utilization of their potential—all these could be much enhanced if we understood that the way deaf people still make language may be the way the whole human race became human.

CHAPTER 2

Chasing the Language Butterfly

IT WAS ASKING for trouble in the early 1960s to argue that a symbol system without sounds was a genuine language, but it seemed to me a good idea anyway. Once my idea was out in the open, other interesting questions followed. One of these was whether the very first languages would have looked like the languages most people today use.

I don't think they would have. I think that language must have begun in one form and changed to another. This is a radical idea, perhaps, but I think it can be explained. All of us use a language (or more than one) in the daily business of living and find it a pretty straightforward process. We make signs that we and others can hear or see or both. Whether we make the signs with our unaided voices or with our upper-body movements or with the assistance of pens or keyboard strokes or microphones, we, and those we interact with, assume that the signs we are making mean approximately the same things to them as they mean to us.

When we talk about these language signs, we call them words and sentences; and for most adults most of the time, they pose few problems. These words and sentences are made out of the sounds we speak and hear every day. They are also represented by markings we see on paper, billboards, television screens, and so forth. We seldom think about how and why the words and sentences mean what they mean. As long as they work, we don't need to worry. Most of us think even less often about what deaf people's words and sentences must be like.

Once in a while, though, something happens to make us think about the way words and meanings get connected. Reading Lewis Carroll's *Alice's Adventures in Wonderland* gives our comfortable belief that words and meanings are solidly connected a sudden jolt. When Alice encounters Humpty Dumpty in Looking Glass Land, Humpty Dumpty tells her that when he uses the word *glory* it means "a knock-down argument." Because she is a stranger there and he has the authoritative manner of an Oxford or Cambridge don, she doesn't argue with him, but we may stop a moment and reflect that, yes, indeed, the words we use mean just what we and others say they mean. There is nothing else to make them mean that.

The words and phrases and sentences we use every day mean what they do because that is what most of us intend them to mean. This leaves us with the mystery of how they got their particular meanings in the first place. The Swiss linguist Ferdinand de Saussure (1857–1913) was noted for saying that language signs are arbitrary, not motivated, not naturally connected to what they mean. He also is credited with saying they cannot be motivated. Before Saussure, René Descartes was even more extreme, concluding that language and thought are quite separate from bodies and the material world.

Language signs *seem* to be arbitrary because they are conventional, and given a convention—an agreed-upon usage—anything can be a sign for anything else. A convention is a tacit social contract. People who regularly interact with each other use the same form-meaning pairs. They never negotiated a contract among themselves confirming the connection between forms and meanings, but the contract holds nonetheless. When people disagree about meaning—in civil disputes as well as in families and in international relations—they often need courts and arbitrators and other intermediaries to sort out the resulting chaos.

∼

The question of how language signs acquired their meanings takes us back to the beginning of life on earth. Without considering that beginning, we could not refute ancient myths that claim language resulted from divine intervention. Even to deal with the thoroughly modern mythlet that supposes a brain mutation initiated language as a strictly human, species-specific instinct, we need the story of life.

Life began as single living cells. Much later, aggregations of cells formed more elaborate living creatures. Still later, central nervous systems evolved. But through all this long time, life proceeded by movement and change and adaptation to change—from the organism's point of view, by interpreting change. All animals, using whatever sensory nerves and brains they have, interpret actions. The one-celled bacteria *E. coli* show by their behavior that they interpret change in their environment. These bacteria tumble about at random in liquid, but if sugar is dissolved in it, they swim toward the greatest concentration of sugar molecules.[1] Interpretation endows actions with meaning. This fact of life is ubiquitous: a lowly fly interprets simple actions, making evasive moves when it sees a flyswatter approaching.

I am suggesting that we should look for the beginning of language in the actions of other living things, even the housefly evading a swatter. The connection is unmistakable. Not just flies but all creatures with functioning eyes interpret what they see to survive. Visible or otherwise perceptible actions are signs, and creatures interpret them as signifying something else. This is as true of the swing of a flyswatter or the presence of sugar molecules as it is of words and sentences. As species evolved, the natural and necessary biological process of interpreting meanings evolved with them. Defining meaning that way, we will try to trace the way form-meaning pairs, an aspect of all animal life, could have evolved into genuine language signs, the words and sentences in common use.

At the start it is important to realize that not all words and sentences have to be made of vocal sounds or their representation in writing, even among hearing people who only use a spoken language. When a shopper tells a clerk, "I'll take a dozen of those," the clerk has no idea what the shopper means without seeing a pointing finger. The visible, non-spoken, sign imparts meaning to the shopper's otherwise ambiguous utterance.

This example demonstrates a common intrusion of visible signs into sequences of normally spoken signs. But in deaf people's languages *all* the words and sentences have to be seen. Deaf signers make words and sentences out of easily seen bodily movement, just as hearing speakers make words and sentences out of vocal sounds. Movements seen by a visual system *or* sounds heard by an auditory system can be the primary symbols of a language. Yet vision may have an advantage, for it is neurologically a richer and more complex physiological system than hearing. Sight makes use of much more of the brain's capacity than does hearing.

What kinds of symbols might the very first languages have used? The easy response to such a question is that first languages originated too long ago for anybody to be able to know, but we can consider the issue with another set of questions: How could vocal sounds have been put together to make words and sentences? Who was there to tell the earliest speakers on earth what the sounds they were making meant? Who could tell them which words were verbs and which words were nouns? And who explained to them how to combine words to make larger-than-word meanings? Expressed this way, it seems that speech alone could not have ushered in language. Speech is a way to deliver language. Language has to be in place, in cognitive systems, in brains, before speech can convey it.

One popular theory of why humans have language proposes that a mutation of brain cells gave them a unique "language organ," but the work of some biologists and other brain scientists who study mutations casts doubt on this.[2] An alternative explanation would need to examine what signs humans or hominids could have used at first to represent and transfer meaning; that is, other than sounds, what signs could have been interpreted as words and sentences without language already being in place, fixed in the brain by a fortuitous mutation?

Visible movements provide a ready answer. Movements are naturally interpreted by many different kinds of animals, although the richness of the interpretation varies according to the nature of the animal. The main argument that ties together the following chapters is that movements, which are natural signs naturally interpreted, evolved into genuine language signs. These movements became, with full metamorphosis, the actual words and sentences that we now, hundreds of thousands of years later, speak and write down. Movements continue to make meaningful signs, but for most hearing people they have become largely invisible, taking place inside the throat, producing sounds to be heard rather than actions to be seen.

The differences between the way we see and the way we hear readily demonstrate that visible signs carry more information than audible signs. At a single glance we see a great deal, usually more than we consciously focus on. We can hear language sounds of great variety and discriminate among them very rapidly, but they have to come in succession—we have to wait until a string of them has traveled through our inner ears to our brains before we can be sure what a particular sequence of language sounds, or a spoken sentence, means.

Although we cannot be sure what dinosaurs and other extinct animals could hear or smell, the available evidence assures us that they too could see and move and use their vision and movements to get food, even living prey that had to be pursued and captured. Millions of years later as the Tree of Life branched, visible movements made by animals were communicating not just the information they needed for getting food but also the kind of information that makes social existence possible for those we recognize as social animals.

Humans use visually perceived movements in the same way as other animals, but we do more: we make movements ourselves to resemble visible things and beings and changes and actions. Clever as we are, however, we cannot make sounds resemble the visible world. Sounds are, and always have been, highly useful in the animal kingdom for giving alarms, expressing emotional states, marking off territory, calling companions, and attracting mates; but only a visible sign can look like something else.

These observable characteristics of sensory perception, as well as the existence of signed languages, tell us that speech is sufficient but not necessary for language. I believe the case is even stronger, though. Visible human movements are not merely sufficient for language but were absolutely necessary for making that first solid connection between sign and meaning. To put it plainly, language could have begun when early humans interpreted more richly than other animals could the movements they saw, especially the movements they themselves made expressly to transfer information.

Gestures, movements of arms, hands, head, and other body parts, as well as visible changes of the appearance of the face, can look like, point to, or reproduce a whole world of other visible things, things that human and closely related species had to do and attend to. Upper body gestures transfer information; they carry meanings between intelligent creatures. Facial expressions and a person's overall appearance, along with arm and hand movements, can reveal what a person feels about what is being represented, as Darwin made clear in *The Expression of Emotion in Man and Animals.*[3] Vocal sounds can certainly reveal feelings as well, but if they are not part of an already formed and agreed-upon language they cannot do so with the complexity and effectiveness of visual signs.

Even more than the composition of language signs, the channel used for perceiving them determines the nature of language. Many animals have a very useful olfactory system for getting information, for example, but a language of odors will not work for humans. We can discriminate too few odors to serve as symbols conveying the complexity of human thought. Moreover, except in animals like skunks, odor production is not under voluntary control. We do not need to make a complete inventory of the human sensory systems to find those suitable for adaptation to language. Only two have the power to detect and process language symbols naturally.★ Only sight and hearing in higher primates have a large enough network of brain centers and neural connections for the enormous task of processing a language.

Seeing and hearing, however, are not equally powerful sensory systems. The nerves connecting eyes and brain outnumber by far all the brain connections to the other sensory organs, the ears included. Visual processing involves so much of the brain that a visual field may convey an enormous amount of information simultaneously, whereas language sounds have to reach the ear sequentially, one by one, until the whole message is received and can be interpreted. This difference is shown by everyday experiences.

Take, for example, the act of driving in a lane of rush-hour traffic. Suppose I notice the car in front of me has its brake lights on and is

---

★Of course, the sense of touch is a language channel for people who are blind or deaf-blind, but the primary symbols of a spoken language, its sounds, first have to be represented by letters, and the letters have to be represented by the patterns of Braille. Languages are acquired natural systems; reading print and Braille has to be learned.

slowing. At the same time I see that the traffic light up ahead is not yellow but green and my speedometer reads 50 miles per hour. The rearview mirror shows that the car following is a safe distance behind. To put these details in speech may take less time than reading them; but even so, saying them takes far more time than I have in which to decide what to do; yet every bit of this visual information is instantaneous, and my reaction immediate. Hence, the old saying that "a picture is worth a thousand words." The following chapter will explore more implications of these physiological and physical foundations of languages without sound.

~

Between the gestural systems that could have been the first true languages and the signed languages in use today, there must have been enormous changes, for cultures shape language. Nevertheless, a close look at modern sign languages can be useful in understanding the first gestural systems.

The choice of sight or hearing as the sensory system for communication directly affects the way that language symbols can signify. The visual gesturing people resort to when they don't know each other's spoken language provides some mutual intelligibility. Gesturing works in this situation mainly because a great many animal species interpret movement as meaning. Birds with their small brains and insects with none at all can interpret a movement they see as a sign of danger and take appropriate action.

Although various human cultures have conventionally linked specific meanings to common gestures, in certain circumstances a spontaneous gesture will be universally understood and signify directly and naturally to humans and nonhumans alike. For example, miming picking up and throwing a stone can scatter a flock of starlings or crows, even as a loud shout may do; but a spoken word (unlike a spontaneous cry from an infant, for example) has no meaning at all until a human community shares a convention associating that word with a particular meaning. Lacking a shared convention, the words of a spoken language convey no more information than a hint about the speaker's emotional state. The fact that many gestures in common use today became conventional long ago obscures this crucial difference between gesture and speech.

Nature and human convention have sometimes been treated as if the two are categorical opposites, as if something conventional cannot be natural and something natural cannot become conventional. Some writers, perhaps taking the lead of Saussure, interpret the universality of human gesturing to imply that gestures cannot be language signs. Others, Cartesians (followers of Descartes), argue that language has to be conventional, that its signs cannot be naturally linked to meaning. I believe they are basically mistaken: gestures may be natural or conventional, but they may also be both.

We can speculate that, as humans evolved, the obvious usefulness of gestures led to their increased use through time. Gestures that at first resembled or indicated what they meant became conventionally linked to meanings understood by the group, just as today's sign languages and spoken languages have to rely on convention. There are not enough natural, transparent, visible signs (nor onomatopoetic words) to provide for more than very limited communication without conventional agreement. People need to say and communicate so much that a vocabulary composed only of natural signs could not possibly suffice in a complex social environment. Natural signs thus had to be supplemented by conventional signs.

The idea that language might have begun with gestures instead of voices is certainly not new. The gestural theory of language origins goes back to ancient philosophers' speculations. Despite its antiquity, though, no one has disproved the theory or its possible alternatives. Indeed, no theory about how language might have begun has so far been very helpful in answering important questions, but perhaps the gestural theory has not yet been given all the attention it deserves.

Support for Gestural Theory

In modern times, anthropologist Gordon W. Hewes (1917–1997) focused attention on the gestural theory and helped bring it respectability in learned societies. His "Primate Communication and the Gestural Origin of Language" first appeared in *Sign Language Studies* (4:1–34) in 1973. Earlier, he helped plan a symposium on language origins at an anthropological society's meetings—the first since the topic was banned from scientific discourse for lack of credible evidence in the previous century.

A generation can bring remarkable changes in thinking. When Hewes and Roger Wescott invited me to join them and eleven others to address the subject of language origins at the American Anthropological Association's meetings in 1972, our session drew a number of the curious. But when we three attempted to have the papers published in book form, no publisher was willing to take the risk of publishing on such a subject. I had received a small legacy, however, and decided to use it to publish *Language Origins* privately.[4] Then, in October of 1976, the New York Academy of Sciences (NYAS) held a conference organized by Horst Steklis, Stevan Harnad, and Jane Lancaster, from which came a volume of 914 pages. Two years later, Charles Hockett wrote a major review article of four books on language origins.[5] The search for language beginnings, ruled out of order by anthropological and linguistic societies for almost a century, was on again.

Over two generations even more changes can occur. The 1998 meetings of the American Association for the Advancement of Science included a symposium, "Darwinian Perspectives on the Origin of Language," organized by David Armstrong of Gallaudet University and Sherman Wilcox from the University of New Mexico. Armstrong began the symposium with a tribute to the late Gordon Hewes. Numerous stimulating presentations followed—all with plenty of evidence for the view that language has indeed evolved. It was well attended and well received, and as it ended, a grand old man of physical anthropology, C. Loring Brace, came up front and told Armstrong and the throng that he had heard Hewes talking about gestural origins for many years and thought little of it, but following that afternoon's session he was taking it seriously. Still, the vast majority of language scholars, even those who favor a gestural theory of language origins, seem unaware that language symbols do not have to be vocal, and that the full reach and power of language can exist without speech. They seem all too ready instead to believe that the way almost everybody (that is, the hearing majority), expresses language is the only way it can be done.

The gestural theory also runs counter to what some call the "standard theory" of linguistics—a theory that language could not have evolved from anything else because language is an instinct or a complete set of highly abstract rules hardwired into human brains before birth. Some proponents of the theory suggest that a powerful mutation changed brain cells and broke forever any evolutionary connection between the brains of other primates and human brains, and between earlier forms of communication and language.[6] Scientific evidence for this radical mutation is lacking, however, and it raises difficult questions. Did the whole human species simultaneously have language thus made available to it by this unique miracle-working mutation, or did it happen to just a few individuals who then became the ancestors of the entire present human population? The following chapters address this and other matters that the standard theory does not explain or resolve.

One weakness in the gestural theory of language origin has been its failure to explain how and why today, and throughout recorded history, most languages are spoken. Yet this becomes less of a problem if we recognize that speech and language are not different names for the same thing, that signed languages are true languages, as well. It is a commonplace for nonlinguistic gestures to accompany spoken languages. In recognizing sign as language, it is plausible to argue that at one time the reverse was true, that is, that nonlinguistic vocal noises accompanied early gesture languages.

Signed languages would have provided a directly perceptible basis for vocal signs to work with. Meaning already linked with a gesture could become associated with a sound pattern if that sound pattern was habitually made at the same time as the gesture. The use of spoken sounds along with gesture-meaning pairs could easily and naturally have led to a new convention, the association of the sound pattern with gesture *and* meaning.

Seen this way, language is analogous to certain other natural systems. Languages may have undergone more than the well-known changes that happen over the years—the kinds of changes we see for example when we compare the English language King Alfred wrote in the ninth century with the English Winston Churchill spoke and wrote in the twentieth. Language, over many hundreds of millennia, may have changed in a much more radical way. It may have undergone a complete metamorphosis.

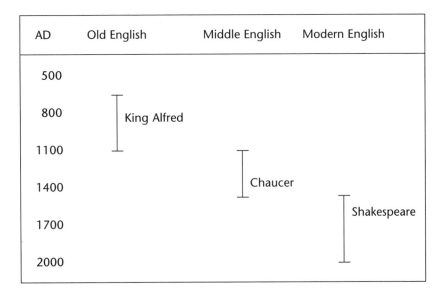

AD	Old English	Middle English	Modern English
500			
800	King Alfred		
1100			
1400		Chaucer	
1700			Shakespeare
2000			

The Evolution of the English Language. English has changed so much in 1000 years that the Old English of King Alfred is unintelligible to modern speakers of English.

Living creatures between birth and death may change in minor ways, or they may change radically. When turtle eggs hatch, the tiny creatures are perfect miniatures of the adults. When chicken eggs hatch, the chicks have two legs and a pair of appendages that will someday be wings, but baby chicks do not look much like adult cocks or hens. When butterfly eggs hatch, however, the many-legged crawling things that emerge look nothing at all like the adult imago. After living as larvae, caterpillars go through a stage of suspended animation as pupae or chrysalises inside cocoons. Only when that stage is completed do they emerge, changed into the delicate winged creatures we know as butterflies.

Language may have undergone a similar metamorphosis.** It may have begun as visible gesturing, passed through a stage in which vocal

---

**The metaphor is not perfect, however, for I would never suggest that speech is in any sense more delicate or beautiful than sign language. It is an equal language in a radically different form.

output loosely accompanied the language-symbolizing gestures (with their natural and conventional meanings), and eventually emerged as (mainly) vocal activity but still accompanied by the visible activity that we now call gesture or gesticulation. If language did begin with nonvocal symbols, this would help explain the failure of attempts to teach rudiments of *spoken* language to chimpanzees, our genetically nearest nonhuman relatives. It would also explain the remarkable success of teaching chimpanzees to communicate and interact with gestural and other tactile-visible signs. Chimpanzees are closer by hundreds of thousands of years of evolutionary time to early humans with gestural languages than to more recent humans with fully evolved vocal tracts. If language underwent a metamorphosis of symbolic form, or channel, this would also accord well with recent discoveries that all infants, hearing as well as deaf, communicate with gestures for some months before they use their parents' language.[7]

New ways to see how cognition and the human mind evolved also present themselves when nonvocal and vocal symbols are given equal attention. Chapter 7 speculates on the early, larvalike stage of this language metamorphosis. It presents arguments and evidence that only visible symbols could have led to the cognitive development needed for language.

Paradigms in Linguistic Science

The linguistic paradigm now in vogue began in 1957 with the publication of Noam Chomsky's *Syntactic Structures*. It describes language as abstract structures created by certain rules genetically wired into the human brain or a "language organ." For the last five decades, linguists have tried to find these rules and formulate them.

The 1957 revolution in linguistics replaced an earlier paradigm. Before Chomsky, linguists working within the older paradigm analyzed the phonology (sound system), the morphology (larger units and their combinations), and the semiology (meanings) of actual utterances they had collected from living people—speakers of particular languages going about their normal activities. This data-based paradigm originated with Franz Boas (1858–1941), and lasted about as long as the current paradigm.

Before Boas, whose work focused attention on data from languages unfamiliar to Western scholars, philology, the genealogical study of languages, had been keeping language scholars busy for almost a century tracing the family connections of Indo-European and other languages.

Sign Language Families

In spite of these paradigm shifts, philology continues as a viable approach, but it has undergone radical change. Morris Swadesh (1909–1967) developed a technique for discovering the family trees of spoken languages and judging approximately the degree of separation of cognate languages (i.e., languages derived from the same parent language). Currently James Woodward is examining the relationships of deaf people's sign languages by using a modification of the Swadesh technique. His work places these sign languages on family trees and gives approximate dates for their separation from parent stock.[8]

This kind of study says nothing about the possibility that any of these sign languages ever metamorphosed into a spoken language. It does show how some of the members of sign language communities move apart, and, just as with spoken language communities, how over time their language habits differ more and more. Even though gestures can signify naturally, there are reasons why no single or "universal" sign language exists.

The sign languages of deaf communities throughout the world are the first or even the only language of many deaf people, but in addition to these primary sign languages there are also "alternate sign languages," as Adam Kendon has termed them. Members of cultures with both spoken languages and signed languages use the two for different purposes but treat them as equally valid alternatives. Kendon has found a very close parallel between one such alternate language (used by the Warlpiri people of Australia) and their spoken language. Anything a Warlpiri may say in one language can be expressed in the other, but Kendon's research does not show any evidence of priority.[9] The same is true of the alternate sign languages preserved in some tribal societies of Africa and North and South America.

David McNeill has examined and compared the gestures and the words of speakers (who may never have seen a sign language being used), and he finds that the gestures and the spoken words may be expressing the same meaning. Although the gestures do not usually translate everything that the speaker says, they sometimes convey things that the words do not. McNeill makes a convincing case that a single central system controls both spoken and gestural output.[10]

Brenda Farnell has found yet another relationship between spoken and signed language. Her book and the accompanying CD-ROM show a formal storyteller using both spoken Nakota (Assiniboine) and Plains Sign Talk in such a way that neither what he says nor what he signs carries the whole meaning. His listeners must look *and* listen; they must know both languages to get the full meaning of his story.[11]

CHAPTER 3

⌒

Gesture to Language to Speech

T HERE IS NO direct evidence as to how language began, but some speculations are better grounded, more susceptible to proof or disproof, than others. Accounts like those in Genesis, for example, may be true; they cannot be disproved. I believe, however, that any scientific theory about the beginning of language has to observe the order given here—gesture to language to speech—if that theory is to stand up to rigorous testing. The crux of the argument lies in the nature of the signs: visible signs can look like what they signify; signs made of sound cannot, but this is not the whole story.

Seeing Language Begin Again

All infants, whether deaf or hearing, use gestures to communicate and interact with others for some months before using their parents' signed or spoken language.[1] This should not be news. Anyone who has raised a child has seen and participated in communicating this way. Parents seem to take their infant's gesturing as something that just naturally happens. And so it does, but most families communicate primarily with speech, and so the infant's gestures get as little attention as the incidental gesturing adults engage in. The scientist's ear, like the parent's, is intently cocked to catch the infant's first attempts at words, the first two-word spoken utterances, and other milestones on the way to adultlike speech, but what of the child's visual signs?

Child gestures have long been the study of Susan Goldin-Meadow. She and Carolyn Mylander reported in *Nature* on children in the United States and China who are too deaf to hear speech, but whose parents, wishing them to learn to speak and lipread, kept them away from sign language users. The study does not focus on the children's gestures as possible clues to language origins. Instead, it treats the gestures as evidence that the children were born with the means of generating language already in their brains.[2] Goldin-Meadow and Mylander's findings and the issue of language innateness were of sufficient interest to be reported in the popular press. Curt Suplee wrote in the *Washington Post* that

> in both countries, the children made up individual sign systems containing three common aspects. They tended to produce far more gestures signifying the object of an action than any other sentence part, less indicating intransitive actors ("mouse" in "the mouse ran") and far less denoting transitive actors ("mouse" in "the mouse eats cheese"). They also almost invariably made gestures for intransitive actors before gestures for the act ("mouse go"), and produced gestures for objects of an action before the gesture for an act ("cheese eat").
>
> [Steven] Pinker [in his 1994 book *The Language Instinct*] called the home sign work very interesting. . . . "Even in that [verbally] impoverished situation, you see signs of the language ability leaking out," he said. "It seems you do get some syntactic ability even with zero language input."[3]

Pinker's phrase "zero language input" has been used often in reference to children born profoundly deaf, and to the American children Goldin-Meadow and Mylander were studying, but what the phrase means depends entirely on how the person hearing or reading it conceives of language and human interaction. Few users of the phrase "zero language input" seem to have considered that there once must have been humans, or creatures about to become human, who literally had zero language input. Yet these prehistoric humans, without anyone to tell them what words or sentences were or what they meant, survived and produced offspring who did possess language. Somewhere along the succession of generations, they created, or happened upon, what we now call language.

The phrase "zero language input" was also used when Noam Chomsky and I participated in a panel at a session of the American Association for the Advancement of Science in 1978. Chomsky used it in referring to children Goldin-Meadow and Heidi Feldman had studied.[4] While Goldin-Meadow was speaking, I scribbled a note to Chomsky, who wrote back, and we engaged in the following exchange:

WS: The Goldin-Meadow children got zero language input but a great deal of face-to-face interaction, and, to me, most significantly, at least one interactant in each taped session who attended to their gestures and was willing to learn their system.

NC: This is a standard fallacy. The fact that a certain condition C is necessary for some function F to develop tells one nothing at all about the biological determinants of F (or virtually nothing).

WS: Right, but most deaf children of such parents get no credit at all for making sense, and the willingness to find innateness coming out is how we got to know that it was there in those kids [in the Goldin-Meadow study].

NC: It doesn't seem to me that the question is one of "giving credit," but of finding out what in fact is innate—i.e., what is the genotype, i.e., what is the function that maps experience into steady state attained. Surely no one doubts that deaf children are genotypical = [equal] in relevant respects to hearing children.

WS: That's the rub—there's a whole literature (mostly in the past fortunately) that relates deafness with mental deficit. Fromkin's "Genie" and Lane's "Wild Boy" were genotypical too, but like Hubel's blinded kittens, they went too long without the complex kind of stimulation that allows the innate pattern to unfold in behavior—True or false?

NC: Exactly. It seems to me that this is suggestive support for the
assumption that the human language faculty is a species-specific
genetically determined organ, much like the cat's visual system.

I think this exchange makes the two positions clear. Chomsky believes
(or believed then) that humans have a species-specific, genetically determined language organ and likened it to the cat's visual system. I cannot
agree. Cats' eyes and brains are organs, but their visual system connects
these organs, the muscles that direct vision, and perhaps other organs.
Seeing is thus the product of the animals' activity and use of the system
with all its components intact. I also believe human infants behave as they
do because of a genetically determined drive, but that drive is to
perceive-and-act, not to create a language according to genetically determined, universal rules. The infant's linguistic system is a product of
its sensory-action system; as would be expected, this system in humans
is considerably more sophisticated than in other species.

It is likely that all human infants act in much the same way as the
deaf children Goldin-Meadow studied. Too young to be able to make
complete sense of adults' spoken or signed languages, infants do what
comes naturally. They first see objects and handle them. Small wonder
then that the researchers reporting their study in *Nature* found the deaf
Taiwanese children's most numerous first representations were gestures
for representing objects. Seeing and holding, dropping, throwing, chewing,
pulling on, and otherwise messing about with objects, infants begin early
on to use their hands for representing objects even when they are not
touching or holding them, although touching and pointing probably
precede any symbolic gestural representation. Infants need no innate language rules to tell them what to do with their bright eyes and busy hands.

Frank R. Wilson's book *The Hand* explains that our hands are potent
keys to what we know and how we know and think and communicate.[5]
We know where our hands are at the same time our hands know and
tell us what they are touching and a great deal about it. Wilson shows
how a musician's or juggler's or mechanic's or surgeon's fingers know
things that cannot be put into words. When eyes and hands work together, we know more than we are aware of. Our vision and bodies tell
us "what's there." This "knowledge" is not inborn; it comes from practice.

Noticing everything around them, infants also see what Suplee referred to as "intransitive actors"—parents, siblings, pets, doting aunts. These living things are relatively large and striking; they move about; they attract attention; above all, they come into the infants' sight and disappear from it. These actors are fewer in number than the objects that first attracted the infant's attention. Naturally, the infant, in this stage of the brain's maximum growth and development of neural connectivity, focuses on, and begins to represent, these actors and to point to them—with hand and eye.

It is literally the infant who does these things—the human infant generally, not just the six deaf children of hearing parents in the United States or four others in Taiwan studied by Goldin-Meadow. All infants, hearing and deaf, communicate gesturally at first, as Volterra and Iverson found in their review of developmental research in several signing as well as speaking language communities. The language or languages used in the infants' immediate environment appear to have little to do with the infant's original communicative behavior. The crucial input to the infants is not the adult language; but they certainly do not have "zero input." Their interactions with things and actors in their environment give their eyes and hands and brains very rich input to work on.

Once infants have begun to represent actors, they make new gestures to represent the actors *and their* activities. Indeed, the connection between a great many actions and the gestural representation of them is entirely natural. It is built into our bodies. The hand's movements reproduce features of the actors' actions. Something else that most infants see and experience constantly is change, especially change that happens to objects. This change is sometimes of their own making. It is also closer to them than any hypothetical, abstract rule of grammar. The order of elements in "cookie eat" is natural. (Perhaps mice eating cheese was something the Taiwanese deaf children saw regularly, but it seems likely that infants in American culture more often eat cookies and see them eaten.) Representing the eating action by the actor, in exactly that order—cookie eat—needs no rules of universal grammar. The cookie is visible for a moment, then it is gone (regardless of who ate it).

After both the actor-action and the object-change relationships have been observed and represented regularly by gestures, the infant is ready to take another cognitive step. This happens because seeing and making representations of things and actors and actions and changes lead to seeing further relationships—those represented by the representations. Once again, the hand is the key or catalyst to this cognitive advance. If something like a pet animal appears for an instant in a doorway and moves out of sight, the infant may point at where the pet was and immediately move the hand to show the direction it went. Within this gesture, the representation of the pet and what it did are joined together; the hand is naturally, physiologically joined to its movement.

In the world that the infant is busily observing, a transitive actor's action often directly affects an object; thus, representation of a three-part relationship begins to appear. The representation may come in stages, as the infant's hand-eye-brain coordination rapidly matures. First, we may see something that we can easily recognize as meant to stand for "cookie"; then perhaps the whole gesture signifies "cookie eat." Not long after that, the hand may be saying "doggie eat cookie"—taking this order from the earlier actor-action representation. A better example would be "dog bite finger." This can be represented in a single gesture: the thumb and fingers represent the open-mouthed dog; the action of closing represents the biting; and a finger of the other hand represents itself.

When gestural representation has reached this stage, it encapsulates a whole transitive relationship in a single manual action, and the child is experiencing the mental, visible, and kinesthetic representation of sentence elements. In short, genuine language syntax has begun. From zero to unlimited possibility in about two years is the normal course of infant language acquisition. We cannot be certain, however, how long it took the "infant" human genus to achieve the same upward progress.

There is a grain of truth, of course, in any language innateness theory. The components of the human visual system are innate (although they have to be used if the system is to form itself fully). Also innate is the massive endowment of human hands and fingers and upper and lower arms with unique, human-only joints, nerves that monitor and move them, and neural mapping and remapping of all these in various centers of the brain. Innate, too, is the potential for using these physical endowments in whatever environment surrounds the infant. Add to this human curiosity, perceptual categorizing, learning, remembering, and the drive to observe and experiment and interact with others, and you get a sum that is far from zero cognitive input.

Language from the Body

If language began with seeing and making physical movements as described above, more than speech and hearing were involved in starting language. Sight and hands—seeing, manipulating, and touching—offer fundamental, indispensable knowledge about the world. The very first knowledge a newborn infant gains comes through smell, taste, and sight. The loudest noises it hears are its own cries. Olfaction and taste guide it to food—all but restoring the direct physical connection of gestation; but once food is ingested, the eyes and brain are ready for new sensations. The whole system of moving and changing the appearance of the body or parts of the body, from brain to eyelids and fingertips, needs to be considered as it relates to the making of language signs.

To understand how language may have begun, we must know more about how eyes and hands work with the brain. Our visual and motor systems are so intricately coordinated that together they are more powerful than their simple sum. There is nothing strange about this. In virtually the whole mammalian order, vision coordinated with movement is essential for survival. One need only think of mountain goats at home on the crags or of monkeys swinging through the forest canopy to realize how the vision–movement connection determines, guides, and preserves life itself.

Before agriculture, before the domestication of animals, before civilization, the everyday life of our ancestral species must have been guided principally by vision and shaped by body movement coordinated with vision. Standing and walking upright gave the earliest humans unique upper limbs and appendages and ways of moving and using them that other species do not have. A hand and arm structure developed that can make movements unmatched in the animal kingdom in their nature, variety, and number. An upright posture also gave humans a new way of observing the world visibly, a new, higher receptor location with a forward focus for vision.

This evolutionary process is also regenerative. Using their hands more and in a greater variety of ways than other primates, hominids generated evolutionary tendencies toward subtle but important adaptations in the bones and joints. Most striking is the way the outer three fingers can close against the base of the thumb. This "power grip" gives its possessor the ability to hold an implement and cut, thrust, and strike with it some distance out ahead of the body.[6] With this in mind, it seems sensible to look for the beginnings of language in the coordination of eye and hand.

Exactly how vocal production and speech perception are connected or coordinated is still an open question. It is not clear whether we understand speech because our auditory system is so finely attuned that it can tell us what the sounds mean or because our own voices can duplicate what we hear. Perhaps when the human perception-action system is given due consideration as a major biological foundation of language, more light will be shed on the relationship of producing, receiving, and understanding language. Perhaps what makes understanding possible are basic brain circuits that connect movement with meaning.

This is not to suggest that other sensory systems are unimportant. The sense of touch, especially in fingertips, which are rich in nerve endings, permits blind persons to acquire literacy.[7] But Louis Braille's invention, those patterns of raised dots, are tertiary symbols. They symbolize letters or numerals, which are secondary symbols invented to represent some of the primary symbols (sounds) of spoken languages. Smell and taste are powerful sensations, and these may affect us deeply, but they cannot make the fine distinctions a language must be capable of.

The sense called proprioception or somasthesia is closely related to movement. It monitors and reports on muscle contractions and limb positions, but it reports on conditions within our bodies, not on information from outside. In nature, the primary symbols of a language must be made either of human movements or of sounds produced in the human vocal tract.[8] The difference between symbols made of visible movements and those made by voices is imposed by the physical difference between sight and hearing, the recognition of visible stimulae versus vibrations in the air. Only vision and hearing are sufficient for the reception and initial processing of primary language symbols, because in human beings the visual and auditory systems have co-evolved with mind or consciousness to serve a specifically human system for modeling and communicating about the human world.

Knowing that both vision and hearing are language channels opens up a new way to look at human communication.[9] No longer can theorists file communication into tight compartments, labeling one "speech" and the other "nonverbal communication." Furthermore, now that we know that signed languages are languages, knowledge about the physiology of speech production and reception becomes much less relevant to the central issues of language.

The Matter of Contrast

Those who believed that language required speech insisted that the vocal tract and the auditory system constituted the only language channel. As part of their argument, they claimed that gestures are incapable of the sharp, clear contrasts necessary for language. They appeared to believe that movements could not make the kinds of feature contrasts made by voices.

There are certainly multitudes of contrasts in speech. Some of these contrasts are treated as highly important, others as dialect variants. In English, for example, the sounds [s] and [z] are important to differentiate because the verb *cease* is very different from the verb *seize,* but they can also represent merely a variation in dialect, as when some English speakers make *because* sound like [*beCAWZ*] and others make it sound like [*be Koss*]. The potential in speech for making such contrasts is often considered unique, but it is not. Arms and hands and fingers can make visible contrasts as well.

Languages as systems for representing information must use contrast. It is absolutely necessary for language signs to make fine distinctions. Speech can do that. Consonants contrast with other consonants; consonants contrast with vowels; and vowels contrast with other vowels. But that's not all. Single consonants and single vowels very seldom amount to words, although combined with words, they can add a contrasting meaning (e.g., *see* versus *seen*). Spoken language words result from producing the consonants and vowels in sequence according to rules that vary from one language—even from one dialect of a language—to another. And this, of course, adds another level of contrasts.

These aspects of speech may make one kind of gesture look crude and noncontrastable. This is the kind of gesture speakers make as they talk, often quite unaware that they are gesturing. Sign language doubters may suggest that such waving of the hands and arms cannot possibly make the kinds of contrast language requires. Yet the human upper body can make at least as many contrasting movements as the human vocal tract can, and human vision can detect not only contrasts in the appearance of hands and upper bodies but also a great many contrasting differences in the movements they make. An anecdote from long ago illustrates this strikingly.

The time was the summer of 1955. Percival Hall, the second president of Gallaudet College, had retired and was still living in the old Kendall farmhouse on the campus, but he was terminally ill. One morning in the college employees' dining room, one of the employees from the lower campus asked another who worked for the Halls in the farmhouse, "How is Dr. Hall?" Both of them were deaf, and so the question in sign language was simply expressed: the sign meaning "how" was followed by the name sign of the former president, while the signer's facial expression made this sentence of two manual signs into a question.

The answer was even briefer, a single sign: the forearms held level and parallel in front of the body, one hand palm up, the other palm down; then both forearms rotated 180 degrees to turn the hands over. This exchange was seen by a hearing employee of the college, the director of public relations. She interpreted the answering sign as "Dead," immediately left the dining room, and phoned the *Washington Post,* Hall's obituary appeared the next day—prematurely. The second deaf signer's movement actually signified "He's dying," not "He died"—the contrast is revealed in the speed of the movement, a slow versus a quick rotation of the forearms (see fig. 3).

Speakers of English need to learn the meaningful contrast between [l] and [r] (which are quite similar in vocal tract operation), but speakers of Chinese do not need to hear or say them as different, and learning English in adulthood they may find it difficult or impossible to produce this contrast. In the same way, signers of American Sign Language and

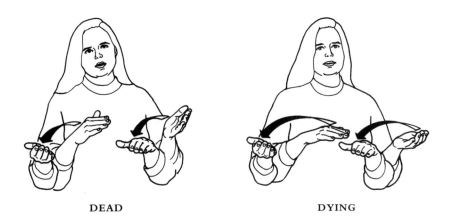

DEAD   **DYING**

FIGURE 3. *A change in the speed of movement will change the meaning of a sign.*

other signed languages need to learn the meaningful contrast (which nonsigners never notice) between a quick and a slow movement and many similar pairs. These contrasts, of course, do not apply to the ordinary gestures made by speakers. Speakers do not depend on their gesticulation to accomplish what their spoken language does for them. They simply need, for example, to make the whole gesture meaning "I don't know" look different from the gesture meaning "Yes, I understand."

Nothing in the physical universe or biology gives audible signs like *die, dying,* and *dead* any more privilege to carry meaning than the corresponding signs of ASL. The Gallaudet public relations director's mistake resulted from language ignorance, not from any defect of the language modality. Those who come to English as a second language often make similar mistakes in understanding English. As long as the reporter of an event makes the basic verb meaning clear and the difference between action completed and action ongoing clear as well, one language serves as well as another.

I believe that the linguistic expression of meaning could have originated with signing but could not have originated with speaking. The same example illustrates an important argument in support of this hypothesis. We might collect translations of the meanings of *die, died,* and *dying* from many hundreds of other spoken languages without finding out very much about which of these languages came first. In some instances, of course, we would find that the forms of one language have been derived from the forms of another, as words in the Romance languages have been derived from Latin words. But no matter how many spoken forms are examined, they will show nothing about why one form represents the action itself, why another represents it as completed, and why another represents it as still occurring. Looking carefully at these verb forms in ASL and other sign languages, however, shows that a slower arm movement is appropriate for signifying something that is still going on and that a quicker, more abrupt movement is more appropriate for signifying something finished, over, done with.

Early humans would have had the cognitive power to grasp important differences between the stages of a process. They could see whether a hunted animal was dying or dead. Representing a process and its differences required only one additional cognitive, manual, visual step. In fact, it can be argued that understanding such different stages in a process can happen only when the phenomena can be represented outside the brain. Once the process is represented, one or more of the major sensory systems can check the representation against what is being represented. All this must have been happening many thousands of years before spoken language representation could have begun. The vocal tract for making human speech contrasts evolved relatively recently, but the ability to perceive the difference between dying and dead must have developed early.

The terms in spoken languages for representing an action and its phases and aspects do not give an indication why they have their particular meaning. Yet the signs for *died* and *dying* suggest a natural connection to the action. The continuous slow movement for the latter accords with an action happening. What the sign DYING signifies directly influences its form, just as the finality of *dead* influences the abrupt movement in the sign DEAD. These signs are symbols, the words of a signed language; but they are also indexes, a most important species of sign.

It may be worth pointing out that just as the English words *dying* and *died* each contain two parts called morphemes (the verb stem and the ending), the ASL signs for the same meanings also have two parts: the hand-arm as described, and its slow or rapid movement. Calling the ASL parts morphemes, however, suggests that signs are structured exactly as spoken words are, but they are not. Spoken morphemes are composed of sounds (phonemes or morphophonemes); the signs DYING and DEAD are composed of a hand-arm and its movement.

Linguistic analysis of a spoken language—breaking it down into morphemes, phonemes, phones, and so on—seldom provides a reliable method for analyzing a sign language. Although the muscle activity for making speech sounds and for making sign handshapes and movements may be managed in the same parts of the brain, hearing and vision are very different physiological systems. Sounds heard and things seen, even if they are interpreted as signifying the same thing, are not the same; and using methods appropriate to one for analysis of the other is like doing dental surgery with plumbers' tools.

It may be useful to consider what early humans would have seen and what they would have heard before language began or was just about to begin. It is reasonable to suppose that when humans first pointed and used other gestural signs they would have done so to refer to things and actions they saw in their environment—exactly as human infants still do. Archaeology furnishes hints of what life might have been like more than one hundred thousand years ago. Bones found in digs show that various kinds of animals were plentiful and vulnerable enough to have been a part of human diet. Digs also show the great manual dexterity and problem-solving abilities of early humans. Tools and implements of stone and wood were augmented with vines, animal sinews, and strips of hides for tying things together. Hearths were constructed and fires laid. Skins and plant fibers were used for clothing. Fruit, nuts, roots, and tubers were gathered, and seeds were separated from husks and pods. And of course hunting must have been an important part of life, and that required manual dexterity.

The environment and everyday activities of early humans contained more stimulation for the eyes and hands than for the auditory system. Even if bird calls and animal cries were common, they would be from a safe distance, for the sounds would have helped to locate their source and attract human hunters. Of course, after the humans had learned which sounds came from what creatures, the sounds would also help in identification. Most of everyday life, however, would have involved things that could be seen. Members of the family, the components of the immediate environment, the artifacts of the normal and special activities—all this and more would have been seen, recognized, handled, and used to best advantage. Such activity, such obviously human culture, would not have gone on for very long, would not have evolved and developed at all, without the ability to represent these activities and the steps and stages of their doing. The practice of representing things and ideas would have made cooperative action possible and indeed significantly changed the social structure.

Understanding the orientation of the human body to its immediate environment would also have emerged early through gestural representation. Other animals "know" directions like up and down or right here and over there, actions like going and coming, relations like inside and outside, and many other matters of place and movement. But they know all this only operationally. Nonhuman animals move about and come and go, but they simply do so; they make little or no overt reference to their actions. However, humans must have discovered fairly early that using a hand and arm to point created an efficient signifier. Another use of gesture, indicating the difference between self and others, represented a crucial cognitive step. This understanding, aided by manual pointing, comes early, as infants' behavior shows.

Visually oriented in a highly varied visible environment, equipped with a unique hand and arm anatomy and neural system, with exquisitely sensitive vision, and with a fully bipedal way of standing and walking, early hominids must have used all these resources constantly. Looked at the other way round, these resources evolved from just such use. Survival depends on using what evolution has provided; its use leads to further evolution. Those hominids most skillful in organizing a group to accomplish social tasks—gathering food, building shelter, protecting territory, raising children, and so on—would have had the best chance of leaving progeny. The advantage of representing things, actions, directions, and selections by gesture to accomplish such organizing is obvious.[10]

Society is a factor in the making of language, but language—or its basic processes of representing and communicating—is equally a factor in creating the characteristics of a society. The hand has a major role in this regenerative cycle of evolution or co-evolution. The hands of primates have a long history of use for above-ground travel, for getting food, for eating, and for grooming, but the hand as a pointer to designate another person or object that the pointer is looking at and has in mind was probably among the first actions to lead toward the development of full humans. The pointing hand couples vision and directed attention with the sensory nerves in the hand and the consciousness of what the hand is doing. Over many generations, this use led to an increased representation of the hand in the brain's neocortex.

An experiment readily demonstrates the extraordinary relationship between the brain and the hand. First read this, and then follow the directions:

> With your eyes closed make a fist with your preferred hand. Then
> extend the thumb to make either the hitchhiker's or the "thumbs
> down" gesture. Open the hand. Use the thumb tip to touch in
> succession the tips of the other fingers on its hand. Still with
> closed eyes, do this again, this time not touching the tip but
> pressing down with the thumb the nail of each finger. Go back to
> the fist formation and push the thumb out between the index and
> middle finger.

If you have moved your hand as indicated, you know you have done it exactly right without seeing your hand. Without looking, you knew how your hand was formed at any instant because a large part of the brain's neocortex is connected to nerves leading to and from the hand. You may have also played the parlor game in which one is blindfolded and asked to identify different objects put into the hand. Another kind of experience can make what the hand does and knows even more surprising. The hand can articulate and receive language even when sight is missing.

In my teaching position at Gallaudet I had to learn to fingerspell English words and also to make signs to translate words (see fig. 4). A few years after beginning there I met for the first time a person both deaf and blind, Robert Smithdas. A noted New York poet, Smithdas visited Washington. When I was introduced to him and found myself conversing with him, I felt as if I had defied a law of nature. He understood me because his right hand rested lightly on mine (just as Helen Keller read Annie Sullivan's spelling hand). But Smithdas understood me whether I signed or fingerspelled. His hand, feeling mine reshaping it-self and beginning to move as a sign moves, also told him what I was about to do with that hand. He was thus able to read my signs of ASL even before they were completed. This ability came from his quick mind but also from a peculiarity of Usher syndrome in his own experience. As often occurs, Usher's had rendered him completely deaf in early child-hood, but it did not impose blindness until his adolescence. During his early years in the Western Pennsylvania School for the Deaf, he became fluent in the ASL that the students and deaf teachers there used—usu-ally out of the hearing teachers' sight. When blindness closed in, his motor nerves and muscles recognized where and how a signer's hand moved for particular signs once the hand gave him the initial cues.

Later, during a sabbatical when I visited a number of deaf clubs and schools in Britain and Ireland, I had to learn to fingerspell the British way, with two hands instead of one (see fig. 5). When I met an elderly deaf-blind man in the deaf club in Edinburgh's New Town, I was able, haltingly, to converse with him. Instead of using my right hand British fashion to touch my left to represent the letters, I used my right to touch his left; and he answered by using his right hand to touch my left. Our conversation, of course, was carried on in the British style of two-hand fingerspelling. Such is the sensitivity of hands and the subtlety of the contrasts they can make.

The appearance of the first humans has been dated variously. Did it occur with *Homo habilis,* also known as "Handyman," some two million years ago, or with *Homo erectus* about one million years ago, or not until *Homo sapiens sapiens* began speaking 150,000 to 50,000 years ago? I will argue here and in the following chapters for the earliest possible date for designating fully human behavior, including the use of language, through sign language, not speech. Visible gestural representation, creating syntax as well as vocabulary, would have created a convention and would even-tually have allowed speech sound patterns to become associated with concepts or meanings.

This study focuses on the way the natural activity of a new species could have begun making visible representations that turned into lan-guage signs; but the converse is as likely. The evolution of *Homo habilis* or a similar species into *Homo erectus* does not seem explainable by

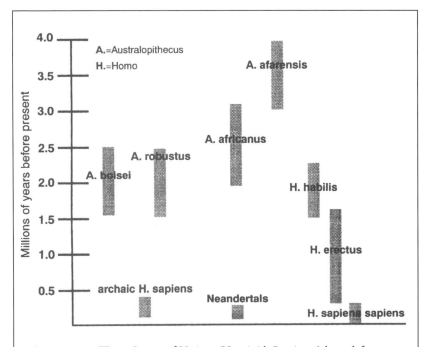

Approximate Time Spans of Various Hominid Species. Adapted from diagrams and data in Michael Corballis, The Lopsided Ape *(Oxford: Oxford University Press, 1991), and Ian Tattersall,* The Fossil Trail *(Oxford: Oxford University Press, 1995). Reprinted by permission of the publisher from David F. Armstrong,* Original Signs: Gesture, Sign, and the Sources of Language *(Washington, D.C.: Gallaudet University Press, 1999), 23.*

changes in the physical environment alone. Developing sign language, which radically changed the way these hominids organized their social lives, may have created the new social environment that encouraged full human development.

Epistemology and child development offer another framework in which to view language growth. Within months newborn human infants understand that they are beings separate from the rest of world. According to some psychological theories, the next step in infancy may

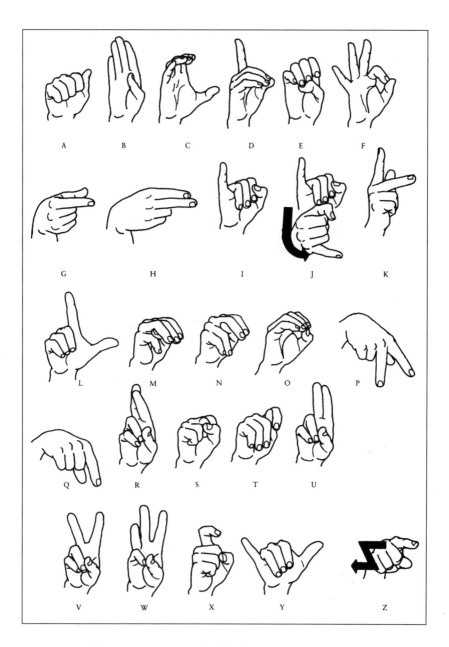

FIGURE 4. *The American Manual Alphabet*

FIGURE 5. *The British Manual Alphabet*. Reprinted from Cath Smith, *Sign in Sight* (London: Souvenir Press, 1992), 59.

be learning conservation—understanding that things out of sight continue to exist. This step is a mix of action and cognition. For example,
the infant holding a spoon drops or throws it out of sight and learns early
that when an adult picks it up it is still the same spoon. What the hand
held and is holding is the object. Feeling and seeing the object together
represent it in neural circuits of the brain; but the hand itself is visible,
and the way the hand is held can be felt, and so the hand, as a perceptible sign, even without holding the object, can represent the object and
its persistence—what philosophers call "substance." No matter how many
times the spoon is dropped and returned, it is the same spoon; the act of
dropping it, by contrast, can be repeated any number of times, but it is
never the same act.

The infant pays close attention to what is going on as it plays the
dropping game over and over. The often-repeated words of the mother
(or her signs if the mother is deaf) may be only incidental.[11] Nevertheless,
some months later, among the first two-word utterances, the sequence
is still there: the hearing child says, "Spoon drop" or "Spoon fall" or
"Spoon gone." A currently popular theory of language ignores all of this
as uninteresting and explains the structure of these utterances as the
operation of innate rules. It postulates that human genes stock each
infant's brain with rules of grammar and syntax before birth. I believe
this theory accords with neither observable physical reality nor everyday experience.

William Calvin has suggested that purposeful aimed throwing may
have been a step taking hominids closer to language and full consciousness. This argument fits what is known about evolution of the hand-arm
anatomy and with observations of child development. Before a stone can
be used to strike a target, it must be found and picked up. Once in hand,
a complex throwing motion involving arm and body and opening of the
"three-point-chuck" grip of the hand follow. A great deal of trial and
error and error correction have to precede successful hits on target, but
the more the better. Like the high-chair baby's spoon-dropping game,
the hominid's target practice would have given vision and proprioception countless instances of object (stone) and act (throw) connected.
Because they are primates, youngsters watching adults practicing or actually hitting targets would have aped the activity they saw. And so

nounlike concepts (stone, etc.) and verblike concepts (throw, etc.) would be represented gesturally, but even more important, so would their natural and syntactic connection.

This kind of speculation might easily be tested: Ted Supalla and Elissa Newport have found a clear distinction between otherwise similar nouns and verbs in American Sign Language.[12] Suppose we hypothesize that this way of making the noun/verb distinction is unique to ASL. This could be tested by examining many other signed languages. I am confident that it would be disproved because the distinction is central to thought as well as to language.

Language requires the cognitive step of distinguishing verblike concepts from nounlike concepts. To take this step, cognition must have had "legs" to step with—a language or a reasonable facsimile of one. Spoken languages constrain us to think in terms of noun and verb. But much earlier than the emergence of spoken language, the visual and manual activity of hominids or humans crystallized the crucial noun-verb distinction out of the hand-moving gesture.

This view of things cannot yet be directly tested; but more attention might be paid to infants' behavior between birth and the beginnings of recognizable speech (or signing if they are deaf). Such study might find that firsthand visible evidence can provide a better explanation for what happens as infants mature than can uncounted abstract rules packed into unidentified genes.

CHAPTER 4

~

Signed Languages
and Language Essentials

ALTHOUGH SIGNED LANGUAGES use attention-attracting visible symbols, and have apparently been used by deaf people throughout history, it has taken a long time for scientists and the public to acknowledge that they are actually languages. Speech and language have usually been equated. Most laypeople, physicians, and religious authorities for centuries claimed that deaf people were languageless, and as recently as 1966 Hans Furth could entitle his treatise on "the thinking-language relation" *Thinking without Language: Psychological Implications of Deafness.*

By the eighteenth century, however, European philosophers and some teachers were reexamining the issue of deaf people's capacity for thought and for language. The most important of the teachers was a French abbé, Charles Michel de l'Epée. Epée conceived the idea of using the visible signs of deaf Parisians, modified by him to accord with the grammar of spoken French, to teach them French language and culture. His method worked well at the Royal Institution for the Deaf in Paris, astounding Parisians with his success. The Abbé Roch-Ambroise Sicard succeeded Epée at the Paris school and continued his method of using signs and fingerspelling in teaching, often with deaf teachers. As the nineteenth century began, schools for the deaf were opened on a similar model in many European capitals, as well as the one in Hartford, Connecticut, in 1817 by Thomas Hopkins Gallaudet and Sicard's former pupil and lead teacher at the Paris school, Laurent Clerc.

A diametrically opposed view of language, deaf people, and deafness was growing at the same time, however. In the seventeenth century Johann Conrad Amman had equated speech with the voice of God, and Epée's intellectual adversary Samuel Heinicke, the German teacher of deaf pupils, argued in the 1780s that without speech a deaf person could have no language. Heinicke and his followers, often called "oralists," believed that language is nothing but speech, that speech, and only speech, is language. Thus they demanded that deaf children be trained to decipher speech by looking at speakers' faces and to produce it even though they could not hear their own attempts. These zealots forbade the use of sign language in their schools, fearing it would inhibit the learning of lip-reading and the development of speech.

By the late nineteenth century, the oralists had gained the upper hand. In 1880 oralist educators met in Milan, Italy, and decreed that sign language had no place in schools and programs for deaf children. They insisted that only speech and lipreading could expose deaf people to true language and allow them to fit into hearing society. Contrary to evidence and experience, they insisted that clear speech could be learned by all deaf people who were not mentally deficient and could be read on the lips with facility. Hearing parents of deaf children naturally believed the educators' promise that their children could be taught to speak. Sign language was banished from the schools and denounced as barbaric gestures, not language. But of course deaf children and adults continued to use a language, sign language, that they were naturally and fully able to express and understand.[1]

This was the situation I encountered in 1955. Signing was permitted and employed at Gallaudet, but as a necessary evil, a "visual aid" to the spoken English we teachers were expected to use simultaneously with our signs. The attitude seemed to be "We know that language is really oral or written speech, but to get our students to understand what we say, we have to resort to cumbersome and inadequate manual word and letter codes to teach them English."

Several circumstances perpetuated these falsehoods about the authentic signed language used by deaf people. First, hearing people resort to gesturing when it becomes necessary to communicate across language barriers or where sound does not carry, but this kind of gesturing is definitely not language. Second, for centuries members of religious communities used manual signs as codes for spoken language when their orders imposed silence; and deaf people do indeed sometimes use such codes for representing the words and letters of spoken languages, a kind of lexical borrowing that allowed some observers to argue that signs were not adequate to create their own language. And third, since the middle of the eighteenth century at least some hearing people have recognized, consciously or subconsciously, that educational use of genuine sign language would logically lead to greater and greater deaf control over deaf education; after all, deaf people, as native users, are more frequently fluent in sign than hearing people. Such a development would challenge the dominance of hearing people, a fundamental characteristic of nearly all deaf education.[2] For all these and other reasons, sign languages were kept well outside the language preserve, and professional educators termed them substitutes or surrogates for "real," that is, spoken, languages. Though hard to believe now, that is the way it was in 1955–1960.

The misunderstandings about signed language were not entirely institutional nor were they entirely the fault of professionals in deaf education. Ordinary people's exposure to deaf people and signed language was and is so infrequent that they have little chance to learn the truth. Furthermore, what exposure hearing people have to the deaf has not always been pleasant, sometimes creating the impression that there is something wrong, certainly inconvenient, and maybe even dangerous in a person who does not hear.

Xenophobia, fear of the foreign and strange, has also helped keep signed languages out of sight and unrecognized. During the age of exploration, world travelers returned and described natives of the exotic lands they had visited as primitive or savage. Some even reported that these people had languages so incomplete they had to supplement them with gestures.

Charles Darwin proposed in 1859 that new species are formed by natural selection; ethnocentrism, xenophobia, and ignorance were compounded in virulent reactions to his suggestion that humans might have descended from animal ancestors. Thirteen years later, his demonstration of the great similarity in the way emotions are expressed in humans and animals widened the gap between science and unquestioned beliefs. Darwin's opponents held that humans alone had language. According to their deeply seated belief, the civilized European was both the aim and the culmination of creation's steady progress from the primitive and savage races to the fully human (Darwin believed this as well).

Despite all this, in modern as well as ancient times, a few philosophers did speculate that the practice of communicating with gestures might have led to language.[3] However, the gestures that hearing persons normally use while they are speaking differ in so many ways from speech that scientists as well as laymen often conclude on insufficient evidence that gestures cannot express language completely.

Ironically, another barrier to acceptance of the notion that gestural signs can be language was the existence of gestural codes, as mentioned. Under a monastic rule requiring periods of silence, monks belonging to some religious orders have long used gestures for necessary (and sometimes frivolous) communication; but their gestures are more or less transparent (and sometimes broadly punning) substitutes for the words of some spoken/written language or languages they share. From very early times the brothers supplemented these gesture-for-word codes with a different sort of manual code. These code systems, called fingerspelling, use one or both hands to represent individual letters. The hand signs are thus tertiary symbols: they represent the secondary, alphabetic symbols, which in turn represent the primary symbols of a spoken language—its sounds. Like the monks' word-translating gestures, fingerspelling depends on having a spoken language and being literate in it. The monastic sign-for-word and the sign-for-letter codes are indeed substitution codes, surrogates for speech. Deaf people's signing, if it was given any attention, was being described even as late in the middle of the twentieth century as a way of encoding spoken language.

Saint Bede (A.D. 674–735), a monk of Jarrow in Northumberland, England, not only provided the Middle Ages with a fount of philosophy that flowed for many centuries but also published drawings of hand alphabets and manual numerical systems, the latter much more convenient than Roman numerals for calculation. While it is possible that Bede himself had problems with hearing and speaking, it is undeniable that of all the remaining copies of his manuscripts, those "containing his description of finger reckoning and fingerspelling language" are the most numerous.[4]

Nine centuries later, two Spanish teachers might have brought together these monastic codes and the signing used by deaf persons. Pedro Ponce de León and Manuel Ramirez de Carrión taught the deaf scions of noble Spanish families in the late sixteenth and early seventeenth centuries respectively, but these deaf children were unlikely to have had any contact with deaf people other than their siblings or to have shared with them a developed silent language. Revolutionary in an era when the Church denied communion to those who could not hear and speak, these teachers did not use the word or letter codes as working sign languages but as tools to help their noble pupils learn enough Latin and Spanish to respond to the catechism and fulfill legal requirements for inheriting. As ways of making written language more or less accessible to deaf pupils, the monastic signs and manual alphabets served a purpose; but they were not thought to be actual languages, and they are not.[5]

In Paris, the work of the Abbé de l'Epée (1712–1789), who opened the doors of his school to any French deaf person, went further toward accepting deaf signing as language. He seemed to realize that his pupils were communicating effectively with their signs, and he learned and used many of their signs himself, but he used them mainly for teaching French. In Paris, of course, French was synonymous with language, civilization, enlightenment, and humanity itself. Epée and his successor Sicard thought it necessary to enlarge their pupils' sign vocabulary with gestures they invented (*signes méthodiques*) to help the signs represent grammatically correct French.

In that period, opinions about the relation of language to mind or thought swung quickly from one extreme to the other. Deaf people were sometimes lumped with natives of Africa and the Pacific islands as incompletely evolved human beings who lacked real language. Then along with a revolutionary shift of political thought, all people, deaf included, were considered to be naturally endowed with liberty, equality, and fraternity. Nicholas Mirzoeff, recounting the philosophic and artistic ferment of the times, quotes from a speech to the French National Assembly in July 1791 made by the Jacobin Prieur de la Marne: "What is more, the deaf have a language of signs which can be considered as one of the most fortunate discoveries of the human spirit. It perfectly replaces, and with the greatest rapidity, the organ of speech."[6] But there were opposing ideologues who had the aim of regenerating what they saw as primitive, savage, and physically and mentally impaired specimens of perfectible humanity. As Mirzoeff writes: "By healing the deaf and restoring them to society [of those who use speech, of course], the revolutionaries sought to complete their wider agenda in which individual physical regeneration would lead to the social regeneration of the body politic."[7]

Whether deaf people were accepted as they were, or were looked on as candidates for healing and regeneration, their language continued to be ignored. Despite conflicting philosophies, the school begun by Epée flourished, and before 1820, others on its model were soon founded. This did not occur without strong opposition. When Epée first published a description of his methods, Heinicke in Germany objected in print, claiming that there is no real language without speech and that unless a deaf person was taught to produce speech and recognize it by watching speakers' faces neither language nor mental competence could be acquired. The ensuing debate conducted in journals of the time was judged at a Swiss university to be won by Epée.[8]

Although it had at first the beneficial side effect of alerting intellectuals to consider the nature of language, this oralist emphasis on deaf education had a negative effect. Under Epée's successor Sicard, the French school included instruction in "articulation." This consisted of training deaf pupils in producing and modifying their vocal output until it satisfied their speech teacher. The rise in oralism was symbolized most dramatically by a resolution taken by hearing educators in Milan in 1880, which declared that speech and only speech could "restore the deaf to society."[9]

The warfare between oralism and manualism has taken different forms through time but continues today in debates on the educational philosophy of those engaged in teaching deaf children.* It still keeps those who

---

Manualism as a term for signing may be an oralist coinage, for sign languages are not made with hands alone. Arms, torsos, faces, heads, and eyes all participate. Neither are spoken languages strictly oral; vocal sounds are noises made in the throat, nose, and the mouth.

will not see blind to the existence of languages without vocal symbols, but fortunately the number of these seems to be decreasing, thanks in part to the growing recognition that signing can be language.

Finding Language in Signs

When Noam Chomsky published *Syntactic Structures* in 1957, he reasoned that grammar is too complicated for an infant to learn from the imperfect samples (he supposed) that it hears, and that therefore the rules of grammar or language must be innate in the infant's brain. This theory did not immediately become the accepted way of looking at language, but it did begin an acrimonious revolution in linguistics, and before long, the majority of linguists worked within this paradigm.

The paradigm that Chomsky's theory displaced is usually credited to the German-born American anthropologist Franz Boas (1858–1941). This older theory took a skeptical, natural history approach. It held that to find out how languages work a linguist must carefully examine the way real people actually use their languages. Field work and data were essential. Consequently, for some decades before 1957 many researchers had focused their attention on Native American languages, which differ in many ways from familiar Indo-European languages. The Indo-European languages had been studied under a still earlier paradigm known as philology—the study, in part through written records, of the relationships and family trees of various languages. Within the later, Boasian, paradigm, linguistics and cultural anthropology were closely allied. Both required field work, substantial amounts of time spent as an observer of, and a participant in, the society of those who used the language. The ideal Boasian language scholar working within that paradigm collected a corpus of users' actual utterances and examined the resulting mass of data minutely to find recurring patterns and other clues as to how the language worked.

By coincidence, it was 1957 when I began to study sign language formally at the Summer Institute of the Linguistic Society of America

(LSA). Its codirectors were George L. Trager, a past president of the LSA, and Henry Lee Smith, both anthropologically trained linguists noted for their work in the naturalistic tradition of Boas. They insisted that it was pointless to study languages alone. Languages, they said, had to be studied along with the cultures of their users. One must examine not just the forms and structures of a language but also its actual use and content. The anthropology (not linguistics) department at the University of Buffalo hosted the institute. Trager, its chairman, saw to it that language was studied not only as a natural system but as part of a larger system, a culture. His definition of language had recently appeared in the *Encyclopaedia Britannica* current then: "A language [note the singular] is a system of arbitrary vocal symbols by means of which members of a culture carry on all the activities of that culture." At the institute I took a course titled Linguistics for English Teachers. This was so rich a learning experience that within two years I had put enough of what I learned from it into practice that I told Trager, rather brashly as I look back on it, that he would have to strike the word *vocal* from his definition of language. He read my manuscript on signed language and replied that although he was not entirely convinced that a language could work without vocal sounds as its primary symbols, he would be happy to publish the manuscript as Occasional Paper 8 in the monograph series Studies in Linguistics, which he edited. It was published in 1960 as *Sign Language Structure* and subtitled *An Outline of the Visual Communication Systems of the American Deaf.*

A bibliographical note is in order here. Studies in Linguistics did not have a wide circulation; Occasional Paper 8 went out of print fairly early. A slightly revised edition was published in 1978; then in 1993 the original was republished complete with a new preface and glossary. However, many sign language researchers seem to be unaware of this 1960 treatise and its reappearances and refer to a later work as the first treatment of sign as language. That work is *A Dictionary of American Sign Language on Linguistic Principles,* which I compiled with the help of Carl Croneberg and Dorothy Casterline, two deaf colleagues, and published in 1965 and revised in 1976.[10] This oversight compounds an error ultimately my own. Our dictionary of ASL uniquely lists signs of the language by their locations, handshapes, and movements and not as translations for listed English words.* For this reason it has suggested to many readers that signs are what the hands do, but five years earlier in *Sign Language Structure,* I had pointed out that manual activity is not all there is to a sign language:

> Having described a sign cheremically [i.e., its location, hand configuration, and movement], the investigator may go to stretches of unanalyzed utterances and look for recurrent patterns [in other words, examine the syntax after the word structure has been analyzed]. One of the first features to emerge from such investigation is that on the syntactic level other signals than the aspectual [i.e., manual] cheremes are operating.[11]

This warns, as the dictionary apparently did not sufficiently do, that moving various hand configurations in various ways does account for most of the vocabulary of a sign language, but to discover the syntax of the language, attention must be paid to what else is happening while the hands are being moved. This emphasis on the strictly manual aspects was unfortunate; it was many years before a thorough study was made of the (grammatical and necessary) nonmanual activity in ASL.[12]

Now, more than forty years after *Sign Language Structure* was published, books about ASL and many other signed languages of deaf populations abound. These vary widely in quality, but together with articles in *Sign Language Studies* (*SLS*) and elsewhere, they give detailed descriptions and furnish abundant evidence that signed languages are languages and also that they differ from one another as spoken languages do.

This book marks the next step in a discovery process, the unfolding of my original idea. Its purpose is to connect gesture to signed languages to speech in a way that inspires the least disbelief and encourages the curious to look for answers where they have not previously been sought. To do this I will not try to describe any signed language fully here—an

---

*The usual dictionary of ASL lists English words alphabetically and supplies photos, drawings, or written descriptions of the gestures used to translate them. Another, older procedure was to arrange the English words by semantic field, thesaurus style, and then provide the sign that the word glossed.

impossible task anyway. As the saying went in the heyday of the Boasian paradigm: "All grammars leak."[13] What is needed is a plausible explanation of why signed languages are languages and how they are related to speech and to gesture. I hope to explain in the following chapters how the kinds of expressive movements speakers everywhere make as they are speaking were in use long ago, before there was language, and that they and the animal communication they derived from evolved into language. Later chapters will fill in the story, but here we will begin with a much simplified description.

What Is Language?

In a lecture entitled "What Is Language?" at Cambridge University in 1977, John Lyons said something like this: "Languages must have a system for making words out of something perceptible, a system for making sentences out of the words, and a third system for settling things when the first two conflict." When I asked Lyons if he would agree that words could be made of gestural as well as vocal materials, he answered in the affirmative; but in work published later, he did not treat sign languages as languages, apparently admitting that some gestures can express meanings as words do but continuing to propound the idea that gestures cannot make sentences.

I identified part of the system for making sentences out of signs in 1960. I found that sign language question sentences often end with a question sign, like WHO, WHERE, WHEN, WHICH (linguists call these *wh*-words). Question sentences in American Sign Language also end with the eye gaze focused on the person being questioned and with the hands held momentarily where they were as the final sign ended. Sentences that tell or state something conclude with a dropped-eye gaze, and the hands return quickly to their resting or relaxed position. Commands or demands keep the gaze and hands up and may add a forward push of hand, head, or trunk. These ways of ending a sign language utterance have been dismissed by some as "nonverbal," or merely "body language."

When these language scholars label a particular behavior as body language they mean that it is not true language, like that rendered by speech.

Yet all language must come from the body. There is no such thing as a disembodied mind. René Descartes claimed that the mind is independent of the body, but that is superstition. Modern science knows no other universe than this one, made of matter and energy.

Darwin showed more than a century ago that other animals as well as humans use their bodies to express questions, demands, and other feelings.[14] Ages before a human species could ask a question with vocally articulated words in grammatical arrangement, members of mammalian species had been communicating feelings—though not consciously—by changes in their appearance, by body language. It may be correct in some sense to insist that the questioning look of a dog, cat, or chimpanzee is nonverbal—these animals don't speak in words. But to say that such a look on human bodies and faces, particularly when accompanied by speech or gestural language, is nonverbal is hardly correct.

The expression of emotions with face and body gives evidence that an emotion was there as cause of the expression. We have no evidence that other animals expressing an emotion are conscious of feeling it, but "conscious thought *includes* feelings," as Graham Cairns-Smith points out. He adds: "It seems to me that it is precisely the element of feeling in conscious thought which makes it conscious."[15]

His conclusion agrees with the way thought and feeling are expressed by the Native American tribe that Brenda Farnell has studied. Farnell reports that Assiniboine people speaking the Nakota language make no sharp separation between intellectual and emotional content in either their spoken language or their sign language. For example, they have a spoken language phrase, *t'wac'i waste* that means both "thinks clearly" and "acts generously." Their sign language also expresses this same feeling-thought by a single gesture. The gesture and the word translate each other; to make the gesture they move the hand outward from the heart not the head.[16]

The evolutionary sequence for emotional expression may have been something like this: first animals with well-developed central nervous systems experience feelings; then these feelings are "globally," or bodily, expressed, as Darwin showed. Later comes the human expression of these or similar feelings. Human hands and arms have been recruited to play a major role in this and to provide more detailed information, more precise representation of the feeling. For example, an early human might have been feeling a desire to know where something went. A quizzical face could express a question (just as it does for other animals), and a rapid shifting of eye gaze, perhaps accompanied with a simultaneous side-to-side movement of a pointing human hand, could signify "where?" Most people today ask such a question visibly the same way.

The next stage in the sequence would have been to indicate what missing person or object was the cause of this feeling of loss and its manifestation. It seems likely that when a question about something or someone missing was originally put in visible form, the one asking would first somehow designate what was missing, and then use the *where* gesture accompanied by a questioning look. Deaf signers today often use this order, first making a sign for the topic (what the signer will be talking about), then following it with signs asking a question or making a statement. Some spoken languages reverse this order. They may put so-called old information at the beginning of an utterance, reserving the new or more important information to be imparted later. This ordering of sentence elements takes advantage of the circumstance that a listener may not have given full attention until after the speaker has begun. Because of the persistence of sounds heard, the hearer usually reconstructs the opening even if it has not been fully attended to. The difference between sight and hearing explains why a signed language sometimes orders things differently. It makes good sense to put the new information up front: a signed language utterance is being received as soon as the one addressed is looking at the signer. Attention to language is "turned on."

This mention of words and order takes us back to Lyons' third subsystem. In addition to a system for making words and a system for making sentences, a language, he said, needs a system for keeping the two from conflicting. The point is easy to illustrate with English. A sentence using either the word *allow* or *permit* in the same place, for example, may be made with the same pattern:

The police will not allow us to park here.
The police will not permit us to park here.

Substituting the word *let* for *allow* or *permit*, however, requires that the sentence change slightly:

The police will not let us park here.

The change cuts a word (*to*) from the sentence.

In a spoken language the form of a word chosen may dictate the form of the sentence, and conversely, the form of the sentence may dictate the choice of a word. This rule does not necessarily apply to signed languages. Signed languages make their words and their sentences out of the same material—visible body parts and their movements (which may be large and salient or small and subtle). But what are words anyway?

Which Came First, Words or Sentences?

At the LSA Summer Institute in 1957, *word* was not treated as a technical or clearly definable term of linguistics. Nevertheless, literate users of the familiar Indo-European languages are confident that they know very well what a word is. For example, although the Latin word *amat* is translated in English as *loves,* Latin *amabat* needs two English words to translate it: *was loving.* The Latin word *amabat* is made of a stem and two suffixes. English uses two words for the same shade of meaning, first the auxiliary verb in past tense form, and then a word made with the stem *love* and the suffix *-ing.* Linguists for a long time have called such stems and suffixes "morphemes" and defined morphemes as the building blocks of words or the smallest units of meaning in a language, but the block analogy is misleading. Languages are not so simple a matter as piling one block on another.

Anthropological linguists inspired by Boas studied Native American speakers and found them using what seemed to the linguists to be a long string of connected morphemes. Some of these morphemes were grammatical markers for such things as gender and number and person, but others were certainly words like nouns and verbs. Often these oversize native "words" needed a whole sentence of English to translate them. The distinction between word and sentence, which had been so clear in the familiar Indo-European languages, became fuzzy when linguists examined very different spoken languages.

As a technical term, then, *word* describes the units of some spoken languages well, but it fails to work with the normal clumping of sounds

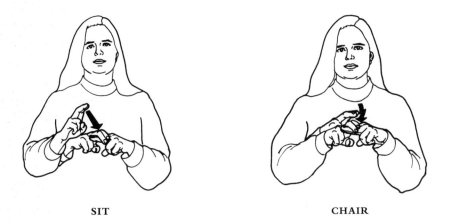

SIT   CHAIR

FIGURE 6. *In certain noun/verb pairs the noun is characterized by short, repeated movements, while the verb is characterized by a single, prolonged movement.*

in other spoken languages. The same kind of misfit occurs in the attempt to make the signs of a signed language equivalent to the words of a spoken language. It is difficult at times to separate words from sentences in signed languages.

Deaf linguist Ted Supalla and his hearing wife and colleague Elissa Newport made a revolutionary discovery about the "words" of American Sign Language. The Supalla-Newport study is first-rate natural history as well as a landmark in sign language linguistics. It describes subtle contrasts that nobody had noticed before but, once having been described, can be seen by everyone. These contrasts make a particular gesture of ASL into either a noun or a verb. The contrasts are easily missed by those who are used to seeing gestures but not to giving close attention to something that looks like a gesture yet is part of a signed language. Once these contrasts have been pointed out, however, their existence is obvious.

Supalla and Newport looked at the ASL signs glossed CHAIR and SIT, which are noun and verb, as these glosses imply. They look alike to a nonsigning observer: the pads of the index and middle finger tap downward on the backs of the index and middle finger of the other hand. The noun SEAT uses repeated small tapping movements, the moving hand descending only an inch or less. The verb SIT uses a single movement, the hand making an arc several inches long and resting a moment on the stationary hand (see fig. 6).[17]

The way in which ASL represents the contrast between noun and verb seems natural. Small, repeated, or checked movements call attention to the handshape, as if to say, "Look at the hand; it is representing something!" The longer, smoother, uninterrupted movement of a verb sign not only suggests the action that is depicted; it reproduces that action on a reduced scale, suggesting some degree of iconicity; that is, the sign, to some extent, looks like what it represents.

In the literature of signed languages much as been made about the iconicity of signs. Research has shown that the iconicity of a sign is not a factor in deaf children's ability to acquire their parents' sign language, for example, and this should not be surprising.[18] A language, whether signed or spoken, is above all conventional, dependent on a tacit social contract. Researchers within the innatist paradigm go further, however, deploring anything that creates a natural connection between a sign and its meaning, as icons do. They take this position because when language is described as innate it has to depend upon the brain's biologically determined universal grammar rules. Being thus arbitrary (by their definition), it cannot depend on anything as un-languagelike as the resemblance between a sign and what it denotes.

The relationship between a sign and its meaning, whether natural or arbitrary, not only gets at the heart of how we know what we know but also illuminates the basic difference between signed and spoken languages. To give it full consideration requires a full chapter, but before that we will look at the way icon and index inform gestures and signs with meaning.

CHAPTER 5

⌒

Language Signs

H IPPOCRATES, a fourth-century B.C. Greek physician, is recognized as the father of semiotics, the discipline that focuses on signs and their ways of signifying. Hippocrates made medicine more of a science when he began interpreting symptoms as signs of what might be ailing his patients. Not just communication and language but all life depends on signs and what they are interpreted to mean. This chapter will examine the ways that arbitrary and natural signs differ, a distinction essential to language.

American semiotician Thomas Sebeok, working from the pioneering studies of Charles Peirce, has identified six major kinds, or species, of signs: *signal, symptom, icon, index, symbol,* and *name.* Sebeok's text introduces and distinguishes them this way:

1. *Signal.* The *signal* is a sign which mechanically (naturally) or conventionally (artificially) triggers some reaction on the part of a receiver. [emphasis in original]
2. *Symptom.* A symptom is a compulsive, automatic, non-arbitrary sign, such that the signifier [is] coupled with the signified in the manner of a natural link.
3. *Icon.* A sign is said to be iconic when there is a *topological* similarity between a signifier and its denotata. [emphasis added]

4. *Index.* A sign is said to be indexic insofar as its signifier is contiguous with its signified, or is a sample of it. The term *contiguous* is not to be interpreted literally . . . as necessarily meaning 'adjoining' or 'adjacent': thus Polaris may be considered an index of the north celestial pole to any earthling, in spite of the immense distances involved.

5. *Symbol.* A sign without either similarity or contiguity, but only with a conventional link between its signifier and its denotata . . . is called a symbol.

6. *Name.* A sign which has an *extensional* class for its designatum is called a name. [emphasis added][1]

These words give us convenient labels for discussing signs, but the names and descriptions come from long study of the whole process of semiosis—how one thing comes to be recognized (by someone or something) as a sign for something else. These six species of signs are the result of sorting out various matters of sign form, sign interpreting, and a world full of possible sign interpretations. Peirce's formulation had sixty-six varieties that went into all the fine distinctions, but Sebeok's six varieties simplify the task. They allow us to examine the semiotic underpinning of signed languages and spoken languages.

To illustrate Sebeok's six species, let us look again at how *E. coli* bacteria interpret the presence of sugar (i.e., cease their random swimming pattern and swim toward the greatest concentration of sugar molecules). It is apparent that sugar in the water is a signal. There is no "topological similarity" between dissolved sugar and the motion of the cell's flagella—thus sugar cannot be an icon. Nothing about the chemical composition of sugar has shaped the bacteria's swimming motion, so sugar cannot be an index. A person's arm movements to suggest swimming would be an index because the normal action of swimming has obviously influenced the way the arms are moved. A swimming gesture would also be an icon, because of the similarity between the gesture and actual swimming. To a human observer, the bacteria's swimming is a symptom. The way the flagella are moving tells an observer with a microscope that the bacteria are finding food. Without sugar in the water, the tumbling action is also a symptom, to an observer, that the bacteria are seeking food.

The remaining two species of sign, the symbol and the name, would seem to be found only in human behavior. Other creatures appear not to use names as we do. A dog may be suddenly all attention when it hears its master speak its name, but the dog is really responding to sounds that it has learned to associate with its master's actions. To the dog the sound of its name is a signal.

Of symbols, Sebeok writes:

> A sign without either similarity [i.e., not an icon] or contiguity [i.e., not an index], but only with a conventional link between its signifier and its denotata, and with an intensional class for its designatum, is called a symbol . . . an intensionally defined class is one defined by the use of a propositional function; [that is] the denotata of the designation are defined in terms of properties shared by, and only by, all the members of that class, whether these properties are known or not.[2]

Sebeok has phrased his definition carefully in the terms of formal philosophy. *Denotata* and *designatum* refer, respectively, to what signs, and a sign, signify, refer to, or mean. Conventional linkage connects a symbolic sign to a meaning through a convention—users and interpreters agree; but a sign may become conventional through use, even though it is an icon or an index (similar to, or naturally shaped by, its meaning).

Clearly, symbols and names do not work quite the way the other kinds of signs work. Symbol and name seem to require a mind to interpret them, a mind capable of making the kinds of distinctions discussed above. Thus, they must have a convention to link them to what they mean. However, it would be a serious error to think that because language and thought operate with symbols and names (both of them arbitrary signs), languages can use no other kinds of signs.

Trager's definition of a language (appearing in a late-1950s edition of *Encyclopaedia Britannica*) relates symbol to language: "A language is a system of arbitrary vocal symbols by means of which members of a culture carry on all the activities of that culture." But the symbols Trager was referring to are not words. They are the sounds that words are made of—vowel and consonant sounds and also intonation differences, even though we represent (inconsistently, in English) only vowels and consonants. These arbitrary vocal symbols are put together in arbitrary patterns forming units called *morphemes.* Morphemes are what linguists call the symbols that our social conventions associate with pieces of meaning. (Thus, *pieces* is made of two morphemes: *piece* means what *piece* means, and the *-s* means more than one.) As symbols of language, morphemes and the speech sounds that compose them may be single consonants or vowels or a whole word; but however they are composed, they depend on a spoken language community's conventions.

Today's signed languages also operate by social convention. Signers, like speakers, have to agree on what their signs mean, and meanings differ from culture to culture: the gesture that is interpreted as "light bulb" by an American signer means "coconut" to a deaf Polynesian islander and to many others living where coconuts grow.[3] The conventional aspect of today's spoken and signed languages, however, does not imply that language signs cannot have, or did not once have, iconic or indexic or symptomatic relations to their meanings.

Kangobai, the first deaf man on Rennell Island in twenty-four generations, and his contemporaries communicate in a unique sign language, as Rolf Kuschel, a Danish anthropologist, discovered. He called Kangobai the Silent Inventor, but of course his sign language was not the invention of one individual. It grew out of give and take, the everyday interaction in that island culture, between deaf Kangobai and his hearing companions. Kuschel's description provides a striking illustration of how natural signs become symbolic language signs, as the following two examples demonstrate:

(8) *te tamana* 'father'—the left-hand index and thumb perform a backward semi-circular motion on the outside of the left hip, beginning at the thigh immediately below the hip and tracing the above described motion towards the hip. . . . (This sign specifically indicated a tattoo on the hip of Kangobai's father, but has been adopted by those Rennellese acquainted with his sign language to mean any father.)

(10) *ta 'okete* 'elder brother'—the motion of pulling out a tooth is performed with the left hand. (Originally Kangobai's elder brother

who had once had a tooth pulled out; later adopted to signify any elder brother.)[4]

Although this language had been in use for only one generation when Kuschel discovered it, its users had already extended and conventionalized the meanings of both these signs. Both are clearly indexes (using Sebeok's definition of *index*). Both signs originally were also names: The tooth-pulling gesture denoted Kangobai's brother, and the hip-touching gesture named his father. However, after being used over and over by Kangobai and his companions, these two signs became symbols. They no longer referred as a name to one person but stood for an entire class, respectively, brothers and fathers.

Seeing Differences

Something can be learned by looking again at the different ways linguists and semioticians have used the term *symbol*. Some linguists seem to have conceived of different kinds of signs as mutually exclusive; believing that the words of a language could only be arbitrary signs. Others have gone further and conceived of language itself as arbitrary, even to the point of its being non-natural, not evolved from anything else. Trager, in the definition quoted earlier, however, was not referring to words as symbols but to their phonetic components. The question to ask is: Why are the vowels and consonants (and the pitch, stress, and juncture differences) of a spoken language arbitrary symbols?

The answer is that the nature of sound and the physiology of hearing demand a dual system of contrasts. Spoken words must contrast to distinguish, for example, what a speaker who says *horse* or *gorse* is referring to. Leaving aside the unanswerable question of how these words got to mean what they mean for English speakers, we can begin to see why they are different words: /h/ contrasts with /g/ in English (though not in some other languages) as both these consonants contrast with /k/ and /m/ and /t/ (in *course* and *Morse* and *torso*) and so on. In fact, each consonant of a language contrasts with the other consonants in that language. English may have only five or six words beginning with a single consonant before the sound spelled -*orse,* but in principle almost any consonant could begin such a rhyming word if one needed to be coined. Moreover, consonants contrast with vowels, and vowels contrast with vowels. The arbitrary sound classes thus formed, *phonemes,* allow a virtually unlimited number of morphemes and words to be formed from them. But the convention of the users of a language allows only some combinations, not others (e.g., *vorse* is not an English word, although *divorce* is). The vocal symbols, then, are arbitrary because they have to be to provide the contrast necessary to construct all the different words a language community needs.

Gestural signs are different in nature. When they look like what they mean, they are icons. When they point to what they mean or touch what they mean or copy direction or speed or manner of movement, they are indexes. When they unconsciously reveal their makers' feelings, they are symptoms. Symptoms by definition are not arbitrary and not yet symbols. How can they be language signs? The short answer is that certain symptoms of our feelings (commonly changes in facial expression) become language signs when these expressions are employed along with a manual gesture used as part of a signed language vocabulary. These symptoms thus add information about the object or action signified by the gesture in much the same way that adjectives add information about what is meant by a noun, and that adverbs add information to verb meanings.

An example of the first kind from American Sign Language would be a nose-wrinkling frown as one makes the manual sign conventionally standing for "apple"—the whole facial-manual sign is interpreted as "sour apple" or "rotten apple." The face (seen at the same time as the manual movement) may be expressing, as symptom, any of a number of feelings and mixtures of feelings about what a sentence says, or about some part of the sentence. In modern signed languages, facial expressions combine with manual activity to convey many nuances of meaning. Again, all this is subject to the conventions of that language community (see fig. 7).

Head movements may also modify a meaning that a manual action is signifying. For example, many years ago, I found that when an ASL user was signing what translates as "I won't go unless he goes," the manual part consisted of the signs glossed REFUSE (thumb–up fist jerked over the

DO YOU WANT THAT?

FIGURE 7. *Facial expressions add meaning to a sign and can, for example, change a statement to a question.*

shoulder) and GO (forearm extended forward obliquely as thumb and finger touch). Next, the important condition "unless" (called a conjunctive adverb by traditional grammar texts) was not symbolized by the signer's hands at all but was clearly expressed by a backward toss of the head. Immediately after this head movement, came the signs for HE and GO. (The index finger pointed obliquely to the signer's right, then the upper arm is rotated inward to point the forearm and hand to the signer's left as thumb and finger closed.) The starting point of their movement indicated that the signer, I, was the subject of the first GO and a third person was subject of the second. A richer translation of the head movement in that context might be conveyed as: "I won't go *unless I understand that* he is going." In fact, seen as the signer made it, the movement was very similar to a common gesture—the head movement that speakers often make while they are saying, "I understand."

Other contributions of nonmanual activity to discourse in ASL and other modern sign languages have been studied in detail.[5] Actual and rhetorical questions as well as many adverbial contributions to the main predicate are signaled by facial, head, eye, and other body movements. Many such questioning looks are interpreted similarly, whether they are part of sign language discourse or are gestures made by speakers. However, there are also facial and other nonmanual signs that only fluent users of one sign language understand, because only they know the conventions of that language community.

All this comes about because natural signs, over time, become conventional. Facial expressions naturally express liking, distaste, astonishment, assurance, doubt, interest, fear, and so on.[6] ASL convention has linked some of these expressions to certain manual signs as regular modifiers. A kind of mental inertia seems to have kept language scholars from seeing that visible gestures can be genuine language signs. The idea that language does not exist without speech persists, and yet the nature of signs and their importance to all life forms shows the universality of semiosis— something gets interpreted by some creature or person as a sign meaning something else.

Language and Instinct

Instinctive behavior, semiotically considered, is an automatic, genetically programmed interpretation of one kind of sign, a signal. Ants instinctively follow a trail left by other ants, but linguistic behavior involves symbols, which may be iconic, indexic, and/or symptomatic. Gestural linguistic behavior and signed languages involve even more: they operate with symbols that *are* iconic and indexic because these naturally and directly combine substantives with action or change. That is, they make sentences. Therefore, to call language an instinct (as Steven Pinker does in his book *The Language Instinct*) ignores the immense difference between humans and other animals.

The formal study of signs sheds light on the operation and the origins of language. Sebeok's sixfold categorization of signs and their different ways of signifying reminds us that semiotics, while a branch of philosophy's subfield called epistemology, nevertheless takes full account of biology. Even one-celled animals interpret signs. Animals with central nervous systems interpret icons and indexes more richly (e.g., birds avoid eating insects that look like sticks), and a whole range of predators correctly interpret, as indexes, the movements of their prey, just as prey animals watch carefully and interpret the movements of predators. Only humans, however, use names and symbols. There appears to be an evolutionary progression from signal and symptom to symbol, just as there is from bacteria to humanity. Physics, chemistry, biochemistry, and molecular biology explain bacterial and insect behavior, which can justifiably be called instinctive.

The interpretations different creatures make of signs are not by any means all instinctive. In animal species with larger brains and more complex nervous systems, much sign behavior has to be learned. In humans, vocabulary must be learned; even theories that posit a discontinuity between language and other animals' communication concede this. There is nothing instinctive to link most words of a spoken language to what a community agrees that the words mean.* The linkage has to be conventional, symbolic. With gestures, however, there is often iconic linkage (visible resemblance), or indexic linkage (the sign influenced by what it denotes), or both. The natural iconic-indexic-symptomatic linkage of gestures to meanings is usually taken for granted, but it makes communication possible when the parties to an exchange have no common language to use.

Many kinds of signs are involved in language, but the heart of the matter is that only the natural kind of linkage (iconic, indexic, symptomatic) can explain how language might have begun. Most writers about language and communication grant that gestures are semantic—they can see that signs are linked to meanings; but they ignore or deny the fact that gestural acts can be syntactic as well, that is, that gestures can form sentences. Syntax can be looked upon as simply another level of interpretation of human actions done and seen, however. Human brains at some time in the past began to interpret gestures as structures containing nounlike and verblike features—that is, early humans saw and interpreted the gestures as sentences.

Signed languages use the natural semantic linkage of gestures to meanings and go far beyond it; but this cannot explain why the spoken language words used to translate the gestures are constructed from the

---

*Presumably it is the grammar, not the vocabulary, that theorists call instinctive; but as is becoming apparent, the bare bones of what is called grammar seem to be prehistoric human recognition—through observation and its representation to vision by movement—that some things act and others change or are acted upon.

sounds they have. The relation of gesture to language, not just to vocabulary, has been largely overlooked, but it lies in the way signs signify. The question to ask, as Sebeok puts it, is "How do particular sign tokens *refer?*"[7]

They refer at least doubly. First, consider a spoken language. A vowel or consonant detected in the flow of someone's speech is a sign. It may signify that the speaker is using a language but not much more than that. Someone who knows the language, however, can interpret a sequence of several such sounds as a sign with meaning—a morpheme or word. A string of such words will be recognized as a sentence with even more meaning, because its structure signifies more complexly than would any random arrangement of the words in it. Of course, the rules for constructing words out of vowel and consonant sounds in any particular spoken language have to be learned. Children learn the words first and then begin to play with the rules, making interesting combinations of their own like "foots" and "getted." But well before this, they have been communicating with gestures in which word and sentence meanings have not yet been separated from their global meaning.

The rules for constructing sentences out of words, however, are another matter. Chomsky said in 1957 that these rules are too complex for children to learn simply by hearing sentences that adults happen to use in their presence, and he concluded that children must have been born with the rules in their brains. Another explanation is that visual signs, like speech signs, can refer doubly, and they do it much more simply.

A gesture can resemble something with its handshape and at the same time be indicating with its movement what that something did or how it changed. Such a gesture, commonly looked at as a single sign, can thus signify what the particular (nounlike) handshape stands for, what the (verblike) action or change it makes represents, and at the same instant what their union means. The gesture expresses a complete thought. It embodies syntax. The gesture *is* a sentence.

We can see things distinctly and at the same time see details of movement, but we use two quite different sets of brain circuits to interpret what we see. Humans (uniquely in the animal kingdom) can also configure and move hands and arms in a great many ways, so that the coordination of vision and physical movement enables human brains to comprehend more from a visible sign than any nonhuman brain seems able to do. Seeing both sentence meaning and word meanings in a gesture amounts to seeing language—syntax as well as semantics.

Accomplishing this double interpretation of a single sign is a large step in semiotics. The sign interpretant (a living creature) has evolved into an interpreter (a human being) and finds the sign to be signifying not just singly but on two levels at once. No longer responding to gestures as other animals do, the human interpreter responds to gestures as language signs—words and sentences.

This was a large step for humankind, indeed; but it required only a small evolutionary step. It amounts to a difference in degree, not in kind, of the cognitive skills that upright walking primates already had. Cave art and early sculpture provide evidence that early humans deliberately made iconic representations. Human skeletal structure and other remains attest to human dexterity and manipulative skills learned a million years before speech. There is no evidence, of course, of when and how the first humans made language; but the necessary pieces—dual vision, mobile human hands and faces, and a playful brain—were all there waiting to be put to work.

CHAPTER 6

~

Descartes Thought Wrong

IT SOMETIMES SEEMS that much of modern science has been carried on as if man was put into the world to have dominion over it, just as Genesis says. But it is an illusion to believe that by being objective we can describe things exactly as they are. Our minds, thoughts, and languages are part of the expanding universe, subject to its physical and biological laws, not separate from them.

What we see is determined by the way we see. In the nineteenth century, for example, James Clerk Maxwell and Heinrich Hertz discovered that light—what we see and what lets us see—is only one segment of a wide spectrum of perceptible electromagnetic energy. Science and technology since then have made it possible for us to "see" something of the vastness of outer space and a long way into the particles and forces of subatomic space. Linguistics, though, is still hampered by an ancient belief, stated by Plato and reaffirmed in the seventeenth century by René Descartes, that mind and language are unrelated to the lowly material universe, and that our souls are likewise independent of our bodies. Cognitive science shows that what we know and think results not just from the way things are but also from the way our thinking and knowing have evolved.

Philosophers over the years have considered many possible relations between the physical universe and perception. These range from the idea that things are just as they appear to be to the belief that the universe exists only in our conceptions of it. And how do we form our conceptions? Our senses and experiences play a major role, but to conceive of our world as science now sees it, we must have not only telescopes and microscopes but also more sophisticated means of extending our senses and conceptions.

The physical sciences have expanded our understanding of the universe because their theories are tested by experiment and modified when experimentation, new observations, and new theories require it. The sciences that study us, however, have had less success. Cognitive science has succeeded in bringing the study of mind, society, language, and culture closer to what is known about brain and behavior; but some people hold on to the idea that language is nevertheless unrelated to animal communication.

If it is true that what we see is determined by the way we see, we should be paying more attention to exactly how we do see. The difference between central and peripheral vision and their respective roles in showing us what we see has been known for some time. Central, or foveal, vision reacts to very small differences in light and therefore can show fine detail. Peripheral vision very accurately monitors movement—its speed, direction, manner, and path. Guided by our ability to see and analyze movement, we may be able to track a flying insect and catch it in a net. Our peripheral vision may also have told us whether it is the kind of insect that zips by in a straight line or one that flits up and down as it flies, like a moth or butterfly. When we catch and hold it still, however, we can focus it on the central area of the retina and make an exact identification.

All this is well known; less well known, less studied is how the nature of vision relates to language and how language relates to it. I believe that language investigators who ignore the physical characteristics of our eyes—and hands—risk being mistaken in their theories. In 1957 Noam Chomsky presented the phrase structure rules of generative-transformational grammar. Its familiar first rule is S $\rightarrow$ NP + VP, or, "A sentence may be rewritten as a noun phrase plus a verb phrase."[1] But this itself could be an index: natural events have the pattern: *Insects fly. Creatures act. Things change.* Possibly this pattern has affected the nature of the sign (in both the semiotic and the signed language sense) that represents them—and the right side of Chomsky's formula.

Natural events, human physiology, and language are related. First, actions occur in the natural world around us—things move or change. Second, our visual system uses one set of neural cells to see things and a different set to see movement or changes. Third, our upper limbs can both change their appearance and move. All three of these and the structure of the simplest sentence, S, share a two-part, ordered structure, which can also be represented abstractly: NP + VP.

We can see, for example, that different insects fly in different ways. Neural networks joining our eyes and brains give us information about their appearance; another such network gives us details about their flight. Being movement in space, these flights, like all creatures' movements, make sense to us because we ourselves have complex ways of moving complexly connected to our senses.* Combined in the brain, all this information is what we see. And as the sentence "Insects fly" shows us, the simplest language expression in sentence form has the same two-part pattern: things—insects and many other things—go into sentences as nounlike language signs. Flying, living, dying, and just about every other kind of action and change go into sentences as verblike language signs.

As Chomsky's first rule is written, it looks something like a formula for a chemical reaction. The rule posits the preexistence of sentence structure "S" as an abstraction and shows its composition; but chemical elements and compounds exist at the same time. For example, the formula $Na+ + Cl- \rightarrow NaCl$ for common salt, is reversible; not only do sodium and chlorine react to form sodium chloride, but we can turn them into chlorine and sodium again by passing an electrical current through salty water. But if we were to write Chomsky's sentence rule the other way around, as $NP + VP \rightarrow S$, we would imply that noun phrases and verb phrases existed first and were put together to make a sentence. This kind of reversal, however, conflicts with what brain scientists like Marcel Kinsbourne believe. They find that the brain does not assemble presorted

---

*It might be argued that by ourselves we cannot fly as birds or insects do, but thanks to the evolution of human upper limbs, our hands can imitate flight very faithfully indeed.

bits, bytes, or pieces. The brain works, as Kinsbourne says, with existing wholes, "carving" or "crystallizing" parts out of them.[2] The evolving hominid-to-human mind could have recognized nounlike entities and verblike entities at the moment it interpreted their union in a manual gesture as meaning what a sentence (the whole gesture) means but separable into the thing that moves and its movement.

What led up to language—the brain finding in existing wholes their essential components—may have been a slow, evolutionary process but one that took a sudden and surprising leap. Given the millions of years since anthropoid ape and hominid lines separated, it is entirely possible that a species in the hominid line, by using their hands and eyes and brains, made visible representations of what they saw and recognized. The first of these manual actions would surely have represented things and creatures in the environment, and the hands' movements would have replicated the familiar actions and changes of everyday existence. Human vision, hands, and arms with their unique joint system lend themselves to just this kind of use far more completely than does any other combination of sensor and effector systems.

This gradual change in behavior, the use of intentionally made signs, would have conferred survival advantages. Sharing sign-meaning links requires a social convention, and a social convention builds social organization, just as social organization is necessary for the conventions to develop. Chimpanzee social order seems to be based largely on who grooms whom, but hominid and human society depends on who signs to whom. Even signs with no more than semantic properties (that is, without grammar) can transfer information. When first used, these sign-meaning pairs could have led to new social ties. But something happened to punctuate this slow increase in social information transfer by visible signs.

At a particular time that may never be determined precisely, some of the creatures that had been developing physically (larger brains) and socially (using more information-carrying signs) saw that their gestures with their global meanings also could be seen as having nounlike and verblike parts. Realizing that, they crystallized parts out of the whole.

The existence of these gestures would have made possible the development of social organizations able to solve problems beyond individual capabilities.[3] Visible signs with syntactic as well as semantic properties would have altered intimate family relationships as well as making possible large-scale undertakings—actually changing the environment, when tools and fire came under control.[4] Social evolution would have been accelerated when manual gestures became both the cause and the effect of changed social interaction. When a group of individuals became aware that a gesture represented nounlike and verblike concepts as well as the relationship between them, they would possess full human potentiality. When handshapes were seen representing subjects, their movements representing predication, and the whole gesture a complete thought—at that point, human culture would have created a new world.

It would have been a world in which one species could see, *and state,* that creatures acted, that objects changed or were acted upon. This literally basic syntactic structure (which I have called "semantic phonology"*) does not so much negate the idea that there is a "universal grammar" as imply that humans first evolved and then created language.[5] Physical beings with complex sensor-effector systems carved language out of earlier primate-hominid gestural communication. Analysis of their behavior as grammar has followed—a million years or more after the fact.

Syntax, the basic structure of language, is a reflection of the natural world where creatures act and changes occur. Even before a human species emerged, chimpanzee-like creatures were using their dual system of vision to parse events they saw into concepts of living beings and their actions, as well as into inanimate things and what happened to them.[6] Animal life and movement (which is central to life) were present on earth millions of years before a human brain and central nervous system evolved in a body equipped with unique upper-limb structure and more highly evolved primate vision. Still later in the story, when there were creatures physically much like modern humans, some of them used their ability to coordinate perception and action to make gestural representations and

---

*Semantic phonology is so called because what composes the sentences and words of this first language is material that already has a semantic component: a handshape looks or points to something; hence it *means* that, and its movement depicts what it did or what happened to it.

Semantic Phonology

Sign phonology can be as complicated as anyone wants to make it; in this respect it differs not at all from phonology generally. As evidence for this I cite a review in the international newsletter *Signpost* of a book that gets to the bottom, says its reviewer, "of autosegmental, metrical, and also lexical phonology." Once highly regarded (by philosophers at least) as a safeguard against unnecessary over-elaboration, Ockham's Razor and even the computer programmers' vernacular KISS rule (Keep It Simple, Stupid) seem to have been forgotten in recent treatments of phonology—treatments that are almost, I am tempted to say, independent of language, certainly of language as laymen use it.

What I propose is not complicated at all; it is dead simple to begin with. I call it semantic phonology. It invites one to look at a sign—i.e., a word of a primary sign language—as simply a marriage of a noun and a verb. In semantic terminology, appropriate here, the sign is an *agent-verb* construction. The agent is so called because it is what acts (in signing as in generative semantics), and the verb is what the agent does. What could be simpler?

Semantic-phonological, or *s-p*, verbs are, like common verbs, transitive or intransitive. For example: when a signer of American Sign Language signifies 'yes', the sign agent (i.e., the signer's active arm including the hand) flexes at the wrist; it is intransitive, it has no object, it acts on no patient. But if the signer signifies 'stupid', the agent action continues until it strikes the forehead; the *s-p verb* in this sign is thus transitive: it has an object (the grammatical term); or it takes a patient (the semantic term).

Source: *From William C. Stokoe, "Semantic Phonology," Sign Language Studies 71 (1991): 107.*

eventually to perceive the structure of these representations and thus make them into language.

The step from primary to higher-level consciousness and genuine language is simple and elegant. Brains discern nounlike and verblike pieces in a gesture that combines them. Gestures have always had meaning for those who made and saw them (including chimpanzees), but gestures at first are global actions with global meanings. Because central and peripheral vision combine in the brain to let us see as we do, these humans of long ago could see that hand and movement together signified a complete idea—and sooner or later would see also that changing either the hand's appearance or its movement could represent a new idea.

The simple difference between a language and any other way of communicating information is that at base level, language represents two different kinds of concepts, the nounlike and the verblike (or noun phrase and verb phrase, as Chomsky saw so clearly) and their natural union (S). For centuries, it was customary to suppose that this syntactic union was arbitrary rather than natural. This thought made man not only the measure of all things but also a special creation superior to the rest of the universe, able to cogitate and assume proud mastery of it all. However, since the time of Darwin, science has been discovering facts that put the human species in a far different relation to the rest of the universe, suggesting humility may be more appropriate than pride. Yet the idea of a human-centered universe persists.

Prominent linguists have argued for several decades that language could not have evolved because it is so special that it requires humans to be born with their brains filled with every language rule—those for syntax, distinctive features, phonetics, semantics, grammaticization, morphemes, lexicalization, phonology, recursiveness, morphology, embedding, universal grammar, government-binding, and so on. The list keeps growing as linguists working within this paradigm keep subdividing the divisions. None of this, however, is necessary. The world's billions of people get along perfectly well using their languages without having any idea what the terms listed above refer to. Perhaps these rules are not parts of language at all but artifacts of grammarians, dimly perceived patterns of actual human behavior that were needed when language became vocal and invisible.

Once gestures had been seen and interpreted as containing nounlike and verblike meanings, they became language signs—visible forms naturally connected to, and connecting, word meanings into sentence meanings. The gestures themselves, physical actions that some primates had been making previously, did not have to change much at first. What changed was the way newly evolved creatures interpreted their gestures. After the change, however, the gestures were being made by creatures whose *brains and upper limbs* significantly differed from those of their predecessors. The emphasis is important; it states something too often ignored when language is studied.

Chimpanzees make a gesture that asks another to share food. They make a different gesture that invites grooming, but there is no evidence that they see or parse these gestures as the sentences "Gimme food" or "Groom me right here." The chimpanzee gestured to nevertheless responds as if the gesture means what our sentence says. Chimpanzee gesture maker and chimpanzee receiver have no need to parse or translate the gestures. They either respond as requested or they do not. But when some early human creatures saw these and similar gestures connecting something nounlike, "you," to something verblike, "do this," they became able to create other sentences—indeed, they had the potential to create an infinity of sentences.

Not by Hands Alone

Simultaneous visible phenomena would have assisted the contribution of manual gestures to "seeing" syntax. Facial appearance and posture, for instance, can change at the same time as manual gestures, giving a basic sentence additional ways of developing and changing meanings. Nevertheless, the simple but profound two-into-one pattern, common to vision, to a manual gesture, and to a sentence, is a beginning from which the rest of language could naturally have developed.

Congruent in structure with the pattern congruence of visible events and syntax, the gesture does not so much connect its components as consist of them. Our two-in-one visual system informs us about the living world, the creatures in it, and what they do; but language lets us transmit and receive that information and speculate about it, even when we are not directly experiencing it. We can see that insects fly and see the different ways they fly. We can also see (and feel) that we have hands with an amazing capacity for different movements. The evolution of our hands—from fingertips and thumb through arms and shoulders to the brain—may have been a small step in physical evolution, but it was a giant step toward human nature and language.

Chimpanzees, humans' nearest relatives in the primate order, have DNA 98 percent or more identical to humans, but human hands and arms and shoulders are significantly different. Furthermore, human bones and muscles and their controls have changed so much that we can keep our balance as we stand and walk on two feet, completely freeing our hands—something that other primates cannot do or do only clumsily. Finally, our thumbs are joined to the hand in a unique way and so have a movement potential quite different from that of chimpanzees. All this uniquely permits our arms and hands to make the intricate manipulations characteristic of human behavior (from painting on cave walls, building mounds, and stone circles to building rockets and space stations). It also permits configuring hands and arms to resemble the appearance and movements of a great many of the things we can see. Carried further, it permits the inception of a language.

Like other adaptations, this one carried a cost; human hands and arms are less well suited than chimps' for acrobatic life in trees, running on all fours, or hand-to-hand fighting. Pound for pound, a human athlete is no match for an aggressive chimpanzee. But hominid upper-limb structure and the eye-brain coordination that evolved with it enabled early humans to throw missiles, wield weapons in a new way, and compete effectively with larger, stronger rivals in the struggle for existence.[7] Human arms, of course, were put to uses other than fighting and food getting. Seeing the flight of insects, humans long ago would have been able, by moving a hand and arm, to depict the straight line flight path of a bee or the ups and downs of a butterfly's fluttering. If an early human actually performed these movements after, and because of, seeing an insect flying, it still may have taken a long time for those who saw them to understand what the hand movements meant.

What could they have meant? "Flying like this." "Bee." "Let's go that way; maybe find honey." We have no way of knowing, but the last of these imagined interpretations is suggestive. Humans, like many other creatures, prize honey as food, and long ago learned to follow bees, as birds and other animals still do, to the stored honey. At this early stage, the meaning of the gesture is still uncertain. Can it be a noun phrase, as the translation "Bee" seems to suggest? Or is it a verb phrase: "Flying like this"?

At its first use, the gesture was probably neither noun nor verb. The distinction between nounlike and verblike would have come later, when hominids or humans saw handshape as representing something and hand movement as reproducing the something's action or change. A gesture prompted by the bee's flight past the observer might at first have been only an idle hand movement, a playful replaying of a movement seen in peripheral vision. But idle, playful? We are talking about something as heavy and serious as language! Of course, playful! If anything about primate and human evolution is clear, it is that playfulness, experimentation, and just messing about lead the way—to maturity, to discovery, and to evolutionary change.

The hypothetical translation of the gesture suggesting "honey" implies that what was seen was a bee, but the gesture's handshape need not in any way have resembled a bee. The three-way congruence is still there: having seen an insect flying by, the watcher's visual system now sees a hand moving. The difference is that the hand was moved by a creature structurally and neurologically different from any insect. The hand's movement may have originally been a random act or a reflex, but it may also have been intentional. If it was intentional, the action might have been to catch the flying insect, but it may also have had a noninstrumental purpose. It may have been, potentially, a sign, performed to put into visible form an impression or feeling—something we might phrase as "Drat the mosquitoes!" or as "Damned bugs!" However, there may have been more going on: the hand's mover may not be expressing inner feelings at all but reporting, "I caught a bug," even though the gesturing hand does not hold anything at the moment. By representing "caught a bug," the second part of the two-part pattern has divided, and the verb phrase contains a second noun phrase, "a bug," connected also but in a different way to the movement, the verb meaning "catch." Seen thus, the gesture hints that a bee or bug might be inside the closed hand.

Disbelief in language evolution means putting language into a Cartesian or Platonic realm of disembodied ideas. Belief in a Cartesian separation of mind from matter requires believing that language never was as simple as noun phrase and verb phrase but came into the world with the myriad rules, syntactic strategies, and the parts of speech intact in a preprogrammed brain. Surely Descartes was mistaken.

From Gesture to Language in Special Cases

A most eloquent refutation of Cartesian separation of language and mind from nature and evolution is a story Roger Fouts tells in *Next of Kin*.[8] The book is a firsthand account of sign communication between humans and chimpanzees and within a family of chimpanzees in their own daily interactions. Naturally, this communication is not in the language of the academy or of the street; it is more like the language of very young children, but the communication and the behavior that accompanies it show these nearest relatives of ours have a similar ability to understand the surrounding world, to empathize with others, to solve problems, and to behave in individual—not in stereotyped "instinctive"—ways.

In the midst of the larger story, Fouts describes two autistic children whose acquisition of language makes an uncanny parallel with the sequence: gesture to language to speech. Interacting with these autistic children, he put his experience of using sign language with chimpanzees to use. He tells first of David, who at nine had undergone all known methods of treatment for autism and was declared by the doctors and psychologists as "too old to respond to psychological therapy or speech therapy." When Fouts first saw the boy,

> David was sitting in a chair, staring up at the ceiling light and waving his right hand back and forth rapidly in front of his eyes. Then he began rocking back and forth, reaching behind himself to run his thumb along the back of the chair . . . meaningless, repetitive behavior. . . . David seemed unable to process auditory stimuli and visual stimuli at the same time. That's why he hid his face in the wall when he screamed; he was shutting out his visual field while he made noise.[9]

Having been given permission to try sign language, Fouts waited until David stopped rocking and ran to the locked door of the room and "be-

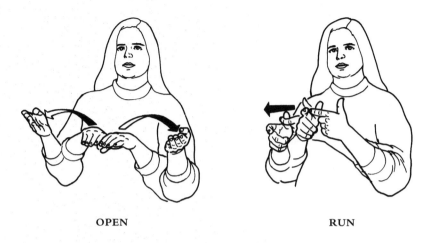

OPEN   RUN

FIGURE 8. *Examples of signs Roger Fouts taught to an autistic child.*

gan turning the locked doorknob furiously." Fouts then shaped and guided the boy's hands into making the sign OPEN of American Sign Language. Fouts then unlocked the door; David opened the door, went into the hall, and began running; Fouts caught him and guided his hands to form the sign RUN (see fig. 8). His hope was that "signing would capitalize on David's two working channels, the visual and the motor."

They met for only one half hour, once a week, "but within two months [David had] mastered a small vocabulary of signs and began combining them into phrases like YOU ME RUN."

> His behavior changed dramatically. There was no more screaming and rocking, and he was actually making eye contact with other human beings, initiating games, and inventing his own gestures to communicate what he wanted. For David's mother, the sight of her autistic son signing MAMA was practically a miracle. The doctors and nurses at the University Medical Center were equally flabbergasted. It was the eye contact, more than anything, that stunned them. They couldn't believe that this was the same child who had never acknowledged their existence. . . .
>
> A few weeks after David began signing, something quite extraordinary and unexpected happened. David began *speaking*.

First, it was only one word at a time: "open," "mama," "drink."
Then, as he began combining his signs into phrases, David also
began putting words into phrases: "Gimme drink."[10]

Roger Fouts's experience with David was not a fluke. Mark, a five-
year-old boy who "had been thrown out of three schools, including one
for learning disabled and emotionally disturbed children," also learned
to sign and then to speak. Fouts writes: "When I charted Mark's progress
in language development, there were four adjacent curves, each beginning a few weeks apart, that traced the same arc . . . one curve for signs,
another for signed phrases, a third for words, and a fourth for word
phrases."[11]

Objectors may say that because they were born with human brains,
David and Mark had all the essentials of language inside them all the
time, all the rules for creating phrases and making sensible requests
like "Let's you and me run." While impossible to disprove, this
explanation is not convincing. It does not explain why Fouts's intervention got results after other methods had failed. Previously non-
communicating, noninteracting boys only used language after Fouts
led them through stages, beginning with gestures, progressing to gesture phrases (of the form NP + VP), then to spoken words, and eventually to intelligible speech.

Whatever the actual neural networks in David's brain, Fouts's observations and conclusions seem plausible. Fouts reasoned that David's sight
and hearing were bombarding him so unbearably with two kinds of
stimuli that he reacted the way a normal person would if exposed
continually to painfully loud noises and rapidly flashing bright lights. He
tried to block out some of the disturbance. Motion—his rocking—
seemed one way of coping; hiding his face and eyes was another. When
Roger showed David how to use his own movements to make sense of
things, improvement began almost immediately. For David and Mark (like
all of us), mind and language are not separate from, but intimate parts
of, their physical being. It also seems likely that in the case of autism and
other neural abnormalities, upper-limb movement is easier to bring under voluntary control than the intricate mechanisms needed for the production of speech.

It is tempting to see in these two brief case histories (and in the description Volterra and Iverson provide of all infants' early gestural communication) a recapitulation of humankind's progression from gestural communication like that of the higher apes to the beginning of a signed language. The normal acquisition of spoken language, the amelioration of autism as Fouts describes it, and the progress from *Australopithecus* to some species of genus *Homo* seems to share a single dynamic pattern: gesture to language to speech.

Fouts's book makes a strong argument that good scientists need to listen to their feelings as well as their intellects. It made sense to consider what David might have been thinking or feeling. He obviously was not happy being locked in a room. His "turning the locked doorknob furiously" was surely a sign that he wanted to get out, a symptom of frustration. David knew and felt what it was to be shut up; he knew what (relative) freedom was; and he was frustrated by the failure of his knob turning to get him out. Fouts intervened in a way that reflected what had become his life work—interaction with humanlike creatures who have shown no propensity on their own to use our languages: "I took both his hands in mine, shaped them into the ASL sign for OPEN (palms down, side by side), and then moved his hands through the sign (opening them up and out as if opening a book). When we got into the hall, David began to run."

Here was a succession of events that David had no difficulty putting together to make sense and satisfy his urgency: (a) the door was locked and turning the knob did not work; but (b) movements of his hands (guided by Fouts) were followed by Fouts's opening of the door. "A week later, we met again. This time David went over to the door and signed OPEN. David recognized that the movements Fouts had guided his hands into making were connected with unlocking the door of the consulting room. At this moment David was demonstrating the same kind of manual and conceptual behavior that has been described ever since the Gardners began moving chimpanzee Washoe's hands to shape signs of ASL. Washoe and many other experimental animals, as the literature of three decades attests, after being shown or taught to make the sign OPEN, regularly and spontaneously use it to ask for opening of a refrigerator as well as doors, food boxes, soda cans, and bottles.[12]

Although apes can take this step, the step that Fouts taught David in a single half-hour visit, the apes' behavior does not minimize the significance of this step in human evolution. Indeed, the fact that apes can use movement to make representations is part of, and necessary to, later human evolution. As the human arm and hand evolved, the ability to use neuromotor activity to represent cognitive connections evolved with it. Human infants take this step early in life. Only later, if they can hear, do they begin to speak. It is reasonable to conclude that when David began speaking, his use of speech was related to the way he had learned to use his hands—the way he could represent to himself and others what he wanted and wanted others to do. Once able to connect thoughts with visible representations, the human infant, like David, can proceed to vocalizations for representing what has been manually represented. David took this step almost eight years late, but only after he had connected Fouts's hand-arm movements and his own guided hand-arm movements with the opening of a door. Hominid evolution may very well have proceeded languageward in much the same way.

Fouts has presented the once unthinkable idea that signing can be language put to spectacular use, confounding experts on autism and its treatment. His account also demonstrates—even though it is based on but two instances—that signing *can lead to* spoken language. Today, in normal circumstances, vocal representation begins when a child hears others using vocal noises and begins to connect these sounds with meanings. *But this connection happens because these meanings for some months have been developing in the child's perception, manual gestures, and understanding.* The autistic child fortunate enough to have a tutor like Roger Fouts may be years late in taking the step from gesturing to speaking, but as these two boys' stories show, after years of autism, after the so-called critical period for language learning had long passed, after psychologists and language specialists had given up, making manual, visible representations did lead to language and normal social interaction, and thence to speech.

Chimpanzees, bonobos, gorillas, and orangutans have not made the step to speech and are unlikely to do so. Given the physical and social environment to which they have adapted, they have no need to, and the vocal equipment for producing speech has not evolved in them. Besides a human brain, they also lack the highly evolved human hand and its visual, cerebral, and musculoskeletal connections. They have not, by themselves, taken the step to a gestural language. However, all the evidence implies that the ancestor we share with chimpanzees must have had the cognitive *potential for language,* the ability to form concepts. Species in the human branch a million or half a million years ago also may have lacked the vocal equipment and brain connections needed for fluent speech, but they had the potential, a larger brain, and above all the hand and upper-limb structure with brain connections necessary for making visible representations and more—a semantic-syntactic gestural language.

Hands, Heads, and Voices

The evolution of human anatomy that made speech possible included changes in the bones and soft tissues of the skull and neck. These developments can be seen when human skulls are compared with skulls of other primates and also when adult and infant human skulls are compared. A full discussion of these changes is not necessary here; a summary of the findings will suffice.[13] Physical changes (ape to man, and infant to adult) lower the larynx or change the position of the foramen magnum (the opening at the base of the skull through which the spinal cord passes) relative to the spine, thus bending and lengthening the vocal tract. This change makes simultaneous breathing and swallowing no longer possible and puts older children and adults at risk of choking. But the change results in a double resonance chamber, enabling the adult human vocal apparatus to produce the range of consonants and vowels a spoken language needs. Babies obviously do not speak like adults because their vocal tract is immature, but this evolution of the throat has a further implication: chimpanzees, though intelligent and able to form concepts and represent and recognize them when represented, seem to have throats incapable of human speech.

It is well worth emphasizing how different babies' earliest attempts at speech are from fluent adult speech—and from the speechlike productions of birds like grey parrots.[14] A baby's vocalizations sound different from an adult's, but there is every evidence that it has the capacity for language and, if able to hear, the capacity for adult speech. Both the human vocal tract and the avian syrinx (with a far smaller resonance chamber) are efficient producers of various sounds, but language requires more than a sound source; it needs a human body, and brain.

The anatomical changes in the throat (species to species, and infant to adult) that characterize adult humans are physical facts, and they certainly seem to be necessary for fully articulate speech. Yet this does not explain why they happened. Physiological and behavioral factors must have brought about their development. Nonhuman primates use their voices, of course; but our nearest relatives, the chimpanzees, have a rather narrow range of different vocalizations, and these are not fully under voluntary control.★ Their natural range of gestures is also limited, but with teaching and example they can acquire, understand, and use a number of gestural representations of things they want to say and ask for.

Suppose that early humans made many more manual representations of their concepts than did their nonhuman ancestors. These gestures would have enhanced their social and individual lives. But, with this enhancement, their hands, arms, and eyes would have become more and more occupied with communicating. If we then suppose that as they were using these gestures they made vocal noises as well, they might have discovered that a particular noise associated with a gesture could be used to represent the gesture *and* its naturally and conventionally related meaning. The next stage would have been the gradual or occasional disappearance of the gesture, leaving the sound pattern by itself to represent the meaning.

At that stage, speech would have been under double pressure to evolve: first, the pressing need to use the hands for other work than making language signs would tend to make producing manual language costly. Second, the need to make more and more such vocal signs would have led to increased use of the throat, mouth, and nose, and thus created the conditions under which further evolution of this part of the human anatomy would be advantageous.

★Fouts gives an amusing account of a chimpanzee's skill at raiding the cupboard only to give herself away by making the instinctive "food-grunts" when she had the cookie jar open.

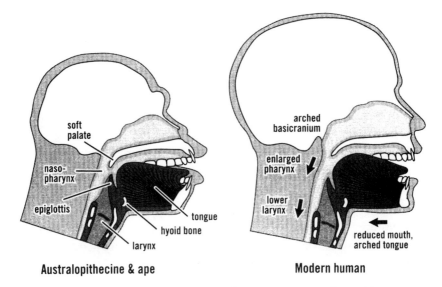

soft
palate

arched
basicranium

naso-
pharynx

enlarged
pharynx

epiglottis

lower
larynx

tongue

hyoid bone

larynx

reduced mouth,
arched tongue

Australopithecine & ape   **Modern human**

FIGURE 9. *Evolutionary changes in vocal tract anatomy made a wider range of speech sounds possible in humans.*

At the period in which this communicative development was taking place, it should be noted, physical changes in human anatomy would also be occurring. As succeeding hominid species used the upper body more and more for representation (as well as for making and using tools, building shelters and traps, preparing hides, cordage, fastenings, etc.), the head-forward posture of earlier species evolved into a more erect carriage. The skull was carried on top of the spinal column instead of projecting forward from it. This could have come about from the evolutionary advantages attained by increased use of visually guided signing as well from the instrumental use of hands and arms, even as it made more space for an elongated vocal cavity.

The fossil record leaves room for different interpretations, but whether the physical changes caused the larynx to descend and form a two-chamber resonator or caused the throat to change in shape from a gentle curve to an inverted L-shape, the result would have been the same (see fig. 9). It seems reasonable to suppose that both the benefits of human manual activity and the need for supplementing (and eventually almost entirely replacing) manual with vocal representation contributed to the evolutionary pressure causing the physical changes in the vocal tract.

The first representation of meaning by deliberately produced gestures would have been a watershed in human evolution but only a single stage in an ongoing process. Gestures indicating directions, sizes, and shapes give social groups using them more control over their physical environment. Gestures used metaphorically for time's passage and to indicate earlier and later time would give their users immensely greater control of all their activities. Gestures would also have given prehistoric social groups more control over their interaction with one another. A change in day-to-day patterns of living caused by representing relationships gesturally (and therefore being able to think about them creatively) would lead to a multiplication of meanings and consequent changes in the way the gestures were made. Obviously, there is very little about three-dimensional space that cannot be represented visibly by gestures. What new meanings could be added to these?

To explore this question it is interesting to look at a parallel process—the acquisition of language by newborns. Herbert H. Clark examined the fit between perceptual space—what everyone needs to know about the physical world—and the terms that an individual's language provides for this knowledge. Logic and nature agree that perception of space must precede the ability to talk about it. Moreover, "the concept of space underlying the English spatial terms, to be called L-space [language space], should coincide with P-space [perceptual space]: any property found in L-space should also be found in P-space.[15]

Clark presents two hypotheses about the relation of language space to perceptual space. The first he calls the "correlation hypothesis [which] claims that the structure of P-space will be preserved in L-space—that is, there will always be a close correlation between P-space and L-space." Clark examines perceptual space and notes that it is asymmetrical or unequally valued. Up is positive, down negative, because although gravity pulls downward, the human "canonical position" is upright. Likewise, forward is positive, backward negative. He adds, "there appears to be no reason, at least perceptually, to choose either leftward or rightward as being the positive direction."[16] But brain laterality and hand preference might tend to make a difference here too.

This perception is entirely cognitive—nonverbal or preverbal. It is the product of multiplying the set of physical features of life on the planet and the set of physiological features of a late-evolved bipedal primate with a large brain. Thus conceived, perceptual space is by no means neutral or valueless. In this it differs radically from space described by the geometer or physicist, who sees only logical opposition between *up* and *down*. For a human, to *get up* is superior to lying supine in order to *get on* with the business of living. To move forward is natural and positive as well. Forward is the direction human anatomy and physiology favors and the direction in which the human binocular visual system is directed. There is in all this a bias imposed not just by physical and animal nature but additionally by human anatomy and functioning. "Up" to quadrupeds must be much like "behind" for humans. It is a direction they are not adapted for seeing or going in directly and easily. Seeing and moving in those two directions is difficult for some and impossible for others. As Clark says, "Man is an inhabitant of a world consisting of objects, people, and time. And because of his biological makeup, he perceives these objects, people, space and time, and their interrelations in a particular way."[17]

After explaining the properties of space and the "canonical encounter" (the face-to-face situation natural for exchange of messages, "both verbal and nonverbal"),[18] Clark summarizes thus:

> When man is in canonical position, *P*-space consists of three reference planes and three associated directions: (1) ground level is reference plane and upward is positive; (2) the vertical left-to-right plane through the body is another reference plane and forward from the body is positive; and (3) the vertical front to back plane is the third reference plane and leftward and rightward are both positive directions.[19]

Clark's detailed description of how infants know perceptual space before understanding and using linguistic terms applies equally well to the perceptual space hominids lived in before the advent of language. Clark concentrates on the child's acquisition of language and not the origin of language, but this makes his analysis all the more impressive as an argument for the latter. The planes and directions in the paragraph above are all part of "man's *P*-space," as he says. And what is more, all of them are easily, naturally, and universally represented by manual gestures. (When there is difference, as when finger pointing is replaced by facial "pointing," it can usually be attributed to the force of cultural norms: "One doesn't point or stare like that at people; it isn't polite.")

Clark's first hypothesis, "that the structure of *P*-space will be preserved in *L*-space," must be true if linguistic space (the spatial terms of a language) was at first represented and understood gesturally. The universal gestures that point up, down, forward, back, and left and right do more than represent perceptual space; they externalize the perception and conception of perceptual space as they transform perceptions into conceptions; thus, they permit humans to act cognitively upon space. Much later in the evolutionary story, if the earliest spoken linguistic space terms were sounds that were used consistently coupled with the original gestures, these sounds would, through the processes of cultural change and sound change, eventually become the linguistic space terms of present languages.

Clark states his second hypothesis, on complexity, thus: "Given two terms *A* and *B,* where *B* requires all the rules of application of *A* plus one or more in addition, *A* will normally be acquired before *B.* . . . [and adds] (1) In antonymous pairs, the positive member should be acquired before the negative member."[20] For example, he notes that infants normally acquire the meaning and proper use of *in* before the meaning and use of *into. Into* includes all that *in* means, but it adds the implication of movement. This is shown naturally in gestural and sign language usage: to hold all or part of one hand within the grasp of the other can signify *in,* but moving one hand into the waiting arc formed by the other signifies *into* (see fig. 10).

Clark's hypothesis about spatial terms also fits well with linguistic hypotheses about marked and unmarked forms. As he writes, "Two of the first spatial terms to be noted are the simple deictic expressions *there* and *here,* which have been reported in most children with two-word utterances" [he cites publications in the 1960s by Braine, Brown and Fraser, and others, and adds] "with perhaps the positive term *there* predominating."[21] The probability that *there* does come first, not just as an acquired word of English but in the form of pointing "over there" as a handle on perceptual space, could be empirically tested. It would require observing not just children's acquisition of the terms *there* and *here* in

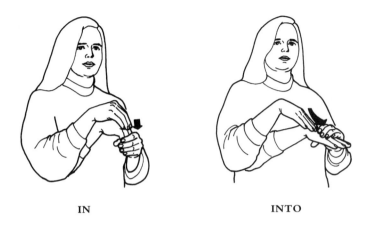

IN   INTO

FIGURE 10. *The addition of movement transforms* IN *to* INTO *and exemplifies the differences in meaning between the two signs.*

many spoken languages but also observing months earlier the gestural activity that precedes it.[22] Thus, the hypothesis to be disproved would be that children will say the words *there* and *here* before they attempt any gestural designation of "there" and "here." This hardly needs empirical testing to show its unlikelihood.

This kind of research might also test a corollary of Clark's complexity hypothesis. It is possible that the child points "there" while still at a stage when getting there or obtaining something from there requires the intervention of an adult. Thus, gestures that mean "go there" or "bring something here from there" might be later to emerge—with the implication that in perceptual space as well as in linguistic space the simpler precedes the more complex.

Although Clark's discussion is more than a generation old, it connects physiology, developmental psychology, and psycholinguistics in an unusually coherent and compelling way. In fact, its date favors the argument here. What the present stage of the original idea—gesture led to language led to speech—adds to Clark's argument is that something else, something visible but not often looked at closely, may operate to develop perceptual space itself and so greatly facilitate the infant's task of mastering linguistic space. In other words, the stages of infant comprehension and communication—perceptual-motor stages—might be shown to precede the acquisition of adult language, and, *a fortiori*, of linguistic space. Gestures and the operating senses, especially vision, enable infants to conceptualize space from their perceptions and the movements they make and see others make. But the infants' natural gestures are also the first representations they make of these all-important directions and other properties of space. Thus, when children hear or see the adults' linguistic space words, or signs, and realize that these tokens are synonymous with their gestures for the conceptions, they do not find it difficult to replace the gestural representations that they have been using for space with the adult terms.

This last step also suggests a testable hypothesis. When infants' gestures representing perceptual space are compared with the corresponding linguistic space terms that they acquire at a later age, there will be more similarity between early and late tokens if the language they acquire is a signed language than if it is a spoken language. The early and late tokens of deaf signing children can be empirically compared. This procedure would resemble lexicostatistic procedures, which look for cognates in vocabulary items for the same concept. If infant gesturing shows very early acquisition of perceptual space, there will be many cognates, many baby gestures similar to adult signs for the same concept. If, however, most of the adult signs are quite unlike the baby gestures, the hypothesis fails that gestures precede speech and facilitate the conceptualization of space.

Inner "Space"

The first makers of manual signs to represent concepts they had formed about the world familiar to them would surely also have made signs that represented their inner states. Use of even a few signs of these two kinds could have immediate effect. Suppose some of the sign makers were engaged in creating stone tools. The ability to point, to imitate movements others make, and to show satisfaction and dissatisfaction would permit useful gestural messages. Or suppose the kinds of scenarios Beaken and Kingdon have developed. Their conceptions complement each other. Beaken argues that the earliest languages arose as human groups pooled their labor to accomplish something for the common good, something that could only have been done with cooperation. Kingdon sees these early human populations as engaged in doing something about and to the environment, and so changing it.

Suppose a group of humans had succeeded in building a corral-like trap into which to drive prey. The work would obviously be done more efficiently if they were able to impart information to one another about the materials used, their placement, concealment, and so on. Indeed, having such signs would be the crucial component; without the ability to sign the purpose and plan it, the task would never have been embarked on at all. Chimpanzees build nests of a kind, but no one has found a fortification that chimpanzees built cooperatively as protection for the whole troop.

After the trap was built, it would have been necessary to organize the hunt to herd and chase the target beasts into the trap. As Kingdon points out, these things did occur; early man did prey effectively on large mammals. And as Beaken indicates, the cooperation needed for this depended on, and also fostered, the development of communication.[23] What could be more likely than that a language of body, head, arm, and hand movements initiated this kind of cooperative, environment-changing activity?

It is not necessary to develop a complete scenario for the success, which archaeology has documented, of early humans in hunting large animals. One example makes the possibility clear: in the building of a trap, materials and their disposition are major components, and whoever supervised the operation might need to tell another: "Bring that [what you are carrying] and put it over here." Such commands would and could have been given long before there was any spoken language—and what's more, they still are. "Bring" is naturally signified by moving the hands and arms toward the body from a starting position farther out. Holding the arms and hands in close imitation of the arm and hand positions of the one engaged in carrying something would strongly suggest what "it" was. And "put it down here" is and always has been naturally signified by movement of the hands and arms.

Far from being separate, mind and body, or language and body, are so intimately connected that each appears to be the other's cause and result. Evidence from several disciplines shows how important representation is—first visible, then audible—in the development of cognition.

As usual in evolution, this process is regenerative. Movement of body parts to represent concepts and their relationship builds mind; but minds—as collections of conceptions of classes, relationships, analogies, and so on— can also lead to changed bodies. The evolution of bodily form from *Australopithecus* to *Homo sapiens* could have been driven in part by mind represented physically. If some members of an early hominid population used manual-visual representation much more than others did, their posture would have become more erect as they focused on one another's signing. With this activity, evolutionary advantage would favor the human placement of the skull atop the spinal column rather than the quadrupedal mammalian placement of skull forward. The hands, particularly thumb placement, changed in the same two or three million years—a result not just of making and using tools but also of hand and finger manipulation to represent a rapidly growing lexicon and grammar.

CHAPTER 7

～

Language Metamorphosis

M Y ORIGINAL IDEA that signing can be language has grown into a belief that language began when a human species interpreted gestural signs both semantically and syntactically. The latter is particularly important, for gestures have syntactic power; they are not just visible movements that represent something else. Early humans saw the hands standing for things or creatures and the movements representing actions or changes. And as hands are physically, visibly, and cognitively connected to their movement, so are the hands' and movements' meanings symbolically (if not quite literally) connected to their meanings—hence, syntax.

A species already in command of language in kinetic and visible form had hundreds of thousands of years to adapt guttural, oral, and nasal physiology for making sounds different enough to represent each visible sign and its meaning. Using this dual-channel system of signs and speech, they would have connected the vocal signs and the visible signs to the same meanings. The conventional association of audible sign to meaning then survived the gradual disuse of the visible sign. Hands were now freed for other tasks, and speech predominated.

The earliest language signs surely referred to their makers and signified objects in the world around them. What they were seen to be doing or had done or should do would make up the primary content of their discourse. To the first creatures with our kind of bodies, they themselves, their world, and what happened in it would have been salient, highly visible, and increasingly intelligible. Less formidably equipped with canine teeth than earlier primates, our ancestors needed to see and understand the world as it related to them in order to survive. By helping each other consciously, they thrived and populated many regions of the world, and they changed the environment for their own benefit. Mike Beaken has conceptualized this pooling of resources and cooperation as a force moving toward the beginning of language.[1] Jonathan Kingdon thinks that early humans may have hunted, trapped, and driven large mammals to extinction and, intentionally or not, burned forests, with the result that grassland replaced woodland and attracted easier-to-capture grazing animals—some of which were ultimately domesticated.[2] It is hardly possible that early humans (before the era of articulate speech) could have accomplished all this without a visible language.

Vision may be the master human sensory system, but in order for seeing to make the difference it did, humans had to be equipped with the means to make use of the information acquired by way of their vision.[3] Early human activity required constant use of uniquely structured human hands and arms. Vision guided this activity, and mental categorization, learning, and memory aided by perceptible representations made this guidance more effective. There is a subtle but important difference between banging noisily with a stick, a threat behavior that chimpanzees engage in, and using a stick to strike a tree branch to dislodge unreachable fruit or nuts or using it to point to various directions that members of a foraging party should take. Vision-guided hand and arm use with a clearly conceived purpose was certainly part of early human behavior.

One cannot overemphasize the significance of human hand-arm anatomy, both for doing things and for representing things.[4] An experiment demonstrates the uniqueness of this anatomy. Hold an arm out supinated (palm upward). Now bend the hand edgewise away from the wrist—it will make an angle of about 45 degrees, leaving the thumb prolonging the line of the forearm and wrist. Chimpanzees and other nonhuman primates cannot do this. Next clamp the fingers against the still angled-out palm. Chimps cannot do this either, but a hand like this can hold a screwdriver or a scalpel, a sword or a plow stilt, a hairbrush or a club. When our ancestors carried this hand-arm configuration to the vertical and the hand was holding a spear, they found that evolution gave them another ability that other primates do not have. Chimps can hold a rod with fingers bent toward the palm, but their thumb is not involved and cannot be used to add strength and direction; likewise, chimps' hands cannot angle away from the line of the forearm as ours can. Human arm anatomy allows the back stroke of a spear throw or stab to reach further, thus imparting more muscle force to the implement's use.

A few purposeful and useful innovations—digging tubers, fishing out termites, and cracking nuts—are in the repertoire of chimpanzee behavior, but they are learned rather than instinctive or specieswide. Each occurs only in a particular population of these animals. What is instinctive in higher primates is not specific behaviors but a tendency, stronger in some than others, to experiment and improvise. Young, inexperienced chimpanzees learn food-getting skills of this kind by watching elders who learned them in the same way when they were young. But while chimpanzee mothers have been observed paying attention to the imitative actions of their youngsters, there is no evidence that nonhuman primate mothers deliberately set out to teach such skills.[5]

From the same ancestor as chimpanzees, our genus evolved perhaps two million years ago, with larger brains, more vertical bodies, and hands better adapted for manipulation than chimpanzee hands. One species in this line, *Homo erectus,* had as much conceptual power and motor-visual skill as chimpanzees, but the erectus' larger brain cases suggest that their cognitive and manual skills were more highly developed. Members of *Homo erectus* apparently spread from Africa to most of the Old World, and what they left behind shows that they performed more and more varied kinds of purposeful activity than did apes. The use of hands and eyes to represent concepts would explain this novel activity.

Manual actions could have become the first way to represent concepts formed within the enlarging brain, giving them visible form where the master sense, vision, could detect and interpret them. Simply by making a characteristic hand-arm action, while holding the hand *as if* it were holding the implement or object used in that activity, an individual would represent, and be seen to be representing or suggesting, exactly that activity. The action becomes a representation as soon as its maker and others see that the virtual action stands for the veritable action. Furthermore, attention focused on handshape and movement could have led to the development of sentence meanings and nounlike and verblike meanings all contained in the whole gesture.

Understanding a gesture and all that it represents as a sentence calls for a cognitive jump, but that jump is made from a solid platform of evolved visual, manual, and cognitive activity. The evolutionary solidity of the platform is dramatically attested by "mirror neurons" in primate brains: "These are neurons found in the monkey ventral premotor cortex that are action-oriented, context-dependent, and implicated in both self-initiated activity and passive perception. They are active both when a monkey observes a specific action (such as someone grasping a food item) and when the monkey performs the same action, where sameness implies not mere grasping but the grasping of a food item."[6]

These neurons in monkey brains, and—because evolution is conservative—in ape and human brains as well, are implicated visually and motorically with food, the hand, and with grasping food. Given the differences between monkey and human brains, the human use of a hand's action not just for food and grasping it but for representing all of that and other events, is entirely too natural to require a mutation of brain cells to explain it.

The course that language took over a million or so years does resemble closely something in biology—a life cycle that transforms itself, as the butterfly caterpillar's does. That a visible human movement could metaphorically be the egg out of which the gesture, as movement with rich meaning, emerged fits well the current understanding of the workings of the brain. So too does the differentiation of the unitary gesture into nounlike and verblike meanings. Neuropsychologist Marcel Kinsbourne writes:

> Rather than being assembled piecemeal and glued (conjoined, integrated) together, the percept, construct, utterance, or intention gradually differentiates out of the preexisting brain state. Diversity is continually being carved out of the existing unity. The operative question is not "How are the details assembled into the

whole?" but rather "How is the whole reshaped to incorporate the details?" . . .

Experience is not a composite assembled out of its parts. The contrary position—that experience is carved out of a less differentiated whole—gains plausibility. While no truly apt metaphor for how the brain works comes to mind, "crystallizing out" seems more fitting than "assembling together."[7]

What Kinsbourne says about experience here applies equally well to syntax, the sentence. Chimpanzee gestures are undifferentiated wholes, and yet creatures only an evolutionary step or two away from us can see that similar gestures may be regularly associated with concepts. Then, in the hands, eyes, and brains of humans, sentences, consisting at least of noun and verb may be said to "crystallize out" of the gesture, though this takes us for the moment away from the butterfly metaphor.

The Larva Emerges

Like the larvae of species that go through a complete metamorphosis, early human gestures must have been voracious, growing rapidly by representing item after item in the visible world. They helped individuals gather together with mutual understanding and work cooperatively to solve problems that could not be solved individually. At the same time, the ideas represented made social action more complex and more efficient. For example, a mother could easily gesture to a child, "Don't do it that way, do it like this," thus accelerating the child's learning of an important skill. The message, "Not there! Come over here!"—which could have been gesturally expressed more than a million years ago—would likewise affect the success of a whole hunting party.

Visually, kinesthetically, and conceptually, gestures can make the first manifestations of language. The kind of social life implied by the fossil record from one to two million years ago suggests a genuinely human means of communication—an early, not vocally articulated but complete, language. Evidence points to an early emergence of *language,* but the emergence of speech and the fully modern vocal tract is relatively recent.

If language had a role in culture earlier than the evolution of speech and the modern vocal tract, as archaeology implies, it had to have used a different channel—the channel prepared by eons of visual evolution and the relatively recent evolution of human arms and hands. Recall that human hands and arms can be configured to resemble many things and that their movements can reproduce the features of many kinds of activity. Nearly all vocal sounds, by contrast, are meaningless without a convention to link them to something else.

If gestures as language signs (arm-hand actions signifying both nounlike and verblike meanings joined) are analogous to the larval stage of insects that undergo a complete metamorphosis, the analogy suggests that, like larvae, gestures may have had to grow rapidly to ensure their successful passage through their next stage. Gestural representation of subject-predicate structure has a natural linkage to what it represents and also the capability of extensive permutation. It is creative. Once a hand pointing has been seen not just as a hand but as a nounlike sign focusing attention on something, that something must be visible. If the hand is representing something else by showing some resemblance to it, the resemblance will be to one or more of the object's visible characteristics. If the hand represents a person, some peculiarity of that person may be represented manually (e.g., a long nose, a scar). Again, if the hand represents an object, the hand will be shaped to show some salient feature of the object (e.g., compact and rounded).

The number of things the gesturing hand can represent grows constantly. Changing the appearance of the hand and arm configuration makes possible an infinite vocabulary. Despite what those ignorant of signed languages have thought and said about them, deaf people's signed language vocabularies are rich and productive. They also offer a challenge to traditional linguistic and grammatical analysis.

A handshape that represents something compact and rounded in a prespeech language gesture does not fit the traditional division of nouns into common and proper. The handshape does not refer to anything unique, so it is not a proper name. But neither does it name what we would consider a single class of objects. It could represent any of several kinds of things: a rock, an apple, a lump of clay, a large egg, or the skull of a small animal. What it does denote is something with a shape and size that a cupped or curved hand can hold comfortably. This handshape thus has the characteristics of both a common noun and a neuter pronoun; but once again, traditional grammars give us only these two choices. Grammarians want a clear answer: Is it this or is it that? Rigorous logic and grammar impose limits too strict. In describing a natural system like language, stating that something is either "x" or "y," however, is dogmatic, not scientific.

When a handshape of this kind, not categorically noun nor pronoun, is part of a gesture sentence, it can still serve as subject of a verb or object of a verb or preposition. Like a noun it can refer to something, but it does not denote as narrow a class as a common noun does. Representing the visible characteristics a number of things have in common, the handshape resembles a pronoun more than a noun because it can refer to something without being as specific as a common noun must. Unlike a pronoun, though, it does not need an antecedent. What could be more natural, in the period when language was beginning and not every last thing had yet gotten a name, than representing visibly the visible features of different classes of objects in order to say something about them?

Gestures or Signs?

Some spoken languages also have words that fall through the cracks of rigid grammars in this way. These words have been called "classifiers," and the term has been applied by linguists to just the kind of sign language signs discussed above.[8] Chapter 12 considers classifiers in detail, but a brief look at them here is necessary, for they provided a natural way for an early visual language (the larval stage) to grow before new vocabulary (noun signs for more specific classes of things) could be invented. Having handshapes that can refer to a number of things not specifically named allows useful statements to be made even when the thing actually meant is not more precisely designated. The way English speakers colloquially use "gizmo" or "thingamabob" or "whatsizname" shows how useful such imprecise markers can be for conversation.

Rigorous logic applied to the natural history of language does not fit comfortably with imprecision, of course, and it seems capable of ruling out any change or evolution. But synchronic logic ignores history. It supposes things as they are to have always been thus; time means nothing to logic. In the world Aristotle contemplated, if a thing was true it was not only true for all time but it also was what it was and nothing else. Such an approach categorizes a communicative system as either language or not language, without ambiguity or imprecision. Questions of how, when, where, and with whom language first began are all out of order, because by this kind of logic if something is not language now it could not have become language.

This kind of thinking allows no halfway. It assumes that, at a given time in earth's history, communication took place, but no language existed. Then, says such logic, at a later time there was language— utterly different from what went before. Grammarians of this mindset, who make categorical opposites of language and not-language, find no link between speech and gesture. In their edifice of formal linguistic logic, nothing could turn other animals' communication into language. This kind of thinking allows for nothing in-between, nothing partly language and partly not, nothing in the process of becoming language.

This way of thinking affects even some signed language scholars. They are troubled by a pseudo-question: How can an observer know whether an action seen is a sign of a signed language or a gesture? This question is really a paraphrase of logical categorizing. In effect it asks: Is that particular act language or is it not? The short answer is that no one knows from seeing a single, isolated action that looks gesturelike. Watching the gesture maker over time, an observer with some knowledge of signed languages should be able to detect whether the action seen belongs to a grammatical string of such actions (and thus clearly is language) or does not. A further test is to determine whether the gesture string is equivalent to, or translatable into, a stretch of spoken language.

The physical characteristics of the act do not determine whether something is a sign language sign or a gesture (such as a hearing speaker might make). The user's intentions determine whether it is language or gesture. Gestures hold the meanings a society's conventions have assigned to them, but sign language strings have more than meanings; they have syntactic force; they can be parsed.

I am often struck by the impossibility of translating everything I see into English when I watch an eloquent user of American Sign Language. This may reflect my own lack of fluency in the language, but native signers who have studied linguistics also characterize some parts of sign language discourse as "sign mime," describing the way that gestures, mime, and facial expression are swept into and become part of a regular sign language.[9]

Some of a signer's visible actions may not be strictly grammatical parts of the accompanying sign language sentences, just as an eloquent speaker's gesticulation, facial expressions, tone of voice, and voice quality are very much parts of that person's discourse but cannot be conveyed when the speech is transcribed in writing. More than four decades after George L. Trager, and Henry Lee Smith led the Summer Institute of the Linguistics Society of America, it appears ironic that they were examining the relation of paralinguistics (voice quality, etc.) to linguistics (morphology, syntax) and kinesics (gesticulation, facial expression) in the very year that Chomsky's *Syntactic Structures* was published, sending paralinguistics and everything not generated by grammar rules into limbo.

Early Growth

We have seen how easy it is to interpret a gesture composed of handshape and movement as a sentence representing something and what it did or what happened to it. It is also easy and natural to see a gesture showing the effect of action. To do this visibly involves only letting the active hand make one of many possible kinds of contact with the other hand or with some other body part. Two phrase structure rules of early generative grammar seem to formalize this larval language:

$$S \rightarrow NP + VP$$
$$VP \rightarrow V + NP_2$$

The usual interpretation of phrase structure grammar seems to be that one takes the first of the elements on the right side of the arrow, adds to it the other, and so creates the structure symbolized on the left of the arrow. Marcel Kinsbourne, Andy Clark, and others argue, however, that what comes first in the brain is something unitary, whole, and undiffer-entiated.[10] That whole, I believe, is a gesture with the "global" meaning gestures generally have. But sometime long ago, human communicators using these wholes could see within them, or in Kinsbourne's terms, could "crystallize out of them," such concepts as "something" and "what that something did" or "what happened to it."

Gestures are a common higher primate activity (e.g., chimpanzee gestures ask for food to be shared or invite grooming); and hominids' gestures, by their appearance, might well have suggested a replay of actions just seen. But if and when gestures became language signs, their users had *seen* that at the same moment gestures represented substance and action *and* their relationship. Noun, verb, and sentence—all three spring into human ken together, but from a tangible visible springboard, the moving hand. Recognizing what the hand and its movement represent reveals more—the whole is more than the sum of its parts. A sentence is a single, complex mental conception, not an additive process like "add VP to NP to get S," or "take S and make NP and VP from it." One might even play, as in elementary algebra, with this formulation:

a. NP + VP = S   A handshape and its movement equal a sentence.
b. S = NP + VP   A sentence is something nounlike and something verblike conjoined (things equal to the same thing are equal to each other).
c. NP = S - VP   Take a verb (movement) from a sentence (gesture) and you get a nounlike sign (handshape).
d. VP = S - NP   To get a verb, start with a sentence and take away the nounlike part, leaving the motion.

The operation described in (c) is not really an operation. A motionless handshape can be neither a gesture nor a sentence. And (d) presents another impossibility: motion with nothing moving. Yet this was the way I first analyzed ASL, considering the handshape or "dez" (designator) as if it were not moving, and the movement or "sig" (signation) as movement and ignoring what was moving.[11] To resolve the paradox in (c) and (d), one holds the hand still or makes small checked or repeated movements so the watcher will focus on what the hand represents. One makes a larger, smoother, continuous movement to emphasize the verblike meaning, directing the watcher's attention to the movement, not the handshape.

All this amounts to conceiving of something as a visible whole that contains visible parts united in a special way. The question needs to be asked thus: Conceiving of things in this way, do we recognize something real and natural, or invent or impose a structure? I believe the former. As a basic principle of language, this conception of a whole and parts seems to have a kind of transcendent truth in keeping with the way the brain works. In a similar vein, Leslie White has asked and answered the following questions about mathematics:

> Do mathematical truths reside in the external world, there to be dis-covered by man, or are they man-made inventions? Does mathemati-cal reality have an existence and a validity independent of the human species or is it merely a function of the human nervous system? . . .
>
> Mathematical concepts are man-made just as ethical values, traf-fic rules, and bird cages are man-made. But this does not invalidate the belief that mathematical propositions lie outside us, and have an objective reality. . . . They do lie outside us. They existed before we were born. . . . The locus of mathematical reality is cultural tradi-tion, i.e., the continuum of symbolic behavior.[12]

While this seems a proper conclusion about mathematical truths, it leaves our question unsettled. White's term "symbolic behavior" may show a way out, and one that is not totally incongruous with the belief that lan-guage is an instinct.[13] Language does require the functioning of the hu-man nervous system, but it also at first requires functioning of the body that the nervous system is an integral part of. My disagreement with the instinctualists lies elsewhere: White equates cultural tradition with "the *continuum* of symbolic behavior." Of course there is a continuum; it was masterfully described by Darwin and successors, and after heated debate, it has become better understood by biological science. It is also a semiotic continuum.

The human nervous system functions the way it does, I argue, not because its neurons are repositories for the rules of universal grammar or any other blueprint of the universe, but because it operates with information (electrochemical impulses) supplied by its perceptual systems. The human nervous system also uses information of a richer, more concentrated kind than that delivered directly by perceptual systems. Working with symbols, the brain-equipped, truly human creature took the few symbolic gestures used by earlier-to-evolve species, added copiously to them, and saw within them (by crystallizing out of them) two important categories of meaning: nounlike and verblike. This pioneer human saw also that these can be symbolized separately ([c] and [d] above). As a result, information, knowledge, and truth about the social and natural world can be shared to become cultural tradition—*symbolic behavior.*

The sequence implied by the butterfly analogy, gesture to language to speech, is only a brief episode in the evolutionary history of semiotic behavior; but it is the one most important to us. It would be a serious error to suppose that symbolic behavior is not part of the biological continuum called evolution.

The Larva Keeps Growing

To return to the development of early gestural languages, it is necessary to understand how basic symbols elaborated into more complex *visible* representations. Vision, which perceives more than one thing simultaneously, was the key. This ability to perceive multiple events at once in itself required little human adaptation. Primates and other creatures transfer information visually, as Darwin demonstrated in great detail, and as others have reaffirmed.[14] For a species using manual activity to represent conceptions, utilization of facial and postural displays of emotions adds qualities usually thought of as adjectival and adverbial. Whether the hand is representing something pleasing or disgusting, enticing or frightening, bloated or shrunken, and so on, the simultaneous facial expression immediately displays information that speakers of languages had to invent adjectives to represent.

Likewise, hand movements, while they can vary widely—quick, slow, smooth, jerky, and so on—convey adverbial information at the same time that they directly designate the action or change. Here too, facial expression and the whole demeanor of the one gesturing give the watcher copious information about the action and its manner and what the one gesturing thinks about it all.[15]

Spoken languages use prepositional phrases to modify nouns, verbs, or sentences to elaborate on basic syntactic patterns. The nature of hearing and sound makes such elaboration necessary. Gestural representation modifies basic meanings more simply. For example, to indicate that someone or something entered a shelter or cave or went under something, a transparent ASL sign pushes the flat fingers of one hand held with fingers gathered together through the curve made by the C-like formation of the other hand with its palm downward. In any appropriate context, this gesture will be interpreted as "enter" or "go into." But such is the nature of things and their manual representations that simply holding the same handshape motionless within the C-formed other hand expresses quite naturally the important spatial concept "in." Moving the dominant hand changes the simpler meaning "in the cave" into the meaning "enters cave." No elaborate grammatical explanation is needed. Both signs are equally simple. What the hands do *is* the difference between "in" and "go in" (see fig. 10 on p. 99).

Alterations in the hand's movement also give expression to meanings that English expresses figuratively; for example: "She edged in little by little" or "She entered in a rush." Gesturally, the first can be expressed with the hand making small, hesitant increments of movement, the latter with a faster and larger than usual movement—quite possibly with a facial display adding further information.

A genuine signed language (and by the present definition, the first sign languages were genuine) uses much more than hands. If the hands are visible, so is the rest of the body. The English description of an action might be: "She entered in a state of shock." Visibly expressing it requires only that the sign maker depicts (i.e., mimes) shock. The English translation refers to "her" first state and her state later, but leaves the timing ambiguous: was she in shock before, during, or after entering? The nonmanual expression in a sign language report makes her emotional state at the appropriate point in the narration. Because vision works differently from the process of hearing speech, the gestural expression can make the time sequence clear.

Languages and Caterpillars

The butterfly analogy suggests that one natural process may be in some ways similar to another. I have no intention of claiming that caterpillars are actual models of language, but the analogy opens the mind to alternatives not often considered. It prompts a new look at the possibility that from the inception of language to historical times, languages may have undergone a metamorphosis somewhat analogous to the caterpillar's becoming a butterfly with radical change in form and appearance. An analogy between two natural systems does not claim that a natural system works like some ingenious human invention (from clockworks to computers). It suggests instead that we look to biology rather than logic or mechanics to understand more about language origins.

Comparing the life history of butterflies to that of languages has the advantage that both are natural. It also reminds us of a most important principle: evolution never makes something out of nothing. A butterfly emerges from a chrysalis constructed by a caterpillar hatched from an egg laid by the butterfly. Spoken languages too must have origins. I believe that they emerged from signed languages when the latter were requiring so much manual activity that other necessary uses of the hands were being impeded. Vocal sounds then became surrogates for the gesture-meaning pair.

One thing is certain: if it happened this way, those who began using voices to take over some of the work done by gestures would have had ready-made a system of concrete, visible representations of concepts and relations. They would also have had a convention linking forms to meanings. They would have had nounlike, verblike, adjectival and adverbial signs and meanings, and above all, they had all of this within open-ended, expandable sentence patterns. They would have had a working grammar, a syntactic-semantic system in order, requiring only the use of vocal sound complexes to associate with, and eventually substitute for, visible sign-meaning pairs. Brains long accustomed to managing a gestural language could easily have developed new pathways to and from the visual processing regions and reconnected them to the auditory center.

The change of muscle control from the upper limbs and face to the tiny muscles inside the vocal tract would have been even easier, because the brain centers that serve speaking activity are virtually the same ones that serve complex manual activity.[16] The following formulation implies that language in the brain would not have had to pick itself up by its own bootstraps when it became preponderantly vocal:

GESTURE : HANDSHAPE + MOVEMENT :: SENTENCE : SUBJECT + PREDICATE

"Gesture is to Handshape and Movement as Sentence is to Subject and Predicate."

The butterfly analogy lies entirely within the animal kingdom and so is subject to biological knowledge; as such, it suggests certain questions: If language did change from visible to audible form, what natural processes would have been involved? Can a pattern of progression from one form to the other be discerned? The analogy and the questions it suggests do not ask for belief but for testing. The answers prompted by the questions, some of them at least, can be tested against present knowledge and discarded if they fail.

The Next Stage

The larva of an insect that undergoes complete metamorphosis enters an inactive state as pupa. Inside its chrysalis, eating and other activity is at an end, but cellular growth and internal change continue. Does the analogy collapse here? Would language, once it had begun to be part of human behavior, ever have become inactive? Quite possibly its outer manifestation might have changed, if the kind of activity is distinguished carefully.

The use of language for communication as well as for formulating one's thoughts (or modeling one's world) is certainly activity of a kind, but here we are considering evolutionary activity—what happened over hundreds of thousands of years, not what happens in seconds or milliseconds. It is conceivable that once language had begun when humans saw complex meaning in gestures, and when the activity of using language had grown and spread among the human species, more and more ways of making and modulating meanings would have developed—enlarging, but not radically changing, language.

As the visible language became ever richer in ways of representing meaning, its uses would have multiplied exponentially. A time might have arrived when use of the upper body's resources for language seriously interfered with other tasks that arms and hands and eyes were needed for. Grammatical pattern growth and proliferation might well have stopped then or slowed down, while a new, no longer gestural but vocal way of representation was developing to take over the main work. During the period when the incidental vocalizations that had accompanied the gestural representation were being refined until one vocal pattern could represent precisely one gesture (or gesture part) with its meaning, the rapid development of the gestural language might have slowed. If this metamorphosis did take place, the replacement of visible representations by audible representations may have been in a sense internal activity, similar to what happens inside a chrysalis.

CHAPTER 8

~

Language in a Chrysalis

WE KNOW that language is able to express more things in heaven and earth than any one person can imagine. Language is also able to express everything that scientists have found, everything that science fiction writers can imagine, everything that poets have said, and most wonderfully, all that we, they, or anyone else may ever say or think. This is the potential of language, but a potential and its realization are not the same thing.

The very first language utterances were probably prosaic stuff. The first signers would have had no suspicion that this new way of representing separate and connected things was opening up infinite possibilities. Surely at first they would have used their gesture sentences to refer to creatures and objects and activities that were right there in front of them—thoroughly familiar sights, the events of everyday life.

Nevertheless, the first language signs would have been epoch-making. No contrast of before and after could be sharper. Before language signs, all the visible attributes of the world were out there—some dimly reflected in early hominid world-modeling systems or concepts—but none was fully expressible. Afterward, all the world was still there; nothing had changed, except that now there was a species with the potential, the power conferred by vision-brain-motor linkage, to see and conceptualize this world *and to represent* these conceptions to themselves and to each

119

other, in natural, easily produced, visible, doubly signifying (wordlike and sentencelike) language signs.

The first language signs would not have raised any barrier between seeing and thinking about these matters and feeling and reacting to them. It is difficult today, after centuries of science and several millennia of Western philosophy, to put thought and feeling or intellect and emotion back together. They have been too thoroughly pulled apart by philosophers and reductionist scientists. Yet there is good reason to suppose that they were once united and that our languages and our Western cultures force us to use two names—emotion and intellect—for one global, holistic engagement of body-mind. We make a division where none exists naturally.[1]

It is not necessary to go far afield to find cultures that unite the mundane and the supernatural, cultures that do not divide consciousness into thought and "mere" feeling. Native tribes of North America have languages with roots as ancient as any, but unlike people in the Hebraic-Hellenic tradition, some of them keep and use signed languages as acceptable alternatives to speech. Moreover, with and within their languages, they preserve a tradition, a view of life, in which feeling and thought are one.[2]

Gender and Early Language

Something else, besides speaking and signing modalities, makes languages different from each other. Author Deborah Tannen suggests that men and women use language differently: women, to make connections and develop relationships; men, to negotiate power and status.[3] This view of gender difference in language use has been criticized by some; but her view is compatible with the gesture-to-language-to-speech hypothesis. If Tannen has it right, men and women would have used language differently from the beginning. It is plausible to hypothesize that making connections and developing relationships was a mother's chief role in prehistoric society. That role may have begun even before her child's birth—when she was choosing its father. Men building shelters, defending territory, or hunting needed to be clear about who "gives the signals" and where each one stands in relation to the leader and to each other. Thus, to understand language in human perspective, it makes sense to think of the uses of language as equally important with its grammatical forms.

The perspective opened by Barbara King, which shows the roots of language in the primate order, indicates that every mother, even before there was a language, had to transfer essential information to her child as quickly and effectively as possible.[4] That information gave her children a better chance to grow and survive. All social animals share the biological drive to produce and foster offspring, but human animals differ radically from their nearest primate relatives. The human baby's gestation continues for about a year after birth. The human brain triples in size during this period, and after the child is no longer within the uterus, the brain requires large amounts of physical nutriment and even more sensory and interactional stimulation.

Human interaction and behaviors that must be learned have added to, rather than replaced, biological drives and gene-driven changes. Creatures who had realized that their gestures could represent relations, and not just things, changes, and actions separately, would naturally have used this knowledge to full advantage. This better way to transfer social information must also have helped the human brain to evolve—to grow larger and more complex as it developed greater and greater new connectivity between its parts. Acquired behavior is not gene-transmitted to offspring, but early humans who had learned to communicate with gestural language signs had already inherited an openness to new ways of doing things and of solving problems. These new ways of transmitting information allowed them to pass on to offspring what they had learned. With their new skill at communicating what they had learned, they would have built societies, cultures, and these would have given offspring with their genes a better chance than more backward populations had to compete and survive. This kind of communication also helps to explain why human beings, unlike other animals, live a long time after their reproductive period; parents may be busy at other tasks, but grandparents make grand teachers.[5]

Many of the connections that other mammals' brains and nervous systems need are developed during gestation. But in our species, the laying down of many of the new brain circuits for representing concepts must occur not in the womb but during the months after birth. Interaction with others *and the use of language signs* allow the infant human brain to develop its full potential.

Farnell's work on social movement challenges the belief that there would have been a sharp separation between mind and body, knowledge and experience, reason and feeling, and verbal and nonverbal, when language first developed. In the distant era when language was beginning, women would have used their language signs to tell their children what they needed to know, to show them how to do essential tasks, and to make them aware that they lived in a social milieu where relationships were crucial. As this kind of language use began, women would also have shared information with each other about these matters. Men would have been using their first language signs as they went about activities that required cooperation and knowledge of who is able to direct operations and who must watch and obey.

The original connection between the language signs women used in child rearing and the language signs men used for hunting and fighting might have been that both sexes saw hands and arms representing persons and animals and things, and movement depicting changes and actions. The actions, agents, and changes referred to by the two groups might for a time have been different—men's and women's vocabularies still differ; but with the common feature of seeing what moved as subject and the movement as predication, women and men would soon have established a common language.

Formal studies of spoken languages prevail upon us to ask whether these early systems should be designated as separate languages or as dialects of one language. Both women and men were using language signs to transfer information. They were moving, doing things with their arms and hands and eyes—all this coordinated in their brains. Farnell entitles a section of her book "Mind Is a Verb."[6] I think that our language itself leads us to make too much of the grammatical markings that speech must have for distinguishing nouns from verbs and to forget the very real, visible, kinetic, and cognitive difference between substance and accident.

Magic and Language

In the basic activity of everyday living, we are likely to think of persons and animals as having the ability to move, to perform the actions we see them doing. But we think of objects as things that are acted upon and are powerless to act. Myth, religion, and magic became possible once a manually represented language could connect different handshapes with different hand movements. When a hand representing something natural but not animate—for instance, a tree or a river—is moved to signify that the inanimate object acted or caused an action or a change, it becomes possible to say that stones speak, that a tree (or the nymph within it) casts spells, and that other impossible things happen. Thus, the difference between what was observable and what could be imagined and represented widened.

People talk constantly about abstractions like life, but how is *life* the name of something? Life certainly has a material component: living things are made out of carbon, hydrogen, oxygen, nitrogen, sulfur, and other elements. But the whole is much more than the sum of these parts. Is *life* then a very capacious collective noun? Or is it actual biological activity? Is life in fact a verb—really essential, incessant movement? Cells are never at rest until they are dead; matter itself is energy transformed; what looks and feels solid is made up of particles moving in microspace. But our spoken languages do not allow free speculation about such things. In English, *life* is a noun and *live* is a verb, and wondering too much whether the distinction is real is uncomfortable. The case is somewhat different in a sign language community, however. The ASL signer brushes the thumbs-up A hands or L hands upward on the trunk, and context and the recipient decide whether *life* or some form of the verb *live* is the appropriate translation.*

Language is also a noun, even though it does not exist except as activity, both internal in brain-body and externally as something accessible

---

*Note that the recipient's intuition may be aided by the signer's ability to make small repetitive upward moves for "life" and a longer, more deliberate upward motion for the verb form.

to one or another sensory system. Life itself surely began not as a thing but as movement, cellular activity. Likewise *language* is something human brains and bodies *do*.

Still, it is worth asking how much languages have in common. And if this question is permitted, what about their differences? Are there languages or just language? Some theorists believe that one set of rules—like the eighteenth-century "laws of nature"—govern all language. Natural laws, though, are few in number and confirmed by centuries of experiment and observation, whereas the rules of "universal grammar" are conjectural. Once observant, upwardly mobile hominids grasped the natural connection of visible signs to what they signify, making these signs resemble and point to things and reproduce actions would have become their way to model the world and to communicate their conceptions of it. The rest—speech and even grammar as we know it—would have grown from there.

Signed languages suggest also that before the evolution of speech and the invention of writing, people did not separate mind and body or thought and emotion; in signed language all representation of thought and emotion comes directly and observably from the body's actions. The person as a whole not only moves in a social setting but also experiences "moving" within as emotions. Visible changes and movements present evidence of this neural, muscular, and visceral movement to others.

Movement in a social context, like dance, religious ritual, and fighting, "make meaning" and so cannot easily be distinguished from language.[7] Placing each such activity in a separate category is the result of a particular way of thinking, a tradition extending from Aristotle to Descartes and farther. Logic, as these philosophers define it, invites examining language and society in the same way that chemists and physicists examine a piece of matter. However, when physicists probe deeply enough, they find that what appears to our senses as a solid, stable thing is really movement also: particles smaller than atoms moving even inside a molecule of hydrogen or a diamond. Physicists cannot determine ultimately whether matter is "wee sandy stuff" or waves of energy.[8] Perhaps we are fated to find the ultimate truth slipping further away from us as we pursue the big questions; but if so, it would be well to remember that our knowledge about the origins of language and languages is still at a stage comparable to that of physics before Newton, or of biology before the microscope. And even this may be giving linguistics more credit than it deserves.

There is no linguistic microscope, no Michelson-Morley experiment to confirm any language theory, though some linguists insist that language is an instinct. Languages and thinking provide our only tools for examining language and thought unless we stop thinking of the body and the mind as separate and look at the growing understanding of brains and neural activity. On the one hand, neuroscience is showing in more and more detail how seeing, moving, gesturing, and speaking are managed by the brain and the rest of the body and its sensory systems. On the other hand, examining movement may show us how human beings and their society evolved and how the knowledge that individuals and cultures possess was gained.

∼

I can imagine readers at this point wanting to ask, "Since all this speculation about the origin and evolution of language rests on bits of circumstantial evidence and on a particular way of arguing from them, what of it anyway? What good can it do?" Such knowledge can do a great deal of good; it can change the way people who hear and speak think about people who do not, as I have known ever since discovering more than forty years ago that deaf people have real languages made of visible instead of vocal symbols. This insight has eliminated the prohibition of sign language in some schools for deaf children and allowed at least a toleration of signing; a few, bilingual, schools even use genuine sign languages, rather than invented codes, for instruction. This knowledge also has opened vocational opportunities formerly closed to deaf people. In a coming generation this knowledge may even prevail to the extent that there will be no teachers of the deaf left who believe what they were taught in special education programs and never tested for themselves. The lie that to be deaf is to be mentally defective may be at last put to rest.

There are other positive consequences of a theory that suggests language signs were first made with visible, naturally signifying icons, indexes, and symptoms. First among these is the change in thinking that could be brought about by seeing how visible language signs emphasize the indivisibility of body and mind in a way that spoken language signs do not. Body movements, especially facial expression change and movements of hands and arms, express feeling and thought and create social meaning, which is a blend of thought and feeling. Recognizing that dance, ritual, and language have a common source in body movement can help restore wholeness to education. Programs in which art and abstract subject matter are in balance have made remarkable gains in test-measured achievement as well as in school attendance and student and teacher morale.[9]

A case could be made that many of the crimes of colonialism grew out of too narrow, too divided a view of language and other behavior. Members of imperial societies argued that they engaged in slaughtering, subjugating, and enslaving "savages," not fellow humans, thus easing their consciences as they made their voyages of discovery to impose their moral standards and to enlarge their wealth. By assuming that their victims had subhuman minds and inferior spoken languages, which they had to "eke out" with pantomime, imperialists justified for themselves their depredations.

Understanding meaningful human communication as a single mind-body complex that integrates individuals into society, and not as language separate from the body and from social context, can open minds to a new understanding of individuals, society, and even of meaning and how it is created. If the scenario presented here captures at least some of the way that language began, there will no longer be any excuse for separating language from all other human activity and locating it in special modules of a hypothetical "language organ" within the brain. A new generation of scientists can avoid the mistakes of the Cartesians. The sterile separation of language theory from physiology and microbiology can end. As long as theorists maintain that the rules of all grammars are in the brain at birth, and as long as neuroscientists studying the brain anatomically and clinically find this unproven, the study of language will be cut off from culture and science and all human activity except speaking. This new way of looking at the movement of interacting individuals is already being explored. Adam Kendon, author of *Sign Languages in Aboriginal Australia,* is now engaged in finding how Italian speech and gesture—two kinds of language from the body—define roles, meanings, and social interaction. David McNeill has shown how gestures accompanying speech are not incidental additions but another manifestation of the same system that organizes the spoken language.[10] Brenda Farnell has pointed out that we use a divided way of thinking when we contrast verbal with nonverbal, and separate gestures from words. Case law recognizes this division but treats both parts as essential: a witness may refer to a person as "the defendant," or may speak the defendant's name; but the judge will still ask: "If that person is in this courtroom, will you point out that person." Although it is traditional to consider what witnesses say as verbal and therefore as a use of *language,* and to consider their pointing as *nonverbal* communication, in this court situation the physical act has more legal standing than the spoken answer. Farnell suggests that her Assiniboine Nakota consultants' "combined use of speech and gesture might indicate choices between two equally available and expressive media according to convention and context [which] was entirely overlooked in this theoretical [traditional linguistic] framework."[11]

Treating speech and gesture as equally viable expressive modes would force language scholars to reexamine the conventions and contexts of language use. Many of us have been taught to think that what someone *says* expresses what the person "has in mind," and that what the person *does* expresses "nonverbally" emotion or "affect." Such a division is not possible in Assiniboine and many other cultures; their spoken and gestured languages do not support it. In such cultures, thought, attitude, intention, disposition, and feeling are all expressed as movement outward from the body.

That some human societies still treat visible movement and vocalizations, or sign and speech, as equally valid ways to communicate suggests that in earlier societies, even after people had discovered how to use their voices along with their visible signs, signing and speaking may have been considered equally valid. What is needed now is a new look at societies and cultures, a way of looking that will be possible once the Cartesian curtain separating verbal and nonverbal territory comes down. Or to paraphrase Hamlet, "There is more unity in our universe, René, than is recognized in your philosophy."

Language and the Natural World

Brenda Farnell notes that Benjamin Lee Whorf "drew attention in 1941 to the fact that grammatical structures of specific languages allow speakers to presuppose certain classifications of experience."[12] This is a respectful and positive way of acknowledging what Whorf argued. For more than fifty years his writing has been interpreted (usually unfavorably) as saying that a language constrains its users' thinking. Consequently, the effect of language on thinking has been minimized by innatist linguistics. But it remains a fact that once our language gives us a name for something complex like life, language, government, or intelligence—when these common nouns are added to all the others—it is easy to think that what they name is something that can be fully defined and analyzed in the same way that the anatomy of a frog can be explored in a laboratory. In a signed language, however, even inanimate objects like chairs and airplanes have to be named with hands moving. Nouns and verbs are dynamic in signed languages. Close observers have pointed out that the movement differs subtly but categorically when signers refer to things and actions; slightly modified manual movement changes American Sign Language nouns like CHAIR and AIRPLANE into verbs, respectively, SIT and FLY.[13] Yet persons, not chairs, sit, and it is human agency that makes flying airplanes possible as well as dangerous.

Sign language signs, because they involve visible movement, allow and encourage us to think of things in different ways. Thus we avoid the hubristic presumption that we already know everything there is to be known about the structure of language, and about human experience and the universe. American Sign Language has a sign that translates as the English word *language,* but that does not make language into something that will stand still while we dissect and analyze it. In fact, the ASL signs that are translated as "language," "story," and "conversation" need only slight changes to mean "communicate," "tell," and "explain." This should remind us that language is not reality; "the map is not the territory." Language is only the best way we have of trying to understand and discuss reality. Looking at a sign language in use we cannot escape seeing that language is movement. In learning more about sign languages, we may even reach the conclusion that thought and emotion are movement also and no more separable than minds and bodies.

Some environmentalists like to say that modern, Western views of the natural world are inferior to those of Native Americans and other indigenous peoples who feel themselves part of nature, even to the extent of praying to the spirit of a tree for forgiveness before they cut it down. Those who profit from clear-cutting forests and selling lumber deride this as naive superstition; and the bottom line favors the developer, not the naive native. The exploiters' attitude can be traced to the mind-body dichotomy: what they have in mind is justified by Descartes and others who find the mind (human, of course) and its ideas not only more important than forests, dumb beasts, and the savages who worship them, but also on a different moral and epistemological level. This attitude is shaped in part by language, as Whorf knew. There is plenty of evidence that Native Americans, Aboriginal Australians, and other peoples, far from being naive, have a coherent and sophisticated way of seeing their world and themselves in it. Their signed and spoken languages, which do not allow separation of movement from life, affect their thinking. But equally, seeing the world as they see it must have influenced the way their sign languages developed.

The Assiniboine Nakotas, when telling a story or talking about important matters, sit or stand facing south, facing the wind that blows from the south and brings life and renewal to a northern people. And the wind, or the great spirit, or "that which moves," like another religion's mantra, "I am that I am," has a powerful shaping influence on myth and cosmogony and language. Wind, like spirit, is movement; only the effects are visible. This view of things also reminds us that while energy may be invisible and matter is only too present to our senses, energy and matter, like mind and body, are one, and that visible movements must have helped to create meaning and the human capacity for knowing and understanding even before there were intricately encoded and largely invisible movements in the vocal tract.

The neural structure of the human visual system coupled with the mobility of human upper limbs and faces provided a natural way for various body movements to *represent* something other than themselves. Human individuals' movements in groups provided social information, but the ability of human hands to point to, and be shaped to resemble, other things enabled humans to make hands and their movements into multitudinous icons and indexes that became symbols. Because of the physiology of human vision and movement, those movements that were seen to reproduce real world events and to unite actor with action, and experiencer with change, could very easily and naturally have become the first language signs. Given the primate predisposition to gesticulate and vocalize simultaneously, it would have been easy for vocal sounds that accompanied the language signs to be taken, after centuries or millennia of incidental coupling, to represent, first, the movement with its associated meaning, and later, the meaning alone.

This brief scenario also reverses a common way of looking at language. Until at least the late twentieth century, vocalizations were generally accepted as the primary symbols of all languages, and only the relatively modern invention of alphabetic writing supposedly made possible secondary graphic symbols for language sounds. Some scholars even imagined that gestures and the gestural signs used by deaf people were tertiary symbols parasitic on the graphic symbols.[14] Sounds alone cannot point to or resemble anything but themselves or their source. Even if a human group had a convention linking vocal sounds to various actions and individuals and objects, there is nothing in the sounds themselves that could have bestowed syntax on a simple system in which a vocal sign represents a concept.

If this new paradigm replaces the old paradigm, which equated language with speech, it may do more than spark scientific rethinking. When gesture to language to speech is seen as a natural progression, it will no longer be possible to suppose, as was once done, that some people have minds and language so impoverished their speech has to be "eked out" with gestures. Instead, the users of spoken and signed languages will be seen (as Farnell has already seen in the Assiniboines) as having an integrated view of the universe and their place in it. Deaf people will also benefit. Already, recognition of, and respect for, their sign languages is having positive social and economic effects.

CHAPTER 9

~

Emerging from the Cocoon

Tʜᴜs ғᴀʀ, these pages have suggested that language began when visible gestures were used to represent the actions of beings or changes in the state or location of objects. This conclusion, in turn, how-ever, raises an equally searching query: How and why would visible lan-guage signs have relinquished their function to vocal signs? Or, as opponents of a gestural origin theory would ask: If there ever was a ges-tural language, why has it degenerated into nonverbal communication? If language is the special part of human nature that we think it is, why would the expression of it have changed channels? Why would visible actions, which can make language signs naturally and show directly what they signify, have given way to the unlikely use of human voices to make language signs arbitrarily?

First, it is important to realize that before humans appeared, animals had evolved with at least a limited ability to conceptualize. Many non-human animals have a clear conception of what is food and what is not, for example, and which situations are safe, which are dangerous. Chim-panzees can go further than this in making sense, for them, of that part of the world they live in. Entirely apart from human intervention they learn to make a few signs, such as the one that connects food with a request to share it. The next step would be a dawning recognition by hominid sign makers that their gestural signs *were connecting*—were making

131

a connection between something that could act and the actions it performed, or between something and the changes that happened to it.

Some of the offspring of the early human line must have been brighter and quicker to *visualize* than others and so been prone to doing things in new ways. What these innovators were doing would have been both visible and invisible. With their hands they would have been doing things that the other members of the troop did. They would have been using gestures to communicate a few requests and demands. But the brighter ones must have been paying closer attention to these movements everyone saw, for inside their developing consciousness they would have seen that their own movements resembled things and actions they were looking at.

At that juncture they would have begun to make these actions intentionally. Such activity would have led to new brain-eye-hand neuronal circuits. And with the new neuronal group mappings of what their hands and eyes were doing—making signs that combined elements and their relations—language would have been born, a language made of visible signs.

Visible language signs are detected by the sensory system that evolved in primates, who for ages had lived in trees above the forest floor. Their way of life demanded vision for seeing and deciding, for example, "Is that branch safe to leap to?" It also demanded vision adapted for judging distance, speed, and depth and the coordination of vision with motor acts (i.e., binocular vision, not vision divided by the muzzle as in other quadrupeds). Vision for primates was a key to continued existence. But vision alone was insufficient. Vision had to be coordinated with the movement of limbs evolved to act in ways compatible with what was seen and felt, grasped and let go.

Most primates' sense of hearing is important too, but it does not need to differ in any major way from that of other social mammals. Mammalian as well as primate infants, if they are to survive, must learn early to recognize and respond with appropriate behavior to a mother's call or cry, a predator's shriek or roar, and to other sounds, like calls to the family or troop to assemble or disperse or repel invaders.

Sounds, actually sound-response pairs, are common features of the life of many species. Sounds facilitated communication and still do for arboreal monkeys and apes. However, after the anthropoid primates came down from the trees, a radical difference in anatomy and its uses occurred. Some of these new primates not only gave up using their front limbs for walking but began to use them in new ways. Chimpanzees use their hands and arms to dig up tubers, make probes to pull out termites, and crack nuts with stones. Hominids must have begun to make more and different kinds of tools for more and different highly practical, survival-enhancing purposes, thereby evolving the subtly but significantly different upper-limb structure of humans.[1]

Upper-limb activities are fully visible and fully coordinated with the proprioceptive sense; that is to say that hominids would have known, just as modern humans do, how it feels to be holding an object with one hand and doing something to it with an object held in the other hand, monitoring the activity by both feeling and seeing it. They could likewise feel and see the action of throwing. Chimpanzees practice indiscriminate throwing too, as unwary visitors to a zoo will discover while dodging what is hurled at them through the fence. But negative, unaimed throwing to chase others away is not the same as purposely aimed throwing to kill or stun prey. At some point after chimpanzees evolved to their present state, humans learned not only how to throw a missile accurately but also how to shape a stone point, fasten it to a carefully prepared straight shaft, and hurl it at edible prey. Skill at throwing develops best when only one arm is used, studies have shown, and thus the differential use of right and left hands, and hemispherical brain specialization known to be involved in language, might have evolved.[2]

Sight and Sound

Visible action is a major conveyor of social information in primates. Barbara King argues that because apes used more of this with better effect than monkeys, hominids must have gone further in the use of visible action for communication than apes.[3] Sounds are important too, but acute hearing is not enough for decoding speech; there must also be a finely honed ability to recognize specific features of sounds as they are heard and a convention for interpreting them. For instance, to decode speech, the hearer has to learn when two different sound patterns are to be understood as identical for the purpose of meaning and when two identical or near-identical sounds must be interpreted as contrasting. ("Tomayto" and "tomahto" refer to the same thing but *shake* and *shock,* or *sum* and *some,* do not.)

In the higher primates, a superior ability to see and interpret complex and varied visible signs had evolved. But to make speech express language, the vocal mechanism had to develop more versatility, and hearing had to make not only finer and finer discriminations but also arbitrarily sort them. This articulatory evolution was completed only about 150,000 years ago. Hence, the questions asked earlier: Why would the more easily detected and decoded visible signs have gone out of use and been replaced by vocal signs, which are more difficult to monitor and can be easily misheard? It is natural, surely, for ways of doing important tasks to become simpler and more efficient, not more complicated.

To compare the relative simplicity of the two modes, consider this: human upper-body gestures look essentially the same whether they are produced by men or women or by adults or children (although secondary sexual differences may tend to make women's sign language movements appear smoother and more graceful than the rougher, more angular movements men make). Human voices vary widely, however. Not only do male and female voices and adult and child voices differ; but they differ also within those categories: a man's voice may lie anywhere in the range between high tenor and basso profundo; a woman's, between coloratura soprano and contralto; children's voices have a still higher upper range. The receptive system for hearing speech—the physiology and functioning that linguists call phonology—has to compensate for these differences. Practice has taught listeners to automatically make the adjustments needed to recognize some language sounds as "the same" even though they may be pronounced by voices octaves apart or different in other ways. But this only emphasizes the relevance of the question about changing modes: Why, when upper-body actions can be immediately seen for what they are, when they often show or point to what they mean, and when speech needs a complex auditory system to interpret difference as sameness and sameness as difference—why ever would there have been a change from clear, obviously transparent visible language signs to audible language signs that require this complicated coding and decoding process?

This is a hard question because there can be no doubt that the language signs most people use today are made with voices. Deaf people form their language signs differently. To possess language is to be human; to be human is to possess language. This seems self-evident, and yet in historical times, it was not the possession of language but the ability to speak and understand speech that most often determined human status.

Four facts suggest that language in visible symbols came before speech:

1. Sign languages still exist.
2. Spoken utterances often require accompanying visible signs in order to be fully understandable.
3. Only visible signs have natural links to concepts and syntactic structures.
4. All human infants use gestures to communicate before they master the language of their caretakers, whether that is a spoken language or a signed language.

A fifth suggestive fact is that vocal and gestural symbolization are closely related. Centers in the brain controlling speech production are the same as, or adjacent to, centers controlling manual movements; thus, the former may well have evolved from, or along with, the latter.[4] When gestures are defined as intentional, willed productions of complex, interrelated, and coordinated muscle actions, it becomes clear that gestures, most of them invisible, also produce speech.[5]

In that long-ago era when visible gestures may have transformed hominids' communication into language, the cultures would have been very different from our modern, speaking cultures, if only because the two kinds of languages are built around very different perception-action systems. Much information that speakers take in by listening, deaf signers take in by looking. This use of different sensory systems for detecting and processing language has a direct effect on brain activity. Brain blood flow monitoring shows that deaf and hearing children of deaf parents process sign language differently, apparently because of the effect of auditory stimulation on cortical organization.[6] Although today the brain's processing of audible and visible primary language symbols can be monitored by scanning techniques, we can only infer the cultural changes that a radical prehistoric change in transmission and reception channels would have caused.

Changing Channels

The consequences of changing from signing to speaking may have been revolutionary, but the causes of the change had to be cultural. In the first place, there has never been a total switch of language channels. Gestures, visible signs made by hands for transferring social information, have never disappeared from human use. They remain not only in the primary sign languages of deaf people, and the alternate sign languages preserved by certain Australian, Native American, and African groups, but also in every-day use by speakers everywhere. Many experts perversely label these gestures "nonverbal," but such labeling manipulates the meaning of *verbal* the way a thimble rigger manipulates the walnut shells hiding the pea: "Now you see it, now you don't." The following tandem quotation, in which Thomas Sebeok quotes Gregory Bateson, presents an example of this:

> [L]anguage-as-a-modeling-system, not speech-as-a-communicative-tool—[evolved] in *Homo habilis.* This ancestral member of our genus appeared, rather abruptly, only about two million years ago. Language, which was an evolutionary adaptation in the genus, became "exapted" . . . in the species *Homo sapiens* a mere three-hundred thousand years ago in the form of speech. It took that long for the encoding abilities of *Homo sapiens* to become fine-tuned with our species' corresponding decoding abilities. Note that, as in human ontogeny, verbal semiosis has by no means replaced the far hoarier diversiform non-verbal manifestations, for reasons that were spelled out and elucidated by Bateson:
>
> "[The] decay of organs and skills under evolutionary replacement is a necessary and inevitable systemic phenomenon. If, therefore, verbal language were in any sense an evolutionary replacement of

communication by [non-verbal] means . . . we would expect the old . . . systems to have undergone conspicuous decay. Clearly they have not. Rather, the [non-verbal sign uses] of men have become richer and more complex, and [non-verbal communication] has blossomed side by side with the evolution of verbal language."[7]

Both Bateson and Sebeok seem to have confused the physiological functions of specific organs with language, which is not the function of any one organ. And besides, those body parts physiology has singled out and termed *organs* are in fact parts of a complex system in which all organs function to maintain the whole physical organism.

Language is a special kind of behavior of the whole organism. It requires the brain's normal functioning to connect sensory, motor, and cortical networks and the brain's coordination of the sensory systems and of larger (skeletal-muscular) or smaller (respiratory tract) motor systems. In plain terms, a heart pumps blood and a stomach digests food, but neither a mouth nor a hand nor a brain nor any other single organ makes language. Hence, "oral language" and "manual language" are barbarisms no matter how often they have been used to contrast the languages of hearing and deaf people. Language, though socially indispensable, is not a physiologically vital function. The use of the terms *verbal* and *nonverbal* simply begs the question of the relationship between spoken and signed language. Bateson and Sebeok seem to use the adjective *verbal* to mean "expressed in and by language" rather than "spoken as opposed to written." They then use the term *nonverbal* to set off from language anything they consider to be nonlanguage or not expressed in language. Because neither Bateson nor Sebeok fully recognizes that language is a system that may utilize either vocal sounds or gestural actions as its primary symbols, the word *verbal* as they use it applies to spoken language only.

When the terms *language* and *verbal* are recognized as true synonyms, referring to the same system, the phenomena that Bateson and Sebeok refer to are very different from reality. Vocal *and* gestural semiosis—the use of sounds and visible actions as signs—has always been part of general primate behavior, which includes the behavior of humans. Neither in human nor in animal behavior have visible signs for information transfer completely replaced audible signs, nor vice versa, except in the case of blindness or deafness.

Gesture and Voice Together

What is more likely than replacement and decay of visible signs is that some million or more years ago, gestural acts became language signs by the steps outlined here. (From the beginning, vocalizations are likely to have accompanied visible language signs. This is certainly true in a child's progress from being without a language to having a gestural communication system to having adult language.) At a later stage, the familiar vocalizations could begin to be used without the gestures they usually accompanied. This might have come about relatively quickly or over millennia during which meaning was expressed by visible gestures with incidental vocalization. Members of a social unit, hearing the sounds that normally accompanied the gestures, would still grasp the meaning even if the gestures did not appear in full. Likewise, if the eyes strayed away for a moment, or if occasionally the one vocalizing while signing omitted a visible gesture, the message would still get through. This is what sometimes happens with alternate sign language users.

Neither speaking nor gesturing needed to decay or disappear. Use of these two modes of expressing meaning and these two sensory channels for reception have always been part of human life and cultures; but they are used in different ways at different times, in different circumstances, and for different purposes by peoples with different cultures. Vocal and gestural communication are not natural adversaries, and only the invention of writing led to the mistaken assumption that speech alone could be language.

Another way to see this evolutionary change with revolutionary effect is to recognize that language signs have always been gesturally expressed, first and mainly by visible gestures, later primarily by internal gestures producing and modifying sound; but visible expression of language signs has never disappeared. No organs, no skills had to decay, conspicuously or otherwise. The takeover of language sign production (in that large portion of the population that could hear) by a physically evolving vocal tract would have liberated the hands for myriad other tasks.

A fully human voice tract and an auditory system finely tuned to decode increasingly complex vocal signs freed the human visual system for other uses—until the invention of writing co-opted vision for the new skill of literacy. Using the eyes for reading, it should be noted, does not lead to the conspicuous decay of the ability to decode speech.

Bateson seems to have fallen into the error of mixing logical types.[8] Although physical skills are used to communicate and to make language signs, these skills are quite different from physical skills used directly and instrumentally, like walking or flying or digging up tubers or fishing for termites or cracking nuts. To be sure, many animals' signs are instinctive, "built in." Leaving a pheromone trail as ants' bodies do is hardly to be counted a skill, but when chimpanzees invite grooming by making a characteristic gesture, the skill is in communicating social information to achieve a purpose, not in the directly instrumental use of the hands. Humans are certainly not less skilled than chimpanzees at transferring social information. It is natural and virtually universal among primates to produce and react to both visible and audible signs. When hominids or humans first used language signs they too would very likely have been producing both movements and vocalizations. The natural relation of visible signs to what they denote would not necessarily have rendered their producers mute.

The change from making language signs out of visible gestures to making language signs with voices might be likened to the shift 150 years or so ago from canals to railroads. Although railroads today carry some of the passenger traffic and much of the freight that was once entirely consigned to canal transport, the canals have not disappeared. Some of them continue to be competitive for carrying certain kinds of freight, and they are increasingly used for recreation.[9] Although gestures inside the neck and trunk produce the sounds that form most people's language signs, visible signs still carry information that is important, even essential, to them. No sudden cataclysmic event would have been needed to alter what actually changed—*the proportion* of language signs produced by "inner" and "outer" gestures.

The change in language channel use probably proceeded gradually, beginning with a few individuals but spreading to make a whole signing community into a speech community. Eventually whole populations would have followed the lead. The later part of the Middle Stone Age, perhaps as recently as fifty thousand years before the present, is the most likely time when such a gradual change neared completion. This is the period in which stone tool technology took off, suggesting a major cultural innovation rather than a gradual improvement of older techniques for working stone. Learning to make stone tools would have proceeded more rapidly when the instructions could be given vocally while the hands were busily working with the tools and materials.

But questions remain: Why would a shift from making language signs for the sense of vision to making them for the sense of hearing have begun? Why and how would speech as a surrogate for signing have persisted and spread?

These are not the usual questions asked about speech. Surrounded by speakers and only minimally aware that there are people and whole communities whose language signs are gestured rather than spoken, most people (language scholars with them) have assumed that language was always spoken, and that drum and whistle languages, ancient rock carvings, sign languages, and the like must all be surrogates for speech.

If speech began as a vocal accompaniment to visibly expressed language signs, it would have been quite natural to discover that the message was understood even when only the sound was heard. The habitual association of a sound pattern with the missing gesture *and* its meaning would fill any visual gap. From that beginning, the growth and spread of vocalization and the lessening dependence on movement and vision would have proceeded as natural cultural change.

This change in proportion within the dual-channel system of communication could have come about simply and naturally. Certain visible signs might be deliberately left out, but if sounds had usually accompanied the visible signs, those on the receiving end would still receive the complete message. Discovering that spoken sounds could more and more often be acceptable substitutes for the visible signs would have allowed unaccompanied vocal expression to increase in frequency until it became the preferred and usual way to communicate. At that point, the visible signs could be put to other uses—as still occurs with speakers. Trying to account, however, for the existence of primary sign languages under the assumption that language began as speech presents obstacles; for example, why, when even ad hoc gesturing can show naturally and at times with superior accuracy precisely what one means, would a primate species have invented and developed the "arbitrary" and "unmotivated" system of spoken language, and yet still keep on using the natural, gestural, system for certain purposes?

The number of people who use primary and alternate sign languages are few enough and their languages so little known that it has not occurred to many scholars to consider whether visible language signs might have been the origin of words, sentences, and syntax. In most human societies, gesture is now used so differently from speech it seems that gestures could never have performed the functions of speech. And yet, though sight and hearing are both important for information transfer in all primate behavior, sight is still the master human sensory system.[10]

Other primates, to be sure, make no separation between language channels, because there are no language signs to be separated out. General primate communication is both audible and visible. Human interaction is also mixed in mode, except that in historical times written language has provided an obvious though questionable sorting principle. Some may feel comfortable in saying categorically: "This is language, this is verbal; that is not language, that is nonverbal." To confront this kind of assurance the American poet Carl Sandburg had an apt anecdote; a railroad brakeman once greeted him as he sat down in the smoking car with the familiar conversation opener of the 1920s in question form: "Whaddya know?—" and then after a pause, added, "—for sure?"[11]

Out of the Mouths of Babes

Children's use of gestural and vocal signs also provides evidence for the evolutionary primacy of gesture. Not only do all children, hearing as well as deaf, communicate gesturally before making genuine language signs,[12] but hearing children's vocal output from a very early age shows them imitating the sound-pattern or intonation envelope of whole sentences before they can reliably produce individual words.

A sentence, whether expressed in a signed language or a spoken language, is a different order of sign (a different logical type) from a sign that in common parlance is called a gesture or a word. A sentence is a syntactic semantic structure; in it something is joined to something else (agent to action, subject to predicate, experiencer to change, or in current linguistic terminology, NP to VP). But a sentence also expresses a meaning more complex than that of the individual words in it. And whether it is accessible to the sense of sight or the sense of hearing, a sentence also signals its function. Over and above what it says, a sentence states something or asks or answers or demands. Writing does not fully represent this highly important function, the sentence's purpose; and speech signals it with changes of intonation. Questions end with rising pitch; statements end with lowered pitch.[13]

In signed languages, the signals that announce a sentence's purpose are as clearly visible as the rest of the sentence. The signals denoting sentence type, like many of the lexical items of signed languages, bear a natural relation to what they mean: To ask a question, the hands and arms that express the questioning sentence remain relatively high in the signing space, as if ready to pull out or grasp the answer from the one being questioned. At the same time the signer's face wears an expectant, readily interpreted "questioning" look. At the end of a sentence stating something, the hands and arms relax and droop downward; the signer is finished and looks down at the end of the turn. To command or demand, the hands and arms move forward as the sentence ends—even so far as to suggest a push on the one addressed (see fig. 11).[14]

Because the articulation of language, both spoken and signed, involves exquisitely controlled physical action, it is obvious that a signed sentence has a beginning, the start of its physical action; a middle, the body of the sentence; and an end, the signals just described. In this there is another strong indication that language behavior evolved quite naturally from animal behavior. Our nearest primate relatives, and indeed pets and domestic animals, express global meanings of the kind that sentence-type meanings like questions, demands, and statements belong to.[15] It seems reasonable, then, to suggest that syntax began when visible gestures linked agents to actions, actions to persons or things acted upon, and experiencers to changes, creating syntactic structures with sentence meanings and creating at the same time meanings in parts of gestures, which, when separated out, became known as nouns and verbs.

HOW MANY DO YOU HAVE?

THAT MOON IS PRETTY.

FIGURE 11. *At the end of a question, the hand (or hands) remain up; at the end of a declarative statement, the hands are lowered.*

Signs are considered differently in spoken and signed languages. In the latter, both word and sentence signals (semantic and syntactic information, respectively) are made visible by upper-body actions. Modern linguistic theorists, drawing from a tradition that recognizes only speech as language, see syntax as the creation of an abstract structure (an imaginary downward-branching tree), and consider sequences of consonants and vowels as mere identifiers of the lexical items selected to replace the abstract symbols at the ends of the branches. They argue that the way the voice produces the intonation patterns is merely an accident of the "surface" expression and not really part of true grammar, which they contend lies deep in the realm of the abstract.

Language utterances as effort-event, with beginning, middle, and end, may from the first have had vocalizations as an accompaniment to their more precisely signifying gestural output. A glance at other human activity is illuminating: a grunt is often emitted by a weight lifter at the peak of the effort; a vigorous throw or a fencer's thrust or a karate kick is often accompanied by an explosive "Hey, la!" or "Hai!" or "Pow!" Other actions and sequences of movement also are performed with characteristic nonlinguistic but synchronic vocal expressions. Perhaps, from the first, visible language signs had some vocal accompaniment. But at first only the visible sign could have shown any natural relation to what it represented. If the vocal output was reasonably stable and regular in its co-occurrence with the visible sign movements, however, it would have been no great matter to take the vocal expression alone as standing for a missing piece of the visible expression.

Children are able to reproduce recognizable sentence sound contours even before they can produce all the words of the sentence within; this suggests that the first stage in the changeover from mainly gestural to mainly vocal production of language signs may have been the use of the vocal accompaniment to signal a particular kind of sentence—a question, or a demand—instead of signaling each part of the sentence.

Speech could then have begun as vocalizations that tended to accompany gesturally produced language signs. There would also have been a natural connection between a few, but only a few, of the vocalizations and what they signified. While visible gestures are by their nature able to point at things, to hold things or imitate holding them, and to reproduce actions or parts of actions, sounds are naturally associated with a limited range of denotata, especially the sound's producers and with certain actions, as above. Creatures that had begun to see the relation of gestural signs they made to things they saw and concepts they had in mind would have been ready to exploit the iconic potential of vocal sounds. One might guess, for example, that because birds fly, a gesture referring to a bird would be made with hand and arm held upward and moved. But some birds also make sounds that can be imitated, so a hand-waving sign for a bird may have been performed with the imitation of a cry or peep or squawk to give more specificity to the general designation "something flying." Other such instances of sound symbolism may have accompanied and reinforced the relations of manual signs to what they represented.

Effects of Channel Change

As a newly evolved way of modeling the world and thinking and communicating, the first use of language signs would have profoundly affected the pecking order of social animals. Physical size, strength, age, audacity, and experience are some determinants of who commands and who obeys in a group or larger society, but ability to make and respond to language signs would have had a direct effect on the social structure of their users. In a species that possesses language, fluent and effective use of it brings leaders to the fore. Although language competence is considered by current language theory as a universal human trait, a "species typical function," something everyone is born with, common experience indicates otherwise: skill and language knowledge, like other traits, vary greatly from individual to individual. Among primates generally, cleverness often prevails over physical threat or force.[16] The addition of language signs to the primate behavioral repertoire would certainly have reinforced the advantage of those hominids adept at sign use.

When a few individuals at the top of the pecking order had learned to use vocal signs and to rely less on gestural signs than others did, they would have gained an advantage. They and their peers could make plans and carry out schemes while keeping those without the extra vocal-auditory skills figuratively in the dark. If the clever and dominant members of a group were more facile at acquiring and using vocal language than others less skilled, their status would be enhanced.

It is difficult to imagine how thousands and thousands of laborers could have been persuaded to build a ziggurat or pyramid or temple unless the persuaders had a spoken language. With a spoken language, in dark caves, on mountain tops, or in holy places consecrated by their own priest-king caste, the early speakers would have been able to convince masses who had inferior vocal skills that they were actually hearing the echoing words of a god demanding obedience to their overseers. Just as in historical times, natives of the Western Hemisphere mistook for gods their first visitors arriving in great ships and armed with superior weapons, early human tribes without the ability to replace gestural signs with speech may well have made a similar mistake about those who had mastered the trick of making language signs invisibly.

The use of voices to make language signs would also have given its users the gift of more time. In the dark, less information is lost by speakers than by signers;[17] thus hours of darkness could have been used by the earliest speakers—perhaps for planning ways to exploit their advantage over the "vocally and auditorially challenged" members of their society.

CHAPTER 10

⌐∽

Families of Signed Languages

ACCORDING TO THE *Oxford English Dictionary* the first use of *philology* as "the study of languages" dates from 1716 and the use of *linguistics* for the same meaning dates from 1855. Linguistics today is a multi-discipline. Cognitive linguists study the relation of language to brain structure and function; sociolinguists examine the effects of contacts among linguistic communities; psycholinguists probe the acquisition of languages by infants. Field linguists study the languages of people in the Third World, devise writing systems for them, and translate scriptures and classics while teaching the speakers to read. Still others try to define what it is that makes language a human trait.

Philology, today, advocates the historical study of spoken and written languages to ascertain how they may be related. After finding that many languages spoken in Europe and the Indian subcontinent come from one family tree (now known as Indo-European), philologists moved on to identify other language families around the world. Some may hope to find the single spoken language that all (spoken) languages might have descended from. The idea that once upon a time all people spoke one language is as old as the Tower of Babel story, but it is unsupported by evidence. However, many apparently unrelated languages have similar-sounding words for common meanings, and this inspires some to search for "the" original spoken tongue.

Some linguists and philologists, however, have taken more interest in natural history than in a universal theory. One of these was Morris Swadesh, who devised a method for assessing the degree of kinship between languages. Simple, as test instruments should be, his is a list of the words speakers of a language use for some two hundred things and concepts that are likely to be familiar in all cultures. Lists from different language communities are then compared for cognate pairs—words in the two languages that have the same meaning and sound enough alike to have been derived from a word in a parent language. In some instances there are written records of the original word's form. Latin written in the time of the Roman Empire helped trace the earlier forms of the modern Romance languages. Sanskrit, with a still older literature, showed how Latin belongs to one of several language subfamilies that branched from proto-Indo-European.

But even without written records, philologists use sound change patterns to follow the lead of Swadesh. They reconstruct a parent language inferentially from the form of the cognate words. Swadesh's branch of science, glottochronology, is a sophisticated kind of language history. It is also known as lexicostatistics when it provides quantitative data on the vocabularies of different languages. His two-hundred-word lists allow researchers to calculate the percentage of cognates between two languages. The higher the percentage, the more likely that both derived from the same earlier language. This procedure also permits estimates to be made of how long ago related languages separated. Related languages with few cognates would have diverged longer ago than languages with many cognate pairs.[1]

Much information about languages and their histories has been obtained in this way and checked against historical records of migrations and invasions. However, these methods have not led to finding a single, original spoken language from which all others stemmed, and if the argument of this book is correct, it will never be found because it never existed. The evidence found so far points to a number of first spoken languages, each of which would have begun among a particular population as their way of representing the sign-meaning pairs of their sign language. At the time when fluent speech became possible (as shown by the formation of fossil skulls), humans were already living in widely separated regions of the world. The speech patterns that different groups used for translating their gesture-meaning pairs would naturally have differed, no doubt relative to the timing and geographical distance of their separation.

Humans apparently began to spread from Africa into Europe and Asia in the early part of the long *Homo erectus* period, roughly one million years ago. The fossil record shows that they had brains much larger proportionately than those of earlier hominid species. There is no evidence that they had and used a sign language, but there is hard evidence that they made and used sophisticated stone tools. "The invention of a tool," as Jonathan Kingdon points out, "has less implication for brain size than the ability to impart knowledge of its effective [manufacture and] use."[2] The skeletons and other fossil finds at *Homo erectus* sites imply, and what they did with their hands implies even more strongly, that long before they could speak humans were using language to plan and guide and direct what they did.

Speech requires a skull shape, placement on the spine, and a vocal tract configuration that appeared with *Homo sapiens sapiens* only about 150,000 years ago. At that time groups of fully modern humans were living in sites as much as ten thousand miles apart in Africa, Asia, and Europe. During this crucial period how could widely separated groups have developed a single, identical spoken language? Genesis 11:1 says that they did, but that follows from its account of the way the world and its creatures were created. Nevertheless, the dominant modern linguistic theory is not essentially different; it supposes that a mutation installed the language instinct in human brains.

Some facts about spoken languages are clear: (a) there are numerous spoken languages in the world today; (b) there were spoken languages in the relatively recent past; and (c) the differences among spoken languages are many. An exact count even of current spoken languages cannot be made, however, because such a count would vary according to whether some systems are considered to be different languages or dialects of the same language. This distinction requires drawing an arbitrary line between a language and a dialect.

As can be discovered readily in urban America, speakers of some varieties of English, a world language, have more or less difficulty understanding speakers of their own language when they come from different regions and social strata. The way speakers put sentences together and the variations in their sentence melody and rhythm create as much difficulty in mutual intelligibility as the way they pronounce the vowels and consonants.

Studies like those of Swadesh show empirically that if a sizable group of speakers of a language becomes isolated from the main population, the words the migrating group uses become, as time passes, somewhat different from the words in the language left behind. After more time has passed with little or no contact, the two populations appear to be speaking separate languages.

Language divergence like this has happened countless times, and philologists or linguists like Swadesh must investigate to reveal the languages' relationship to each other. For example, tribes of people from Germany's North Sea coast invaded Great Britain in the fourth and fifth centuries, but by the ninth century their languages (Anglian, Saxon, and Mercian) spoken in Great Britain differed from the German spoken in the part of Germany they came from. In the eleventh century, Normans—speakers of a variety of French influenced by their native Scandinavian—conquered Britain. Their Norman French forever changed the nature of what we call the English language.

Some things are also clear about signed languages. First, there are many signed languages, not even counting the numerous manual signaling systems used for specific purposes;[3] and they fall into two major classes: the signed languages of deaf people and the signed languages preserved and used by tribal peoples as alternatives to their spoken languages. Counting only the signed languages of deaf populations may be even more difficult than counting spoken languages. Manual signs look much alike to hearing/speaking people, and because few hearing people are aware that some of the movements they see may be the words of an actual sign language, they may suppose that all gestural signs have guessable meanings. They are mistaken on two counts. First, although the meanings of some gestures are nearly unmistakable, the same or similar gestures may, through convention, mean different things in different cultures. Second, signed languages that serve deaf people as their primary languages differ from population to population.

For the same reason that there are different spoken languages, there are different signed languages. Different cultures and different circumstances of life in different places impose differences in language. When the methods of Swadesh are applied to signed languages, however, family relationships, if they exist, can be discovered. Before looking at this evidence, however, the methods of lexicostatistics and their application need discussion.

Swadesh's *Origin and Diversification of Languages* was published posthumously in 1971. In 1978 Charles Hockett reviewed it and four other books about language origins in a long essay in *American Speech*. Hockett concluded that "the inference is inescapable: the channel for prelanguage was not primarily vocal-auditory, but multimodal, with a slowly changing balance between modes. . . . But some of the most important features of language arose long before the vocal-auditory mode became ascendant, and were only subsequently transferred."[4] This states the case well, but might do so even better if Hockett had said that the gestural-visual mode was originally the dominant mode.

Hockett also thought that the gestural system may have lacked the power of language (i.e., spoken language): "The early hominid primarily gestural system was *only* reasonably serviceable [his emphasis]. It could not have had the power of language or of such modern signages [a term he introduces] such as Ameslan [ASL], or the switch of channel would never have taken place, and perhaps the Upper Palaeolithic technological revolution would have begun earlier than it did."[5] If by "*only* reasonably serviceable" Hockett means that the early hominid gestural system worked well for those people in their time but would hardly work for modern humans today, there can be no disagreement. However, I define certain gestural systems as languages, not signages—not reserving the term *language* for spoken systems only.[6]

Modern signed languages as well as modern spoken languages have power—the power to deal mentally, socially, and cooperatively with every part of the lives of their users. Of course, modern signed and spoken languages will seem more powerful than the gestural languages of prehistory because modern life is more complex. To take just one example, our means of getting from place to place are much more various and powerful. Ancient humans walked or made and used boats. Modern languages keep requiring new verbs for new kinds of locomotion. They also need many times more nouns because there are more things in the world of today than there were in the world of *Homo erectus*. They need more verbs of all kinds because there are more processes and actions that we have to think and talk and write about. As Hockett implies, a modern sign language like ASL has that power too. His words may seem to rate signing inferior to speaking, but I doubt that he intended to do so.

If humans had not largely replaced their gestural symbols with vocal symbols, the world would not have become as we know it today. The shift to predominantly vocal language freed the hands, arms, and visual attention for important other uses. It also facilitated social and political changes. The phonetic nature of spoken language made possible the replacement of written or drawn pictographic signs with relatively easy and efficient alphabetic writing systems. Vowels and consonants of speech are produced in virtually linear time order; but the many manual, brachial, and facial details of signed languages, as well as the dynamic features, are visible simultaneously. Thus, sign notation, though experimented with for hundreds of years, cannot yet be rendered in any linear script. Like an orchestral score, several lines are needed to represent the various movements that are visible at the same time.

Written languages brought consequences that only signed or only spoken languages could not. Writing and reading conferred immense power on the elite classes who mastered these skills. With this power the ruling classes organized societies and built, maintained, and expanded cities, states, and empires.

The very earliest gestural systems with syntax would certainly have differed from modern signed languages, but the major differences would have been vocabulary. Differences between life then and now—not differences in language channels—impose vocabulary differences. The power of a language lies in its users' ability to exploit it for anything they need or want to say. The most important difference in visible language interaction from the prehistoric past to the present would have been that most of the events and objects of life in the hominids' environment would have been visible, immediate, quite obviously capable of gestural representation. Users of modern sign languages—at least in most cultures—must talk about things like government, education, prejudice, taxation, income, credit, discrimination, rent, interest, and dozens of other matters that can be neither seen nor handled.

Culture—life as humans see and understand it—makes the difference in languages. In his foreword to *The Origin and Diversification of Language,* Dell Hymes explains that the first of the key facts Swadesh used in developing his argument was, "Certain structural differences among languages spoken today seem related to certain sociocultural developments."[7]

Many writers on language tread cautiously around this fact, perhaps because of the way it was sometimes interpreted. The idea that languages and cultures could have evolved became linked in the popular mind as well as in scientific circles with earlier characterizations of aboriginal people as savage, barbarous, or primitive, and with allegations that they and their languages lacked fully human status. But this error has been righted, even overcorrected. The doctrine of cultural and linguistic relativity, which asserts the equal value of all cultures and languages, sometimes obscures differences that might be illuminating.

Edward Sapir once wrote that "when it comes to linguistic form, Plato walks with the Macedonian swineherd, Confucius with the head-hunting savage of Assam."[8] No doubt these two pairs, philosopher and rustic, could have walked together, and if they did talk, Plato and Confucius would have used words of their respective Greek and Chinese languages just as the rustics would do. But do we imagine that they would have talked about the same things and made the same statements? Sapir's point is that to converse together peasants and philosophers must use the language they share. He neglected to note in this passage that their vocabularies and the way they phrase and order their sentences will differ because philosopher and peasant talk about very different matters. Speaking the same language is not the same thing as thinking alike about the same topics.

Spoken languages and signed languages are used in societies with high civilizations and also in hunter-gatherer societies, but this in no way implies one language is inferior to another. In short, it is just as unscientific to read value comparisons into language evolution as it is to do so with the evolution of species.

With this caution about the implications of cultural and language relativism and change, we can consider the application of the Swadesh

methods to signed languages. James Woodward and his associates have
pioneered in this. Woodward found lexicostatistical evidence that ASL
was influenced by French Sign Language (after the arrival of Laurent
Clerc in the United States in 1816), but that ASL has noncognate signs
in great enough number to prove its independent earlier existence.[9] More
recently, Woodward has been surveying the signed languages of deaf societies in Asia. He finds not only family relationships among some of them
but also, in a relatively short time span (using informants of different
generations), a strong influence of ASL on local languages, due to the
presence of Americans with a knowledge of sign language.

This ASL influence is a clear instance of how cultural factors can drive
linguistic diffusion. The adoption of ASL signs into the signed languages
of other parts of the world would seem to be fueled mainly by the perception that the social and economic status of deaf people in the United
States is superior to that of deaf people in the home country. In a country
where signing deaf people can be university presidents and members of
other professions and not confined to unskilled occupations or beggary,
it may well seem to deaf people elsewhere that there is something special about the language American deaf signers use.

Woodward modified the two-hundred-word Swadesh list of culturally common items and came up with a list of one hundred items. Half
of the original two hundred proved useless for showing sign language
relationships because all signed languages have signs that simply point at
certain things, like body parts (an important group of items in the two
hundred), or that represent something transparently, as does the hand near
the mouth for food. Signed languages now in use have no need to in-
herit these natural signs from an earlier signed language.

Natural signs make up the small domain of form-meaning agreement
that has led to the popular myth that sign is a universal language. So it
would be, if all human needs for language could be met with only a few
iconic movements. Thus these "universal" gestures are useless for deter-
mining the age or relationship of signed languages, but they are sufficient to meet communicators' needs in certain situations, as Gordon
Hewes argued: "Encounters between people ignorant of each other's language are frequently described in the narratives of travel and exploration prior to 1492, although explicit reference to sign-communication

is rare, not because it did not occur, but because resort to it has been usually taken for granted."[10] This does not mean, however, that *sign languages* or the gestures familiar within a community are understood universally. Rather, some gestures can serve for limited communication when spoken languages cannot.

Woodward's investigation of the way various signed languages are related shows that they become diverse, as spoken languages do. Social contact and interaction create a language community and keep community and language together. When a large group of the language users become separated from the rest, however, and when interaction between groups declines or ceases, the systems used by the two populations undergo the normal day-to-day and generation-to-generation change that happens to all languages. But the changes will be different in the two groups. In fact, many of the things and events to be talked about may be quite different in their two environments. As time passes, the two populations will appear to be using different dialects, and after more time, most observers will describe their systems as different languages.

French signs were imported into ASL mainly by Laurent Clerc, a deaf protégé of the Abbé Sicard, who succeeded the Abbé de l'Epée as director of the National School for the Deaf in Paris. Clerc taught his signs to Thomas Hopkins Gallaudet and helped Gallaudet found the American School for the Deaf in Hartford, Connecticut, in 1817. Clerc also had a hand in the establishment of many more American schools for deaf children in the early nineteenth century. He instructed their founders and teachers in the French method pioneered by Epée and Sicard and used signs from that method.[11] This one deaf man's influence seems to have been sufficient, Woodward's lexicostatistics show, to introduce into ASL a large number of French signs and sign-formation principles, such as using a handshape from the French fingerspelling alphabet to form the ASL sign for the English translation of a French word (see fig. 12). Widespread use of the French one-hand alphabet with its ready-made handshapes for word-sign borrowing also resulted from Clerc's activity.

My own personal knowledge gives me confidence that the kind of other-language influence Clerc exerted can happen easily, quickly, and naturally. On a visit to a first-grade class of deaf children, I watched as the teacher asked several pupils in turn what they liked best about the

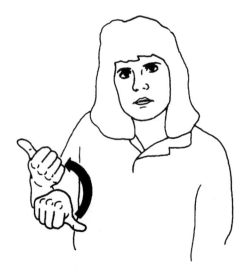

FIGURE 12. *Some ASL signs were adapted from French Sign Language and so use the handshape of the initial letter of the French gloss. The sign for "other" (*autre *in French), which uses an A handshape, is an example of this adaptation.*

field trip they had taken the day before. The instructional method used in that school was called "Total Communication"; the teacher spoke and signed, and the pupils tried to speak as they signed. The first child to respond pronounced haltingly the words "wheel Ferris" as she moved one hand in a W handshape and the other in an F handshape of the manual alphabet, making vertical circles with them. One or two others, taking her lead when it was their turn to answer, repeated her signs with more or less intelligible pronunciations of "wheel Ferris." Then the teacher called on a boy in the back row, just in front of me. He did not speak, though he moved his hands in alternate vertical circles as the others had done. But his hands were not in letter formations. He held them both with the first two fingers forward and bent—icons for seats and their movement indexes to the Ferris wheel's rotation.

The others turned to watch while he was signing. He was the only child in the class with deaf parents. When I left that classroom some minutes later I saw several children repeating his sign to themselves with beatific facial smiles. I interpreted these smiles to myself as meaning: "Oh, that's the way to sign it!" I expect the children, or most of them, may continue to make the W and F handshape signs again for the teacher who taught them this name for the ride. I expect that the teacher may be successful in getting some of them to change the order in which they speak the English words. But I have no doubt that every one of them, in their spontaneous conversation, uses the revolving-seats sign they learned from that signing son of signing parents.

Cultural and Language Change

Social interaction and migration bring change to both signed and spoken languages. Equally if not more influential is change in the culture of the language's users. Deaf people in cohesive social groupings use their own language to communicate about their own inside world, about what they know and cherish—their heroes, their history, even some of the material things in their daily lives, like TTY phone terminals, and doorbells that do not ring but flash a light. The details of deaf cultures differ in many ways from what hearing people know and value. This difference has been collectively termed "Deaf culture," but of course deaf people live within much larger communities of hearing/speaking people; their cultures cannot be completely independent and autonomous. Edward T. Hall has called such a cultural microcosm "a microculture," a term that avoids the pejorative connotations of the more familiar term "subculture."[12]

Being surrounded by a majority of hearing/speaking people, deaf people have had to adopt, and adapt to, the culture of that majority; consequently, their languages also grow and change as the users deal with the surrounding culture. This interaction of the microculture with the general culture can lead to the coining of new sign language terms or to borrowings from the surrounding spoken language. A nice example of coinage is the indexic-iconic ASL sign for a Linotype machine (familiar in the twentieth century when printing was a major source of employment for deaf men). It is made by holding the hands one above the other at waist level with the fingers fluttering as if on the superposed banks of keys. (The sign for "typewriter" or a computer keyboard uses the same finger action but with the hands side by side on the same level.) A newer sign, that for "carburetor," uses metaphor. Because this device, which fuel injectors are making obsolete, mixes fuel with incoming air, the sign is made by tapping a C handshape at the throat.

Borrowing from a spoken language by American, British, French, and other national signed languages takes one of two forms. The first is fingerspelling—the use of hand configurations and movement to spell out the borrowed word. But even this does not work the same way everywhere. Signers in the United States and France and many other countries use a one-hand manual alphabet, while British and some Commonwealth deaf signers use two hands to form their signs for letters. A second method of borrowing is more subtle. It is a longer process, and it remained largely unsuspected as borrowing until Robbin Battison described it in *Lexical Borrowing in American Sign Language*.[13] This kind of borrowing shortens the full sequence of manual letters, usually preserving only the first and last more or less recognizably. It also adds a movement of the hand, which makes the whole into a genuine sign instead of a sequence of handshapes representing letters.

For example, when the open spread hand abruptly closes to produce a fist with thumb tip protruding between the index and middle fingers, the sign means "what"—the sign begins with the palm facing in and moves a short distance downward as it closes (see fig. 13). The meaning "but" results when the same handshape change occurs as the hand moves across the front of the body, maintaining a nonrotated forearm. These signs are recognizable as naturalized borrowings because their initial open handshape approximates, but does not show precisely, the manual alphabet W and the manual alphabet B, respectively. The final handshape of both is the manual alphabet T.

Approximates is the operative word in this. Fingerspelling itself is not a precise production of the manual letters forming a word; it does not require the kind of precision necessary for playing the piano, for example. Sherman Wilcox has used video techniques as well as myographic recordings (with needles in his own arm) to show what a speller and watcher do and see in fluent fingerspelling. The actual performance is quite different from the handshape for the letter as it is formed, drawn, or photographed in isolation. Instead, the muscular action for forming

#WHAT (W-T)

FIGURE 13. *A lexicalized sign results when the letters of a fingerspelled word are reduced, or blended, so that only some (usually the first and last) letters are distinct.*

the previous and the following handshapes has an effect on each hand-shape produced by the hand. This effect is known as co-articulation in speech; the sounds coming before or after a sound modify it. The same thing happens in fingerspelling; a handshape for a letter will be different according to what letters precede and follow.[14] This is not surprising, for the same center in the brain coordinates, times, and sequences fine move-ments of the hands and muscles in the vocal tract.[15]

With these borrowing processes for bringing new items of the in-tellectual and material culture of the larger language community into the sign language of the deaf microculture, deaf people easily keep pace with cultural change. In the industrialized nations, deaf people's signed lan-guages epitomize the culture just as the spoken languages do. It is also unsurprising that these signed languages are causing major changes in the signed languages of younger deaf people in emerging nations—as the example of Clerc's influence and as Woodward's lexicostatistics have shown.[16]

The way that ASL and British Sign Language naturalize vocabulary from spoken (actually, written) language differs. British deaf people use a two-hand manual alphabet; so their signs borrowed and adapted from English are unlike American signs derived from the same words. For example, British signers tap the first two fingers of the right hand once on the backs of the same fingers of the left hand to represent "F"; but they tap twice to sign "father."

The American borrowing practice, and its older initialized signs (e.g., using a B handshape for "blue") follow the French practice accelerated by Sicard when he succeeded Epée as director of the Parisian institute. These French *signes méthodiques* were created to give the deaf pupils visible equivalents of important French words. Even in the nineteenth century, deaf writers were deploring the contamination of their natural language with signs invented by hearing persons as translations of their words, but Battison points out that borrowing is also done by and within the deaf community itself—as the following example shows.

> Many years ago two students at Gallaudet from a midwestern
> residential school for deaf children showed me the sign used in
> their school for "toast." Their guess was that it might have origi-
> nated as a way of showing with the fingers the crisp, granular
> texture of toasted bread. (With the hand closed, the thumb rubs
> the tip of the index finger in a small circular movement.) When
> they were shown its possible fingerspelling origin, they were
> surprised—I am not sure whether they were convinced.
>
> In the first place, to feel something like crumbs or flour or
> sand one rubs the thumb's pad against the pad of the index finger,
> but not in a circle all the way around the fingertip. In the toast
> sign, the thumb's circuit of the fingertip is continuous, but if one
> halts it at stages in its circuit, it spells T-O-A-S-T. Step by step:
> when the thumb is on the ulnar side of the index finger, it is
> forming the manual "T." When it is directly under the end of the
> index finger, it closes a circle, making "O" (or the way very young
> deaf children make it).[17] The thumb against the radial edge of the
> index finger makes an almost canonical "A." Having moved across
> the nail of the index, to place the thumb between that finger and

the next, the hand spells "S." And, of course, as the circling continues, it spells "T" again.

All this shows how modern signed languages inevitably, because of cultural change, differ from each other as well as from the earliest of gestural systems that became language. Nevertheless, a different gestural treatment of nouns and verbs is likely to have been a feature of any signaling system that evolved into language. Objects and persons as well as animals can be pointed at, or a salient feature can be resembled by a hand's posture and placement. In the same way, activities or various aspects of activities, especially of the kind likely to be found in a Stone Age community, can be directly reduplicated by movement of a hand or both hands. These are basic features of all gestural systems worthy of the name language. With them as beginnings, and with the use of nonmanual activities to modify what was represented (in ways we would term adverbial and adjectival); these systems were ready to develop more of the features found in languages from historical times. Such language development would require no more genetic endowment than the obvious human qualities of "mental quickness, adaptability, and aptitude in the teaching and learning of new skills for the greatest survival value."[18]

CHAPTER 11

~

Languages in Parallel

BEFORE SPOKEN LANGUAGE carved in stone or written on parchment and paper helped to make cities, states, and empires possible, persons in the act of speaking conveyed meaning with more than the vowel and consonant sounds their voices made—which is all that writing records. During the long period before writing, speakers' facial expression and hand and arm movements were attended to, because the whole meaning of an utterance is distributed (though not evenly) among all these signs and speech. Even those who can hear get additional meaning if they are also able to see a speaker. Listeners interpret a speaker's appearance and performance as well as the words being spoken and the way of speaking. The invention of writing centuries later brought changes, however. In many kinds of language use—especially academic, legal, bureaucratic—the spoken words were considered to carry the whole message; visible signals were suppressed or disregarded. But in the give and take of ordinary everyday life, what can be seen still carries meaning.

In classical Greece and Rome, live oratory was highly prized as indispensable to democracy. A Roman liberal education began with the trivium—grammar, rhetoric, and logic—the first three of the seven liberal arts. Instruction in arithmetic, music, geometry, and astronomy followed when the first three were mastered. This beginning curriculum thus sorted language into three compartments. It implied that words and sentences belong to grammar, their delivery to rhetoric, and their truth function to logic or philosophy. Surviving treatises on Roman rhetoric do not tell the pleader or the politician what to say, but they give a great deal of instruction about how to present it. They discuss ploys for gaining favorable response from judges in court proceedings and for capturing the attention and approval of an audience in the forum. The tradition lingers: we still treat gesture, general demeanor, tone of voice—everything that would have been part of face-to-face communication before the invention of writing—as rhetorical flourishes, optional features. Most people think of them as add-ons to speaking, some even as nonverbal.

In preliterate societies, because communication had to be carried on face to face, what could be seen could be just as important as what could be heard. We, as heirs to several thousand years of literacy, find this difficult to understand fully—almost as difficult as understanding that signing can be language. The availability of written records has much reduced the kinds of data that linguists take into account, while expanding the number and direction of their abstractions. Written languages dominate formal education and have almost completely eliminated from consideration as part of language any of the visible information in a live utterance. Much of what can be heard is also treated as unrelated to language. Some go so far as to call what writing does not capture "nonverbal." And yet it cannot be denied that language is older than writing, and that communication is older than language. Before writing gained its dominant place in human cultures, language and communication were richer by being multimodal.

Preliterate societies exist today, and a century ago there were more of them. Fortunately, some of them still retain their ancient cultural traditions. One of these traditions is just beginning to be recognized for what it is and what it implies. It cannot be described in a word or phrase, for it is a whole way of looking at animal, human, and spirit life as part of a seamless whole. It is also too large a subject to cover in a single chapter, but one aspect of it is most pertinent to the progression from gesture to language to speech.

One special feature of some surviving preliterate cultures is that their languages are not constrained by the conventions of alphabetic writing. In some of these societies, speech and visible signing are equally valid ways of communicating. It is not surprising then that in these communities both the spoken language and the signed language are treated as language.

This fact has taken even longer to be recognized than the fact that deaf people's signed languages are languages. Of course, early explorers reported that the natives they encountered used gestures, but usually such gestural displays were taken as evidence that the natives had not yet evolved into full human status and that their spoken languages were not complete. Later writers have a more enlightened appreciation of these gesture languages, but the signed languages used by tribes in Aboriginal Australia did not get the scholarly recognition and treatment they merit as real languages until Kendon's work of 1988. The signed languages of native North Americans still await a study similarly comprehensive and unprejudiced by centuries of identifying language only with speech.

Alternate Sign Languages

Adam Kendon has suggested the term "alternate sign languages" for the languages used by Australian tribes because "these systems are typically developed for use as an alternative to speech in those circumstances where, for whatever reason, speech is not used." Kendon also describes them as "not fully autonomous systems and . . . better thought of as systems that *represent* spoken language, rather than as languages in their own right."[1]

I question this characterization, even though I have no firsthand knowledge of these Australian sign languages and have the greatest respect for Kendon's skills as an ethnographer and linguist. Fortunately, the difference in our views can be tested by field study. To explore the possibility that language began with gestures and only later used speech as its major expressive system, a working hypothesis could easily be put to the test: In societies like the Aboriginal Australian and Native American tribes, which preserve alternate sign languages, do their signed languages show more dependence on the spoken language, or do the spoken languages show dependence on the signed? Surely there are linguistic methods sophisticated enough to determine the direction of dependence.

Let us begin with a question that looks rhetorical but is real: Is it possible for users of a spoken language to invent a surrogate system of visible signs that will represent that language's lexicon and grammar completely and accurately and still be as fluent to use as speaking it is? The most generally used, most developed system for representing speech is alphabetic writing. Writing fails this test. Writing leaves out much of the information contained in face-to-face communication. And writing is not nearly as rapid as speaking; hence the need for the invention of shorthand and mechanical and electronic devices to record live speech. Writing evolved over millennia from a skill possessed by few to a near universal accomplishment in some cultures, but literacy is still beset with difficulties. Even in the most prosperous nations, massive educational efforts and expenditures do not achieve universal success.

One motive for inventing a code of gestures to try to represent a spoken language is to give deaf people access to that language. This presumably was the motive for the Abbé de l'Epée's *signes méthodiques* in France, the Paget-Gorman sign language in England, and a number of sign codes invented in the United States in the late twentieth century. These strive for what Kendon finds that the Australian systems have achieved—fluency and unquestioned acceptance of the gestural system as an equally valued alternative to speaking.

Although invented sign-codes for teaching deaf children have been tried in schools managed by hearing persons, and although some of these codes are still in use, deaf people have not accepted them as alternatives to their own primary signed languages.[2] The main reason these codes have not met their inventors' expectations is that real languages—including the signed languages of deaf communities—have a history of natural evolution, meeting both social needs and physiological constraints determined only after long use.

The convention needed by every language grows from social intercourse; it cannot be invented. Codes, however ingenious, reflect the limited knowledge of individuals or committees. The inventor or the inventing committee decides what meaning each of the forms they propose shall have. In the present context, all these inventors of sign language codes make as much sense as Humpty Dumpty in his conversation

"I don't know what you mean by 'glory'," Alice said.

Humpty Dumpty smiled contemptuously. "Of course you don't— till I tell you. I meant 'there's a nice knock-down argument for you!'"

"But 'glory' doesn't mean 'a nice knock-down argument'," Alice objected.

"When *I* use a word," Humpty Dumpty said, in rather a scornful tone, "it means just what I choose it to mean—neither more nor less."

"The question is," said Alice, "whether you *can* make words mean so many different things."

"The question is," said Humpty Dumpty, "which is to be master— —that's all."

Source: *From Lewis Carroll,* The Complete Works of Lewis Carroll *(London: Nonesuch Press, 1939), 196.*

with Alice. Real languages contain the wisdom and knowledge of those who share, and have shared, a culture.

Writing evolved over a long period as a way of recording speech, but invented gestural codes are usually devised with the tacit assumption that only a spoken language, for which they offer visual surrogates, is truly a language. These invented gestures are therefore treated as nonlanguage substitutes, as they are—like the dits and dahs of Morse code or the flags for semaphore signaling. Genuine sign languages, like speech languages, are simply languages. Their symbols are primary.

According to Kendon, "The systems in use by the Aborigines of central Australia are probably the most complex alternate sign languages ever to have been developed." His study of these systems shows them to be not only complex but remarkably parallel in structure, both in form and meaning, to the accompanying spoken language. Kendon does not speculate, but there would seem to be only two ways these alternate sign languages of Australia could have originated and attained this parallel structure—either as faithful copies of the tribes' spoken languages, or as primary languages that were later translated—by substituting speech sounds for certain sign-meaning pairs—into spoken languages. The demonstrated failure of attempts to make a deliberately invented code into anything like a real language argues against the first alternative. The complexity and serviceability of the Australian tribes' sign languages implies a development different from that of modern sign codes. The Australian systems, which differ from tribe to tribe, were noticed by the first Europeans to reach the continent. They can only be a true socio-cultural development.

The difference here between an invented sign code and a naturally evolved sign language is analogous to an experience common to many. For generations, schoolteachers in the United States have scolded pupils for using "ain't," telling them, "There is no such word in the English language." Yet speakers of English have been using this venerable contraction for centuries, and in some communities it has never gone out of use. Sicard in the nineteenth century and Sir Richard Paget in the twentieth, with more authority than classroom teachers, did not succeed in making a major change in deaf people's language habits; neither have the inventors of the various codes in use in the United States, such as SEE I, SEE II, LOVE, Cued Speech, and Signed English.[3] In Aboriginal Australia, it seems, speakers sometimes are signers because their culture requires them to be. No outside authority, no well-meaning educators, no Humpty Dumptys are involved. If we ask why this should be so, we have to consider another possible origin for the tribes' alternate systems. Because visible signs can represent naturally, while vocal signs depend on a convention to link them to what users take them to mean, it is probable that representing concepts and their relationships with visible signs enabled systems of vocal signs to develop later—the thesis of this book. Thus it is also possible that in cultures with alternate sign languages, these gestural systems for representing meanings emerged earlier and never went out of use.

Part of the attraction of alternate sign languages is their apparent novelty. There is something exotic about seeing a Native American—even if only portrayed by an actor on film or television—using gestures that are treated as saying exactly what the voice is saying (or the dubbed sound track is carrying). Natives of Aboriginal Australia and their cultures and mythology raise this exotic quality to an even higher level. And yet, the difference between them and us may be only a difference of degree.

We also, in our everyday contacts with others, seldom listen and speak only; we look and gesticulate as well. The difference is that our normal gesturing does not have—does not any longer have—the systematic organization or grammar found in languages. The sign languages of the Native Americans and Aboriginal Australians, however, do have the kind of organization that every language has. Their handshapes and movements make sentences, not just words, and so their sign discourse is as translatable as their spoken discourse in Warlpiri or Nakota.

An Alternative Provenance

All this suggests that it may be time to revise the conventional way of thinking about language. Starting with the idea "what if language began as gesture," a number of assumptions about cognitive and language evolution can be reexamined.

Brenda Farnell suggests one way that visible representation is likely to have been first: she points out that movements—dance, ritual, gestural, and vocal movements—all "make meaning." Making meaning with movement therefore came first; languages then grew out of visibly, actively represented meaning. The Assiniboines of the Fort Belnap Reservation that Farnell studied have an alternate sign language, but one of its uses differs markedly from what Kendon observed in Australia.

Farnell points out that in order to understand a renowned storyteller's account of the tribe's history it is necessary both to look and to listen, because neither his spoken Nakota nor his signing by itself fully expresses the story. Obviously both kinds of expression are culturally acceptable, and the Assiniboine worldview explains why this is so. Farnell points out that their prime cosmological and decorative symbol is the circle. They do not see the circle as bisected by a straight line from north to south and cut into quarters by an east-west line at right angles to that. Instead, by pointing and looking, they refer to four full quadrants of the circle:

> [W]ihinap'e "east" refers to the sunrise—literally it means "the sun comes up"—and it is the direction from which the grandfather spirits come. . . . *Wiyotaha* "south" refers to noon, literally "the sun in the

middle." . . . *Wiyohpeya* "west" refers to "the sun going down."
Waziyata "north" refers to "where the snow comes from," the home
of the old man "who lives in cold and makes the cold and rarely takes
pity on anyone."[4]

In formal orations the narrator faces the southern quadrant (whether
outdoors or inside a building) and refers to the scheme above and much
that is thematically related to it by sweeping a hand to the left, forward,
to the right, and behind successively. This is very different from the Western imposition of geometrical abstractions on our surroundings. It comes
instead from a deep-seated orientation to the natural world. As Farnell
reports:

> I found that despite a lack of vocal reference in everyday contexts,
> the cardinal points [actually quadrants] nevertheless provide a con-
> stant frame of reference that all use, whether they speak Nakota or
> English only, and regardless of whether they know the sign language
> or not. It is through indexical spoken expressions and gestures that
> this frame of reference is utilized.
>
> Today, even though few people are fluent in the sign language
> proper, there remains a use of gesture that is coincident with it and
> undoubtedly stems from a very different view of language than that
> held by Euro-American people. For example, I found that speech and
> gesture are equally important in giving route directions, regardless
> of whether Nakota or English spoken language is used.[5]

One hypothesis would state that members of this and similar cultures first
possessed only a spoken language and then, for some hard to imagine
reason, they proceeded to describe the world they saw by pointing and
inventing other gestures to represent what they made of it and the way
they had been referring to it with their spoken words and phrases. It is
equally absurd to ignore the fact that children learn to express their dawning ideas in gesture first and only later learn to speak.

Perhaps in the whole history of the Assiniboine and similar cultures
with alternate sign languages, the signed and spoken modes have existed
for a long time side by side. Along with this goes the possibility that long

before this parallel structure and use came to be the norm, the visible representation was the more complete, more structured system, while the vocal representation was not yet fully up to the same level of discrimination and organization.

At present, and apparently in the historical past, peoples with both signed and spoken languages put them to, or reserved them for, different uses at different times; but this does not imply that signing and speaking are coequal. Hearing children communicate gesturally for some months before they can use their adult caretakers' language. Farnell points out that even speakers in the Assiniboine community who do not know the sign language use its gestures appropriately. This suggests that if any symbolic behavior is innately human, it is the use of our perception-action system to orient ourselves to space and point out directions to others.

∼

Accounts written by Meriwether Lewis, among others, of early-nineteenth-century cross-country expeditions, report the use of sign languages by Indians of the Plains, the Northwest, and the Southwest. Seven or eight decades later, the use of sign language throughout the natural range of the bison herds was known far and wide, and it was not confined to the Native American tribes. Traders, trappers, mountain men, homesteaders, Indian agents, cavalry officers, and other non-natives also learned a few, or many, of the hand signs. Lord Baden-Powell introduced these signs to the Boy Scout movement. This sign language was also hailed as a possible international language to promote world peace. Its proponents realized, however, that while it served buffalo hunters' needs, it lacked terms for parliamentary proceedings—for motions, seconds, amendments, and the like. Not discouraged, these enthusiasts for a universal sign language imported terms from the signed languages of the deaf to eke out its vocabulary deficiencies for their purposes.

In the *First Annual Report of the Bureau of American Ethnology,* published in 1881, Garrick Mallery gave these matters scientific scrutiny. His three-hundred-page treatise *Sign Language among the North American Indians,* in the report's first volume, compared the languages used by American tribes with the "language of signs of the deaf" (at Gallaudet College of which his friend Edward Miner Gallaudet was president) and with a number of sign languages described by earlier writers. While Mallery stressed the universality of gesture use, he did not make the mistake of assuming that signs and sign languages are universally understood.[6]

In fact, his monograph includes a lengthy table listing different tribes' sign vocabularies. This table shows that some common objects and actions are represented by a half dozen or more different signs in as many tribal languages. Even the horse, an ever-present feature of the buffalo hunt, was represented by three or four very different manual signs in different tribes' sign languages.[7] If the sign language arose, as some believe, from polyglot contact on the plains, where the hunting was done on horseback, there should have been only one "Plains Indian" sign for "horse."

Differences among tribal sign languages suggests a need for rethinking what is usually called Plains Indian Sign Talk. It is well known that when the wealth of the buffalo herds attracted Native American tribes and white hunters from distant places, members of this ethnically diverse crowd communicated when necessary with gestural signs. It has also been usual to suppose that the lack of a common tongue, combined with the universality of gesturing, led to the creation then and there of this silent lingua franca. Typically, white observers supposed that the native tribes had invented "the" sign language, because their spoken languages lacked the precision of Europeans' grammar, and the richness of European vocabularies (which of course had terms for many things foreign to the native cultures).

Mallery's listing of different signs for the same meaning shows that various sign languages existed before the arrival of Europeans. If the use of sign language was traditional in many tribes prior to the buffalo hunting frenzy, there is no way of knowing how old the tradition might be; it could go back to the original immigrations into the Americas.

The migrations from Asia into North America across the ancient land bridge and the successful spread through the Western Hemisphere would surely have needed the degree of social organization that only efficient communication makes possible. Like communication in all preliterate cultures, the communication of the migrating tribes is likely to have been both audible and visible. The early date of some migrations might suggest that the first representation of nouns and verbs syntactically joined was gestural, with the vocal signs used mainly as attention-getting signals and modifiers of various kinds. If the use of speech to represent the gesture-meaning nexus became dominant only after the groups had become widely dispersed, major differences among the Native American language families in the Western Hemisphere would be easier to explain.

Scholarship has identified cultures in North America and in Australia that use sign as well as speech for language and accept both as valid alternatives. While this circumstance may seem unusual, it differs only in degree from that of all cultures: face-to-face communicators everywhere use both voice and gesture. One way of looking at the facts would be that the people Kendon and Farnell observed have a highly organized gestural system. The question then is: Does this degree of organization come about because speakers invented a manual sign code to, as Kendon put it, "*represent* spoken language"? Or does it result from the preservation in these cultures of a language-bearing system of gestures—with the implication that the gestures most of the world's speakers make use of today are the ruins of a once fully linguistic edifice? Certainly there can be no doubt that the ideas we represent in words such as *here, there, in, out, above, below, up, down, go, come, mine, yours, drop, pick up,* and many more must have been represented gesturally long before there were any vocal signs for them.

The preexistence of various sign languages among the different tribes that converged on the American prairie to hunt the bison would have helped the creation of a widely understood sign language. This statement cannot be tested with data from tribal languages and descriptions of Plains Sign Talk made before the invention of cinematography, but research has been done on a similar dynamic that suggests the statement is true. Hundreds of deaf signers from many countries came to Washington, D.C., in the summer of 1975 for the Seventh Congress of the World Federation of the Deaf. Robbin Battison and I. King Jordan (who later became the president of Gallaudet University) interviewed fifty-three of them from seventeen countries to seek answers to the following questions:

1. Do deaf people around the world use the same signs?
2. Can signers understand each other's sign languages?
3. Can signers from different countries communicate with each other even if they don't know each other's sign languages?

4. Do signers have a clear idea of the separateness of different sign languages, or do they feel and act as if they are all basically the same thing?
5. What attitudes do people have about their own sign language and about foreign sign languages?[8]

Not surprisingly, interviews, observations, and personal reports yielded negative answers to the first two questions and positive answers to the fourth. About the third question, the authors write:

> The fact that deaf signers can and do communicate despite not sharing the same sign language is interesting, and it bears more investigation. While being skilled in sign language may prepare one for dealing with mime and for communicating in difficult cross-cultural situations, the two should not be confused. Signers consider them [using sign language and using ad hoc gestures] separate tasks.
>
> The data we have gathered gives us little reason to believe that sign languages are much different from spoken languages as regards cross-cultural communication.

Taken together, these conclusions are not paradoxical. Whether two languages are signed or spoken, differences in vocabulary and grammar between them prevent easy communication. However, signers and speakers differ in an important way: signers experience language as something gestured and seen; speakers experience language as something spoken and heard. Moreover, whether the cross-cultural communication is between signers of different sign languages, between speakers of different spoken languages, or between a speaker and a signer—whatever their usual practice—there is only one channel open for use in any of these situations: vision and gesture, including mime. This channel is *the* language channel for deaf signers just as it is *a* language channel for alternate sign language users. But for most speakers, using this channel for language is something quite different, unfamiliar, and often uncomfortable.

Speakers are not unfamiliar with gesture and mime, of course; but they are used to seeing people make gestures to illustrate something said or to make a silent comment or to emphasize a point or to beat out a rhythm—not to make connected sentences. Speakers' experience of mime may be only passive—seeing professional mime artists. Even if they have played charades, however, they have linked what they saw or did with specific, limited meanings; and of course the whole point of the game is to identify the visible activity with a specific word or phase. Speech communities also have a convention for connecting gestures to meanings, but very few speakers have experienced deaf people's use of gestures for discourse. Signers, on the other hand, have plenty of experience in seeing just this kind of phenomena. Such experience helps them in cross-cultural communication in the visual-gestural mode.

What Jordan and Battison did not note, because it had not yet been mooted, is another, deeper experience that all signers have. In signed languages generally, as in a conjectured first sign language, the handshapes are likely to be bearers of nounlike meaning and the movements to be bearers of verblike meaning. So, even if the other person's sign language is different, both signers will share this most important structural or grammatical feature—signers are conditioned, as speakers are not, to find noun-verb language structure and meaning in actions they see and perform. As in deciphering coded messages, knowing which signs one encounters are nouns and which signs are verbs goes a long way toward understanding. Knowing this difference even subconsciously gives sign language users a considerable advantage over spoken language users in cross-cultural communication.

If some or all of the tribes hunting buffalo on the plains already possessed a long tradition of signing, this would explain why all contemporary observers spoke of the interactions as taking place in "the Indian Sign Language." The Euro-Americans took their communicative cues from the natives, many of whom may never have lost the ancient ability to communicate linguistically without speech.

It is possible to show how some primary sign languages have added to their vocabulary by borrowing, via fingerspelling, from the written words of spoken languages; but when it comes to distinguishing nouns from verbs and making sentences, it is possible to show that the borrowing proceeded in the other direction. Handshape and movement, central and peripheral vision, and basic syntactic structure are congruent two-in-one structures, as has been noted; but speech sounds have no such direct and natural way of signifying. Likewise, locations, space relations, and directions (not just "that way" but also "he told me" versus "I told him") in perception and gestural representation owe nothing to vocal representation.

Kendon proposed the useful distinction of primary and alternate sign languages; the former serving as the first or only language of deaf populations, the latter as acceptable and serviceable alternatives to a culture's spoken language. The presence of alternate sign languages in a few tribal cultures might be thought to have resulted from constructing a language of gestural signs to represent faithfully the vocabulary and grammar of the spoken language, as Kendon has suggested, but known efforts to construct such a gestural language have failed. Australian Aboriginals have both signed and spoken languages; so either they knew ages ago how to do something that sign code inventors of modern times have never learned, or their alternate sign languages exist alongside their spoken languages because the signed languages were there first.

CHAPTER 12

~

Visible Verbs Become Spoken

M ANY MOVEMENTS that humans see naturally suggest something other than themselves. This is a legacy from the remotest time. Among animals, movements of prey and predator give each an indication of what may happen next and a basis for choosing their own actions. As species evolved, the movements that could be made and the meanings that could be suggested in those movements became increasingly sophisticated. Among the higher primates, grooming, aggressive and submissive displays, begging, and other movements regulate complex social interactions. Humans also interpret movements; they inform us of what others do, what happens to things, and how a movement maker feels—all this is instinctive.

It has been understood for a long time that movements, gestures among them, have semantic interpretations. The argument of these chapters, however, is that syntactic interpretation has also evolved and is also eminently natural. Humans not only make, see, and interpret movement but also discern patterns in it: "Something dropped," "That one leapt," "She took it." Movements, when they become the primary symbols of a sign language, have a syntactic structure that can represent these patterns and many others that grow out of them.

Sounds can alarm, warn, beckon, threaten, and so on; but unaided by convention they cannot represent nounlike or verblike concepts.

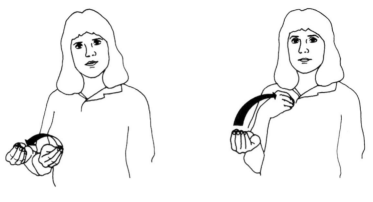

I-GIVE-YOU   YOU-GIVE-ME

FIGURE 14. *The direction of movement of a sign can be crucial to understanding the meaning of the sign.*

Powerless to make even this fundamental grammatical distinction, sounds have no natural, direct way to show concepts linked in the relationship called predication or syntax. Only convention can link sounds to word meanings and sentence meanings.

Primary sign languages are more natural than spoken languages because a visible sign often carries a visual clue to what it signifies. For example, the meaning of "I give" reverses the meaning of "I was given." Gestured, the two meanings are clearly opposite: the former sign moves outward from the signer; "I was given" moves toward the signer (see fig. 14). But when meanings like these are spoken in English, one must know the language to understand the crucial difference between them. To a speaker or reader of English, the auxiliary *was* signals the difference. Using *was* reverses the direction of the giving, but neither the vocal sounds that compose *was* nor the word itself refer to the direction of transitivity. In a sign language, however, what is given goes *from* the giver *to* the receiver; no rule is needed until language becomes spoken.

Humans possess an innate, clear understanding, gained early in life, that movement (of anything) toward self differs from movement away from self. Infants acquire this understanding when activity around them and their own hands and eyes and brain circuitry bring it into their ken. Later, of course, well beyond the period of infancy, they learn that a speaker's use of active or passive voice signals this basic reversal of direction, which was clear to them previously.

Speakers of languages have had to come up with various devices to indicate the difference between giving and being given and the whole active/passive distinction. Signers simply make opposed movements to signal the reversal of direction. This relationship of language sign to meaning is not derived from abstract rules. We first understood the active/passsive meaning difference by seeing, moving, feeling—by physical experience cognized. Observing the direction of physical actions is so simple and obvious that one may wonder why spoken languages need complex active-passive rules; but the explanation is obvious: sounds that voices make can no more directly *indicate* the difference between *give* and *receive* than that between *to* and *from*.

As the previous chapter revealed, alternate sign languages used by hearing people may differ from primary sign languages used by those who are deaf, but whether the difference is deep-seated or only one of degree has yet to be determined. If an alternate sign language fully represents a spoken language, it is just as correct to say that the spoken language fully represents the sign language. However, to know which is the original and which is the copy, we need to know whether signed or spoken language appeared first or whether they evolved together. Knowledge of physical evolution indicates that humans developed the anatomical capacity for speech relatively recently, but visible movements have carried meanings for millions of years; the present form of upper limbs has been a human possession for at least one million years. Hence a gestural, visual language is the likely candidate for first.

The first language sign to weld a nounlike and a verblike component into a single act—and the first signs to be so interpreted—had to be something visible moving. Suppose vocal sounds came to be uttered at the same time as the sentence-making hand-arm movements, however. In time the sound patterns could have become regular accompaniments of visible actions and meanings. The next advance would have been gradual refinement of the sounds or sound patterns until they differed according to which gesture-meaning they accompanied.

In this way, meanings that had long been conveyed gesturally could be more or less precisely represented by speech. This sequence accords with the nature of visible and audible signs. And even if gesturing and vocalizing were always done together, only the gestural representation could have a natural connection to what it signified. It hardly seems necessary, then, to ask whether signed languages could have preceded and given rise to spoken languages.

There might be yet another way to determine if signing came first. We could start by finding evidence disproving what some opponents of sign language have suggested—that signed language representations are derived from "the human universal of spoken language." It has seldom been thought profitable to spend time looking for such evidence. Ancient philosophers found it self-evident that humans communicated with gestures before they used speech. Once speech became a synonym for language, however, any such search became unthinkable.

In the first half of the twentieth century, many linguists considered gestures, voice quality, and tone of voice to be paralinguistic; that is, as integral parts of human communication and therefore as part of communication, though peripheral to language. Since midcentury, however, linguists have been more likely to think of gesturing as crude and animal-like and, therefore, as unrelated to language. The currently standard theory holds that language is innate and anthroposemiotic (peculiar to humans), while animal communication (including human gesture) is nonverbal or zoösemiotic (common to animals).

Once the opposite thought is entertained, however, there may be evidence worth searching for, and that evidence can be found. Kendon has shown the similarity of spoken and signed languages in Aboriginal Australia. McNeill has found evidence that vocal and gestural output come from the same inner process. Recently, additional evidence has come to light. Certain spoken-language verbs in their structure translate *quite literally* the structure of a gesture with the same meaning. Such verbs are found in two Penutian languages of the American northwest, Klamath and Modoc; and other languages are being searched for because there are hints that there is "a belt" of Native American languages with identically constructed verbs.[1] New questions and a more open way of thinking thus can lead to reinterpreting old facts as well as to finding new, and above all to looking in places that have not been seriously considered before.

Klamath and Modoc have verbs with morphemic, or syllabic, structure that appears to be copied directly from sign language verbs—or from the kinds of gestures any speaker might make. In the following discussion, some of the sign language verbs cited come from ASL, not of course from any prehistoric gesture language. Nevertheless, signs that look like what they represent obviously have a robustness of form. Because many sign language verbs represent what they mean naturally and directly, and because the structure of certain Klamath and Modoc verbs is exactly the structure of these natural gestures and sign language verbs, it follows that the vocal representation began as a literal translation of the visible action. The alternative—that the gestures were intentionally made to copy the structure of spoken verbs—is absurd.

Classifiers

It will be useful to look at one area of linguistics in which researchers have come close to discovering what we will be looking at here. ASL has been called a classifier language, and writers have identified about a dozen signs of ASL that fit Keith Allan's definition for classifiers:

> [C]lassifiers are defined on two criteria: (a) they occur as morphemes in surface structures under specifiable conditions; (b) they have meaning, in the sense that a classifier denotes some salient perceived or imputed characteristic of the entity to which an associated noun refers (or may refer).[2]

Applying the first criterion to ASL is difficult because of the different way that signed and spoken languages are expressed. The physics of sound and the nature of speech require using discrete vocal sounds to construct rule-governed structures called morphemes. Morphemes are the minimal meaning-bearing units of a spoken language. Thus, it is not the sounds as sounds but the particular combination of them within a morpheme that convention has linked to a meaning. In a signed language, however, differences in meaning can be made by altering a movement—but not enough to make it into what most observers would call a "different" movement, sign, or morpheme. In addition, since the earliest description of ASL as a language, some have considered a morpheme in ASL to be composed of at least a hand, its movement, and its location; others treat the hand, the movement, and a location as separate morphemes.

In addressing the "phonology of ASL," some researchers have suggested additional "parameters" (a term from engineering). These include "orientation," "point of contact," and "contacting part"; but none of these can be considered homologous to the consonant/vowel or other phonemic distinctions in speech, because an ASL sign-word often does not use contact at all, and the movement of a handshape usually makes it impossible to fix its location and/or orientation with precision.[3]

Suppose, however, that we specify a "neutral" or undifferentiated place, the space directly in front of a signer, where the hand or hands can be comfortably held (elbows bent to bring the hands up to chest level). Suppose then that a particular handshape is simply held there or "presented." The hand had to be moved to be presented there, so the movement really amounts to "stop-the-movement," but the stop may cause a perceptible rebound or shake. The handshape thus presented is a meaning-bearing unit, comparable to, but physically unlike, a morpheme composed of sounds. The handshape may have some natural relationship to what it means. It is not then an arbitrary collection of features as a spoken morpheme must be. When sign language users present a hand, its meaning may owe much to convention, but its whole appearance may also represent, as Allan suggests above, "some salient perceived or imputed characteristic" of the thing or class of things it represents (see fig. 15).

This "presented" handshape does not denote action, but often it does represent something likely to be associated with a particular kind of action. Recall again Supalla and Newport's discovery that the same handshape presented (or very slightly moved) is nounlike, but when saliently moved it becomes verblike. Characteristics of the kind or class of things that "sit"—the two bent fingers of the moving hand suggest the legs of a sitter—are naturally adapted to the action depicted: the movement places them across the extended fingers (the "seat") of the stationary hand. Similarly, the ASL classifier handshape that represents the class of things that fly is adapted in different ways for the noun PLANE and the verb FLY.[4]

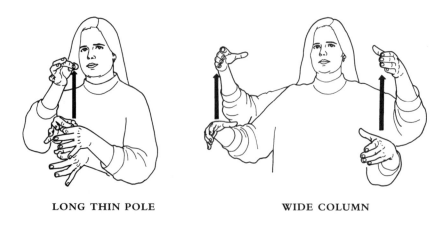

LONG THIN POLE   **WIDE COLUMN**

FIGURE 15. *Classifier handshapes are used to convey a particular meaning that cannot be conveyed by any other handshape.*

In his study of more than fifty "classifier languages," Allan categorizes the languages as belonging "to one of four types—(i) numeral classifier languages, (ii) concordial classifier languages, (iii) predicate classifier languages, and (iv) intra-locative classifier languages."[5] ASL uses numeral classifiers, but it seems to be mainly the third type, a predicate classifier language. It fits Allan's criteria well. Allan cites Hoijer, who "drew attention to the fact that Navajo verbs of motion/location consist of a theme such as 'give' or 'lie' and a stem which varies according to certain discernible characteristics of the 'objects or objects conceived as participating in an event whether as actor or goal.' "[6]

Verb Structure

In ASL, to relate that someone gave something, movement expresses what Hoijer calls the theme; that is, the hand moves from the assumed location of the giver toward the recipient. The handshape making the movement often appears as it would if it were actually holding the object being given: a book, a glass of water, a ball, a basket with handle, or something tall and thin like a staff, and so on. Thus the sign verb's handshape is a stem. It is also a classifier because it denotes a salient characteristic of what is being given or held or thrown or whatever.

Because the handshape can assume configurations suggested by the characteristics of the objects represented, there will be differences in the movement as well. Both classifier (handshape) and movement, as stem and theme, show visible characteristics of the object.[7] Thus, it would be equally correct to say that ASL verbs are composed the same way: *a handshape is moved.*[8] In verbs, the movement expresses the "theme," which also may be influenced by the nature of what the handshape (Allan's "stem") is denoting.

This two-part structure is easy to see when a verb's theme denotes "throw." English often uses this one verb to designate a fast, directed movement of dice, a stone, a spear, a glass of water, or a softball, and figuratively a contest or "a curve." But in ASL, as in any spontaneous gesture of the "illustrator" kind, a different hand-arm movement will be used to represent the theme, because each different kind of object calls for a different kind of throwing (an underhand swing with palm outward for shooting craps or releasing a bowling ball; an overarm arc for throwing a spear or a rock). Thus, the gesture and sign language verb use the appropriate arm movement as well as the appropriate handshape for the action represented. The physical action of the sign maker is directly influenced by what the sign denotes; in other words, the whole sign is an index. The two parts of the ASL verb (or an "illustrator" gesture) visibly suggest both the object and the action, the stem and the theme in Allan's terms (see fig. 16).

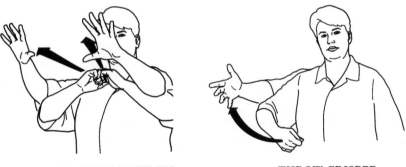

THROW-BASKETBALL   **THROW-FRISBEE**

FIGURE 16. *The verb* THROW *is an example of an ASL verb that incorporates both the action and the object of the verb.*

Some ASL verbs, however, instead of using the handshape as an object-representing classifier, use it to indicate number. ASL thus qualifies to some extent as a numeral classifier language. For example, compare the following English sentences with their corresponding handshapes when translated into ASL:

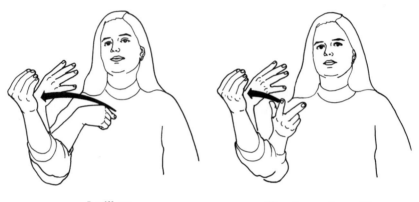

I will go.   **The three of us will go.**

With a singular subject, the handshape of the sign GO briefly extends the index finger (a universal symbol of singularity), but with a plural subject, the handshape indicates exactly how many subjects there are.

Allan defines seven categories of classification: material, shape, consistency, size, location, arrangement [arrangement classifiers in English are *row* or *tier*], and quanta [*heap* or *bunch*]. He writes, "The last two occur in languages like English which are not classifier languages; but so far as I can judge, the first five occur only in classifier languages."[9] Allan also notes that they "intermesh." Material can be wood, water, plastic, and so on; consistency may be solid, liquid, viscous, or sticky; and both material and consistency may be represented in one classifier. All these characteristics are readily represented with hand activity. After all, the look *and feel* of most materials is the way we still distinguish them. The first humans to take note of them must have done likewise, using their highly developed senses of sight and touch.

Classifiers in all of Allan's categories occur plentifully in sign languages. What he calls "discernible characteristics" are salient to vision, the master sense, and to touch and proprioception (muscle sense). The users of the earliest sign languages would not have been selecting rules from universal grammar to create a vocabulary. They would have been doing what comes naturally.

First, in order to represent an object in use, the first humans to use language would certainly have imitated closely (with an empty hand) the look of the hand actually using or handling that object. They would also have imitated the action they wished to associate with that object—for example, picking it up, throwing it, or striking with it. Having discovered this way to call attention to the whole thing, they would also have found a way to focus others' attention, either on the object (hand) or on the action (movement). Thus, separating out of the representation of the whole action signs for a nounlike and for a verblike concept gave them a visible language with syntax as well as the wordlike meanings. Permutations and combinations of handshape and movement (noun and verb) would immediately have opened up the creativity of language.

Signers' use of space—in the abstract geometrical sense—has often been written about as a grammatical feature. It is worth considering, however, that it is not abstract space in front of a signer that is significant. What is significant is the movement (in any and all directions) made by the signer. Yet because they are visible, locations that signers point to may function somewhat like predicate classifiers. A signer who has been telling a story about an animal in a tree will point up and outward when first designating where the animal was seen. Then, in referring to it and what it did later, the signer need only point to the same location and smoothly move the pointing, animal-designating hand classifier in the movement of some such sign verb as CLIMBED-DOWN, JUMPED, or FELL (see fig. 17).

Color

Allan was surprised to find "not a single color classifier in any language."[10] This may be surprising to a linguist or semanticist, but it is not surprising at all to a student of sign language and gesture. Sign languages and gestures make no *direct* (iconic or indexic) representation of color. How could they? Color, though visible, has no shape or form, it cannot be directly represented; it must be denoted by inference. Although color has

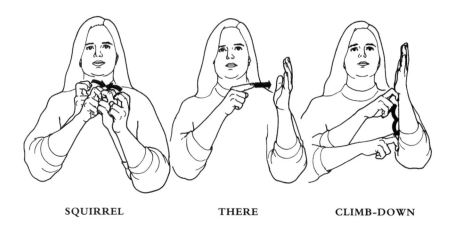

SQUIRREL   THERE   CLIMB-DOWN

FIGURE 17. *Signers designate a location in space as a reference point for sentence subjects or objects.*

obvious visible characteristics, it does not exist as an entity, only as a feature of something else.

A long time was probably needed for early language signers to establish the convention that when they pointed to the sky they meant "blue" instead of "up there," or when they pointed to a leafy tree they did not mean "tree" but "green." The sky and foliage are so pervasive in many cultures that using specific words for "blue" and "green" never became necessary. Researchers have actually found societies with languages that lack color terms for "blue" and "green." But gestures can easily represent dark and light. Appropriate handshapes and movements (including handshape change) in front of the eyes suggest obscuring and revealing sight. And, as it happens, terms for "dark" and "light" are the only color terms a few languages have.[11] Unlike the blue of sky and green of jungles, however, blood when seen must have had, as it still does, a sudden startling effect. Small wonder that red is the first term after black and white, or dark and light, to appear in languages with only three color terms.[12]

In ASL, French Sign Language, and others related to them, signs for some colors have been derived by directly borrowing a spoken language's color word. The manual alphabet handshape for the word's initial letter is presented; for example, moving the manual alphabet B for *blue, bleu,* or *blau* (see fig. 18). But in another cultural setting, color may be treated

The Evolution of Color Words

If a language encodes fewer than eleven basic color categories, then there are strict limitations on which categories it may encode. The distributional restrictions of color terms across languages are:

1. All languages contain terms for white and black.
2. If a language contains three terms, then it contains a term for red.
3. If a language contains four terms, then it contains a term for either green or yellow (but not both).
4. If a language contains five terms, then it contains terms for both green and yellow.
5. If a language contains six terms, then it contains a term for blue.
6. If a language contains seven terms, then it contains a term for brown.
7. If a language contains eight or more terms, then it contains a term for purple, pink, orange, grey, or some combination of these.

Source: *From Brent Berlin and Paul Kay,* Basic Color Terms: Their Universality and Evolution *(Berkeley: University of California Press, 1969), 2–3.*

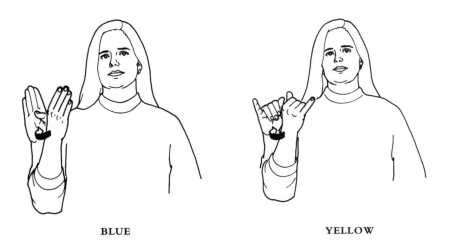

BLUE   YELLOW

FIGURE 18. *The signs* BLUE *and* YELLOW *are initialized signs.*

differently. Kuschel and Momberg, in an essay about Rennell Island's Polynesian people, used one of the islanders' sayings for their title: "We don't talk much about color here."

Kangobai, a Rennell islander, is deaf and uses a sign language with his peers, but the islanders who told Kuschel and Momberg they don't talk much about color are hearing speakers of a Polynesian language. Kuschel points out that two otherwise identical-looking fish that the islanders routinely catch are quite different in color. One is wholesome, but eating the other brings on ugly visions or hallucinations. Nevertheless, the Rennellese don't use any terms for their difference in color when referring to them but differentiate them by other characteristics.[13]

Much of the variety in the modern use of color terms becomes comprehensible when we understand that the first languages were seen rather than heard. If the use of color terms developed only after languages had shifted their major work of making language signs from hands to voices, the wide variation in the nature and number of color words becomes clear. That color words are not used as classifiers would seem to result from the impossibility of directly representing colors gesturally. The characteristics discerned by appearance and touch and manipulation are the ones most likely to be represented in the earliest signed, and spoken, languages—and to survive as classifiers.

Noun Classifiers

By contrast, shape as a feature for classifying differs sharply from color. Allan notes that "Amerindian languages seem to have more shape classifiers than other languages, and Tarascan has only this type."[14] This too will not surprise anyone who has followed the argument thus far. Hands and their movements are particularly useful for representing shapes (Harpo Marx may come to mind). It is not surprising either that tribal peoples who now have or once had a sign language as part of their culture would have many shape classifiers in their spoken languages. Shape classifiers by their nature refer to visible things that nouns designate. Indexic movements in sign verbs and gestures take their "shapes"—as tracing in air of their movement—from what they signify; but Allan is talking about the shape of the objects, not of the actions. His conclusion begins thus: "The recurrence of similar noun classifiers in many widely dispersed languages from separate families, spoken by disparate cultural groups, demonstrates the essential similarity of man's response to his environment."[15]

He might have carried this point further. Human response to the environment depends first on seeing, touching, and manipulating things within it. Along with vision, using the hands for representing these things makes the resulting brain circuits and neural maps increasingly more effective for their possessors' control of the environment. To take one example, the way one grasps a club and wields it to ward off an attacker is built into not just the hand but the whole brain and body.[16]

But that sequence of actions performed is easily represented by actions of the empty hand, the arm, and body—the handshapes and movements of the representation are simply copies of the original action. Small wonder then that classifiers meaning "something clublike" or "something paddlelike" or "something basketlike" would be common manual representations. It seems also that certain spoken languages in various parts of the world have classifiers, words or morphemes that originally referred to such gestures and their general meaning. Certainly response to experience with the environment brings forth manual representations, but grammatical categories cannot explain the actual form of different spoken language classifiers for classes of objects. However, if we posit an intermediate stage of manual representation, between the experience and the token formed by the voice, the similarity Allan notes is easily explained.

There is more in this than similarity of response to the environment. Finding in many languages similar noun classifiers demonstrates the importance of hand and eye for first representing the environment and human responses to it. Spoken languages and spoken language families show almost unlimited variation in their use of sounds to represent meanings. This is to be expected. Virtually nothing in the nature of vocal sounds ties them to visible characteristics. However, the practice in classifier languages of grouping things by shape, consistency, and size, while it seems logical after the fact, must have begun when hands and vision were first used to classify. Classifiers that denote visible features and features recognized by seeing movement predominate in all the classifier languages. This strongly implies a gestural beginning.

Sign languages unite noun classifier and verb theme in signing in a way that speech does not necessarily follow. In English, for example, *stone, spear*, and *apple* are nouns, and *throw, lie,* and *fall* are verbs. In a language like ASL, the classifier furnishes the handshape that denotes the object, and moving that handshape in the appropriate way expresses the verb's theme. When these elements—object and action—began to be represented vocally, the morpheme (pattern of sounds) uttered to stand for what the handshape signified and the morpheme to represent the action would initially follow the same order: first the handshape, then its movement. Once it became common practice to speak and as the practice of using the gestural representations at the same time gradually went out of use, classifier and theme would no longer be held together in their original sequence by the look and feel of the original sign or gesture. Once verb and argument (subject, object, instrument, etc.), become represented vocally there is nothing to keep them in their original order.

In any spoken language, the meaningful signs (morphemes) must assemble certain vocal sounds in prescribed order, but only the convention of a particular language community prescribes the ordering of the morphemes themselves. When only two morphemes are joined, the grammar of the particular spoken language determines their order; for example, "throw spear" or "spear throw." Nothing in the nature of speech itself imposes any order.

In any sign language, however, the order is determined naturally by "body-sense": it is hard to imagine throwing a spear that one does not have hold of. It might be possible to sign "throw" and then "spear" in a hypothetical sign language, but the sign for "throw" would, like any manual sign, need a handshape, and it would make no sense and be a waste of time and energy to use a noncommittal handshape (if there is such a thing) for "throw" and then to represent "spear" without any characteristic hand configuration. (People who invent sign codes for representing English vocabulary and sentence structure make such errors.)

When a spoken language not only keeps the natural order of the gestural representation but also composes its verbs with a first part expressing what a handshape would represent and a second part expressing what the movement would represent, the implication is clear: Klamath and Modoc and other languages that preserve the natural gestural-visual order in two part verbs appear to have taken at least this much of their structure from an earlier sign language. The implication is made stronger by the persistence of alternate sign languages in many of these indigenous cultures.

If this close scrutiny of only certain verb forms in just two languages seems to yield findings too meager to impress many scholars of language, the objectors would do well to reflect on the paucity of fossil evidence on which our present understanding of biological evolution is based. More human and hominid fossils have been found since Darwin's time, but these still constitute a smaller fraction of the whole of hominid and human population than the fraction these few verb forms constitute of "the whole of language," whatever that may be.

Allan also points out that "other commonly recurring noun classes designate bladed or pointed objects, body parts, food, implements, liquids (often including rivers, creeks, and the like), and boats. Boats are perhaps the original vehicles, and the 'boat' classifier is more widely used than any for vehicles in general."[17] The ASL vehicle classifier—very widely used in our mobile culture—looks as if it might at first have been an iconic sign for a boat or ship: the hand as hull and the extended thumb and index and middle finger resembling spars. (The ASL "boat" sign uses two hands to imitate a hull-like shape, but two-hand signs in time often give way to one-hand signs.) Today, of course the thumb-and-two-finger handshape of ASL can be a classifier for any land or seagoing vehicle (see fig. 19). Languages, sign languages included, are subject to cultural change.

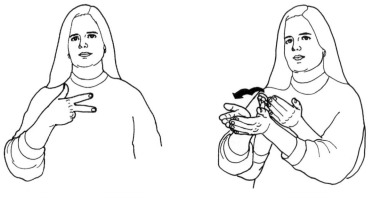

VEHICLE CLASSIFIER   **BOAT**

FIGURE 19. *The 3 handshape vehicle classifier can be used to represent any kind of vehicle, whereas the sign* BOAT *has one specific meaning.*

Sign languages apparently have little need for the full panoply of grammatical rules and devices that grammarians have inventoried, or invented, over the two and one half millennia since Pānini. Given the power manual gestures have to represent nounlike, verblike, and sentence kinds of meaning, given so plastic an organ as the human brain and its cognitive powers, given truly human bodies and the unique human hand, those in the first species so equipped would have had no difficulty showing each other what they could see and contemplate and experience. And the gestural language they used would have had no difficulty keeping up with the growing complication of events and relationships inevitable in a language-using human society.

CHAPTER 13

❧

A Difference That
Makes a Difference

THE ARGUMENT PRESENTED so far may be summarized this way: mimetic representations would have externalized human conceptions of creatures and things and happenings. One kind of representation—a hand and its movement—serendipitously connected active creatures with their actions, or things with the changes that happened to them. Human vision does the same. Thus represented, the sentence meanings, and the nounlike and verblike meanings that crystallized out of the gestures, could have led to full development of a language that would express any conceivable thought of its users. Consequently—millennia later—vocalizations that had been uttered incidentally with the visible language signs at first became more precisely differentiated. At that point distinctive sound patterns made with different gesture-meaning pairs could gradually have taken over from the gestural signs more and more of the language-representing function. Only the outward form of language, its mode of expression and the sensory channel for its reception, would need to change. But this summary fails to point out what might be gained by such a view of language evolution. One may ask: What advantage comes from supposing that language began with visible signs? Giving serious consideration to the idea that manual representation plays a major part in human evolution could revolutionize educational programs for people who cannot hear. Years of teaching deaf undergraduate and graduate students showed me the results of miseducation—the inevitable consequences of a widespread belief that only speech can be language.

For centuries, persons with charity and good intentions developed educational methods for deaf (and hearing children as well) based on the false assumptions that language is speech, that literacy is the sole aim of education, and that the inability to hear speech is associated with mental deficiency. Thus, willingness to accept the present language metamorphosis theory could have beneficial effects on the way children are educated.

In the past, and to some extent still, the accepted way to treat deaf children in school was to make "every lesson a language lesson," as older teachers loved to repeat. To teachers in the United States "language" was exclusively the English they spoke (or thought they spoke), the English of their grammar books. Immense amounts of time and money were devoted to the goal of training deaf children to make sense of what they saw on the faces of speakers whom they could not hear. As much or more resources were devoted to training them to speak sounds, words, and sentences they themselves had no direct way to monitor and correct. To be sure, a degree of success at speech can be useful to deaf people, especially when they have some residual hearing. But when they are taught nothing else and the training continues long after positive results fail to be obtained, they gain nothing and lose much.

This attempt is driven largely by the belief that language is speech. If one person can be singled out as responsible for beginning this miseducation of the deaf, it would be Johann Amman of Holland. Assuming the persona of Laurent Clerc, Harlan Lane has written in *When the Mind Hears*:

> The "German system" . . . oralists urge upon us now began at the dawn of the eighteenth century with Amman, the perpetrator of a particularly evil and self-serving thesis I call the God's breath flim-flam: "The breath of life resides in the voice, transmitting enlightenment through it," Amman wrote. "The voice is the interpreter of our hearts and expresses its affections and desires. . . . The voice is a living

emanation of that spirit that God breathed into man when he created him a living soul."[1]

Even without the religious fervor of Amman, however, the identification of enlightenment, mind, human understanding, and language with the human voice continued to dominate attempts to educate deaf persons in many places. The Abbé de l'Epée and some of his successors disagreed. Those (including Clerc) who helped found schools like Epée's all over the Western world made good use of their pupils' understanding of manual signs. For two centuries the debate, sometimes an open battle, about how deaf persons should be educated and communicated with has continued under the name of "The Oral-Manual Controversy."

One consequence of the argument here is to refute not only Amman's thesis that spirit, speech, God's breath, and language are all one and indivisible but also the nineteenth- and twentieth-century secular version of oralism. That version was based on the belief that unless deaf persons could be trained to read speech from speakers' faces and to speak intelligibly themselves, they would remain not only without language but defective mentally.

The contest between oralists and teachers who use and welcome sign languages has continued for centuries. Not solely a theoretical battle, it has been waged also on pragmatic grounds—each camp parading its successes and keeping its failures out of sight. However, in more than four decades of teaching deaf students, I encountered a great many of those dubbed "oral failures"—dropouts and pupils dismissed from oral programs. And I have seen many of them succeeding in settings where they and their teachers use their sign language. There may be some truly deaf persons who have dropped out of programs where signing is used without restriction, who have given up signing, and who have succeeded in an oralist program, but I have neither seen nor heard of any.

It is not ironic but sensible that some deaf parents of deaf children send them for a time to an oral school. Having acquired a sign language practically from birth, these children may well be in a position to benefit from rigorous training in how to speak words they cannot hear; but were I in the parents' place, I would visit the school to ascertain that dislike and distrust of deaf children do not underlie the teachers' attitudes.

The time has come to move this debate from speculation to science. Once it is understood that vocal sound production can have no *natural* connection to nounlike and verblike concepts, let alone sentence meanings; once it is understood that every infant grasps and uses the natural connection of body movements to meanings on the way to acquiring language; once it is realized that our species emerged by going through the same stage of representing concepts visibly—only then will the falseness of the claims of oralism be seen. When not just specialists but those who vote for school boards, pay taxes, and serve in PTAs take in fully the arguments presented here, respect for the power of gestural representation could help many educational programs succeed, and not just those for deaf children.

If vision and movement, the perceptual-action system, are natural and necessary for the first representation of mental conceptions, then vision and movement must form the foundation on which cognition, mind, and language are built. Thus, it would make sense to see that all young children's visual-motoric readiness for language gets the attention and emphasis now given to their early attempts at speaking. Positive results of such support have been reported in the press. At the University of California Davis Center for Child and Family Studies, hearing children whose parents communicate with them in "baby signs" have been found to score "significantly higher on standard IQ tests" than children without that experience.[2] Similar communication experiments at Ohio State University are also having success, according to reports.[3]

Teachers of the deaf, instead of grudgingly accepting their pupils' signing as "the best they can do," can now go forward, confident that they are not only justified in accepting and using sign language but are in harmony with the natural history of language. The good work these teachers are doing will become more satisfying when they know that by working from a visible language toward a spoken and written language, they are not going against nature but are following the course of human history. They may even look at those of their charges who do not attain fluent mastery of the community's spoken language in written form not as lacking something but, because they are fluent signers, as having something very much worth having—a genuine language with a naturalness and directness that deaf speech often lacks.

In this connection, I recall an evening spent many years ago with a prominent sociolinguist from the Center for Applied Linguistics (CAL). There were two or three deaf teachers and an interpreter also in the group, and the talk was mostly shop. Partway through the discussion the CAL guest remarked: "This is fascinating; there seems to be a far smaller nonsense quotient when sign language is being used than is usual in such discussions." Here, indeed, the theoretical side may be lagging behind the practical: the number of hearing persons in the United States who are taking courses in ASL in high schools, colleges, and universities keeps growing. Perhaps these students have intuitively grasped what this theory of language metamorphosis encapsulates. As Andy Clark puts it: "Perception and action [not speech], on this view, form a deeply interanimated unity."[4]

Back to Basics

Improved education of deaf people is by no means the only benefit that could come from seriously considering speech as a later, changed state of language. A great deal of attention and many resources are expended on education generally. But the untested belief that language begins with speech directly influences the way we raise our children. A key question for parents and educators is, When are children ready for school? First grade at five or six was the norm seventy-five years ago when I entered school, but kindergarten at that age has been the starting point for decades, and preschools now commonly enroll three- and four-year-olds in formal educational programs. Head Start makes some impact on this general pattern but not enough.[5]

The question of when to begin formal, institutionalized education is complex enough, but there are also uncertainties about what and how to teach very young children. There continue to be questions, yet it was clear to John Holt and others many years ago that teaching is inappropriate for infants and young children. They are driven to learn by being human. What they need is not "teaching" but the opportunity to learn. They are too often turned off by attempts at teaching them what someone thinks they need to learn. Willingness to entertain the possibility that language began long before there could be speech might make a difference in the way these questions are addressed.

Biologists, neuroscientists, and cognitive scientists have been acquiring new knowledge rapidly, and one thing they have discovered applies directly here: the human infant's brain at two years of age contains more neural connections (synapses) than it will ever have again, at any age. The electrochemical circuits of the brain can grow and to some extent replace themselves; but when they are not used, they die and disappear. Another fact of biology is that the uniquely large ratio of brain to body size in humans has led to a unique epigenesis in the mammalian order: the human infant after nine months in gestation is born completely helpless, with its brain only incompletely formed (otherwise its head could not pass through the birth canal). Then, for a year or more the infant is dependent not only on complete physical care but on sensory and mental stimulation if it is to survive and develop.

Add to these physiological facts what Volterra and Iverson point out—*all infants communicate first gesturally*—and the conclusion is clear: the real foundations of language, both social and biological, are the infant's interactions with the environment and with others. These interactions for months during the period of maximum brain growth are mediated by gestural communication. Researchers have found that the *amount* of direct, positive, and encouraging parent talk with children from birth to the age of three is the one variable that fully predicts their placement on all kinds of tests; and these results remain when the same children are tested again at age ten.[6]

It would be interesting to study longitudinally more than the effect of parents' talk with their children—we might look also at the effect of parents' visual-gestural, hands-on interactions with their children (as seems to be happening at UC Davis and OSU).

Volterra and Iverson undertook their study to test the claim made by some (I was one of them) that deaf infants in deaf, sign-language-using families might reach various milestones in language acquisition earlier than hearing children do within hearing families. What they found is that the general timetable for language acquisition is the same for both deaf and hearing children. That, together with others' results, makes it likely that the parents who talked more with their infants may also have been engaging in more eye contact and gestural activity with their infants.

This too is a testable hypothesis, but experiments are hardly needed. Humans are not just social but supersocial animals—we have a special mode of communicating and socializing that other animals have not so far been found to possess. It has been argued that this special mode, language, is a highly abstract set of grammar rules stored in the brain; but it is beyond question that language is both cause and effect of human socialization.

Over the centuries, language has been taken out of the normal context of use to become an object of study by itself. This is not surprising; language is a highly complex and endlessly fascinating behavior or system. But when language is studied as a self-contained system, apart from individuals, society, culture, physiology, and the uses it is put to, the descriptions of language become more and more abstruse and complex. When language is studied in human society—where it comes from, where it belongs, and where it is used—however, we find that language is far more than writing can record of speech. Language is also more than what parsing, diagramming, and linguistic rules make it out to be. Language may not be the literal breath of God, as Amman thought, but it is surely very close to the essence of human nature.

Recognizing that only visible signs can *naturally* represent the relationships of visible objects, creatures, and events; recognizing that each infant has to invent language anew by moving from gestural to genuinely language representations; recognizing that the emerging human species in all probability moved along much the same trail—recognizing all this, we could, I believe, do better than we are doing for all our children. Day care, before a child is old enough to be in preschool, could become the most productive part of the child's education. If day care providers were aware of how important direct interaction (with gestures as well as language) can be, day care could become preparation for success at every stage of schooling and life.

Developmental problems have sometimes been treated by taking the child back through the very early phase of crawling on all fours. This treatment is based on the idea that the neural timing required by language and other higher-order functions is initiated by the proper sequencing of alternate arm and leg movements (and of course by the associated asymmetrical brain circuitry). Perhaps the gestural origin theory could also become the basis for therapy: the evidence that all children communicate gesturally before using the parents' or caregivers' language suggests that understanding gestures first and then understanding words is a perfectly normal and natural progression—as Roger Fouts found it to be with David and Mark, two autistic children (see chapter 6).

Although children can be said to be born with the potential to walk and talk (or sign), these activities are by no means simple gene-driven instincts. Walking and talking emerge only in the continual presence of others who already walk and talk (or sign), and who more unconsciously than consciously help the infant toward acquiring these skills. It could certainly do no harm to be attentive to infants' visual interests and attention, to interact with them as if they understood more than we usually think they do—surely they do—and to look on visual communication as at least as important as vocal communication. It could do no harm, and it might do much good.

New Directions

A better start in life for all children, not just deaf children, is a benefit that could accrue if spoken language came to be understood as the changed form of language originally signed. When this hypothesis about language origins is entertained, the direction of scientific research might also change. Language sciences might become more empirical and less formalistic. Psychologists might find new ways to discover what children really know and understand. Psychometrists might come up with new instruments for examining mental abilities. Cognitive and brain scientists might find that the relationships of vision and movement to knowing, thinking, and using language are closer than they have heretofore imagined. Instead of searching for precise brain areas or particular genes for particular grammatical functions, linguists and psycholinguists might take more notice of current neuroscience, which finds that brains work with broad connectivity—integrating vision, physical movement, and cognition, and finding intricate patterns within existing wholes. Paleontologists' ability to date and differentiate human and hominid species might also be sharpened by knowing that language could have begun long before speech emerged, and in its visible form could have been productively used and its patterns elaborated, giving them a full range of sentence patterns. Individuals might also benefit, simply from realizing that when it came to skills for survival, our ancestors back as far as a million years were hardly our inferiors in survival skills and innovation.

Notes

Chapter 1

1. William C. Stokoe, *Sign Language Structure: An Outline of the Visual Communication Systems of the American Deaf* (Buffalo: University of Buffalo Department of Anthropology and Linguistics, Occasional Papers 8, 1960; reprint, Burtonsville, Md.: Linstok Press, 1993).

2. William C. Stokoe, Dorothy Casterline, and Carl Croneberg, *A Dictionary of American Sign Language on Linguistic Principles* (Washington, D.C.: Gallaudet College, 1965; reprint, Burtonsville, Md.: Linstok Press, 1976).

3. Thomas A. Sebeok, *Signs: An Introduction to Semiotics* (Toronto: University of Toronto Press, 1994).

4. Noam Chomsky, *Syntactic Structures* (The Hague: Mouton, 1957).

5. Andrew Clark, "Where Brain, Body, and World Collide," *Daedalus* 127, no. 2 (Spring 1998): 267.

6. Ted Supalla and Elissa Newport, "How Many Seats in a Chair? The Derivation of Nouns and Verbs in American Sign Language," in *Understanding Language through Sign Language Research,* ed. Patricia Siple (New York: Academic Press, 1978), 91–132.

7. Adam Kendon, *Sign Languages of Aboriginal Australia* (Cambridge: Cambridge University Press, 1988).

8. Brenda Farnell, *Do You See What I Mean? Plains Indian Sign Talk and the Embodiment of Action* (Austin: University of Texas Press, 1995).

9. Scott DeLancey, "Lexical Prefixes and the Bipartite Stem Construction in Klamath," *International Journal of American Linguistics* 65, no. 1 (1999): 56–83. Scott DeLancey maintains a Web site on his research on Klamath and other Indian languages. The information is available at *http://darkwing.uoregon.edu/delancey/klamath.html.*

10. Virginia Volterra and Jana Iverson, "When Do Modality Factors Affect the Course of Language Acquisition?" in *Language, Gesture, and Space,* ed. Karen Emmorey and Judy Snitzer Reilly (Hillsdale, N.J.: Lawrence Erlbaum, 1995), 371–90.

Chapter 2

1. Graham Cairns-Smith, *Evolving the Mind: On the Nature of Matter and the Origin of Consciousness* (Cambridge: Cambridge University Press, 1996), 91–94.
2. See Chomsky, *Syntactic Structures;* and the Spring 1998 issue of *Daedalus* for a discussion of this topic by eleven scientists.
3. Charles Darwin, *The Expression of Emotion in Man and Animals* (1872; reprint, New York: Appleton, 1983).
4. Roger W. Wescott, Gordon Hewes, and William Stokoe, eds., *Language Origins* (Silver Spring, Md.: Linstok Press, 1974).
5. In "In Search of Jove's Brow," *American Speech* 53 (1978): 243–313, Charles Hockett reviewed Morris Swadesh, *The Origin and Diversification of Language,* ed. Joel Sherzer (Chicago, Aldine, 1971); Philip Lieberman, *On the Origins of Language: An Introduction to the Evolution of Human Speech* (New York: Macmillan, 1975); Stevan Harnad, Horst Steklis, and Jane Lancaster, eds., *Origins and Evolution of Language and Speech* (New York: New York Academy of Sciences, 1976); and Wescott, Hewes, and Stokoe, eds., *Language Origins.*
6. See Chomsky, *Syntactic Structures,* and Steven Pinker, *The Language Instinct: How the Mind Creates Languages* (New York: William Morrow, 1994).
7. Volterra and Iverson, "Modality Factors."
8. See, for example, James Woodward, "Historical Bases of American Sign Language," in *Understanding Language through Sign Language Research,* Patricia Siple, ed. (New York: Academic Press, 1978), 333–48.
9. Kendon, *Sign Languages of Aboriginal Australia.*
10. David McNeill, *Hand and Mind: What Gestures Reveal about Thought* (Chicago: University of Chicago Press, 1992).
11. Farnell, *Do You See What I Mean?*

Chapter 3

1. Volterra and Iverson, "Modality Factors."
2. Susan Goldin-Meadow and Carolyn Mylander, "Spontaneous Sign Systems Created by Deaf Children in Two Cultures," *Nature* 391: (1998) 279–81.
3. Curt Suplee, "Turning to the Deaf for Signs of Innate Language Ability," *Washington Post,* Jan. 18, 1998.
4. Susan Goldin-Meadow and Heidi Feldman, "The Creation of a Communication System," *Sign Language Studies* 8 (1975): 225–34.

5. Frank R. Wilson, *The Hand: How Its Use Shapes the Brain, Language, and Human Culture* (New York: Pantheon, 1998).

6. Ibid., chapter 1.

7. People who are both deaf and blind find Braille useful too, especially if they suffered hearing loss before loss of sight and acquired language by means of signs and fingerspelling.

8. African Grey parrots can imitate these sounds with uncanny accuracy, but they are reproducing sounds, not language. Machines that synthesize human speech are of course becoming common. It is also arguable that chimpanzees can use linguistic signs.

9. The use of vision for reading is not the same as deaf people's use of vision for communicating with other people. Literacy is the process of seeing secondary, graphic symbols and understanding them as the primary, vocal symbols of language. As a channel for one who knows a sign language, vision takes in its primary symbols directly—just as hearing takes in the primary symbols of a spoken language for one who knows it.

10. In *The Making of Language* (Edinburgh: Edinburgh University Press, 1996), Mike Beaken fully explores the contribution of social organization and cooperation to the emergence of language and of fully human nature.

11. For the story of how a deaf infant learns language and much else from a deaf mother, see Judy Williams, "The Bilingual Experiences of a Deaf Child," *Sign Language Studies* 10 (1976): 37–41.

12. Supalla and Newport, "How Many Seats in a Chair?"

Chapter 4

1. See Harlan Lane, *When the Mind Hears* (New York: Random House, 1984), and Nicholas Mirzoeff, *Silent Poetry: Deafness, Sign, and Visual Culture in Modern France* (Princeton: Princeton University Press, 1995), for a review of these developments, particularly in France and the United States.

2. For a discussion of paternalism in both manual and oral traditions, see Douglas Baynton, *Forbidden Signs: American Culture and the Campaign Against Sign Language* (Chicago: University of Chicago Press, 1996), particularly the epilogue, "The Trap of Paternalism."

3. For a review of Western philosophers' thoughts about sign language and deaf people, see Jonathan Rée, *I See a Voice* (New York: Metropolitan Books, 1999).

4. George Montgomery and Arthur Dimmock, *Venerable Legacy: Saint Bede and the Anglo-Celtic Contribution to Literary, Numerical, and Manual Language*. (Edinburgh: Scottish Workshop Publications, 1998).

5. Teresa Chaves and Jorge Soler, "Pedro Ponce de León, First Teacher of the Deaf," *Sign Language Studies* 5 (1974): 48–63; Susan Plann, *A Silent Minority: Deaf Education in Spain, 1550–1835* (Berkeley: University of California Press, 1997).

6. Mirzoeff, *Silent Poetry,* 47, 50.

7. Ibid., 50.

8. Christopher Garnett, *The Exchange of Letters between Samuel Heinicke and Abbé Charles Michel de L'Epée: A Monograph on the Oralist and Manualist Methods of Instructing the Deaf in the Eighteenth Century* (New York: Vantage Press, 1968).

9. Lane, *When the Mind Hears,* chapter 5.

10. Stokoe, Casterline, and Croneberg, *Dictionary of American Sign Language.*

11. Stokoe, *Sign Language Structure,* 72f.

12. Charlotte Baker-Shenk, "A Microanalysis of the Nonmanual Components of Questions in American Sign Language" (Ph.D. diss., University of California, Berkeley, 1983).

13. Edward Sapir, *Language* (New York: Harcourt, Brace, and World, 1921), 38.

14. Darwin, *Expression of Emotion.*

15. Cairns-Smith, *Evolving the Mind,* 154.

16. Farnell, *Do You See What I Mean?* 251–61.

17. Supalla and Newport, "How Many Seats in a Chair?"

18. John D. Bonvillian et al., "Language, Cognitive, and Cherological Development," in *SLR '83: Proceedings of the Third International Symposium on Sign Language Research,* ed. William Stokoe and Virginia Volterra, 19–22 (Silver Spring, Md.: Linstok Press, 1985).

Chapter 5

1. Sebeok, *Signs,* 1994, 22, 24, 28, 31, 33.

2. Ibid., 33f.

3. Rolf Kuschel, "The Silent Inventor," *Sign Language Studies* 3 (1973): 1–27.

4. Ibid., 15, 16.

5. Baker-Shenk, "A Microanalysis of the Nonmanual Components of Questions."

6. See Darwin, *Expression of Emotion,* and Paul Ekman and Wallace Friesen, *The Facial Action Coding System* (Palo Alto: Consulting Psychologists Press, 1978).

7. Sebeok, *Signs,* 19.

Chapter 6

1. Chomsky, *Syntactic Structures.*

2. Marcel Kinsbourne, "Unity and Diversity in the Human Brain: Evidence from Injury," *Daedalus* 127, no. 2 (Spring 1998): 233–56.

3. See Beaken, *Making of Language.*

4. Jonathan Kingdon, *Self-Made Man: Human Evolution from Eden to Extinction?* (New York: Wiley, 1993), 156–219.

5. William Stokoe, "Semantic Phonology," *Sign Language Studies* 71 (1991): 107–14; David Armstrong, William Stokoe, and Sherman Wilcox, *Gesture and the Nature of Language* (New York and London: Cambridge University Press, 1995).

6. Gerald Edelman, *The Remembered Present: A Biological Theory of Consciousness* (New York: Basic Books, 1989), chapter 9.

7. Wilson, *The Hand.*

8. Roger Fouts, with Stephen Tukel Mills, *Next of Kin: What Chimpanzees Have Taught Me about Who We Are* (New York: William Morrow, 1997).

9. Ibid., 186.

10. Ibid., 188.

11. Ibid., 188, 189.

12. Ibid., 187. See also R. Allen Gardner, Beatrix T. Gardner, and Thomas E. Van Cantfort, eds., *Teaching Sign Language to Chimpanzees* (Albany: State University of New York Press, 1989).

13. See Philip Lieberman, *Uniquely Human: The Evolution of Speech, Thought, and Selfless Behavior* (Cambridge, Mass.: Harvard University Press, 1991), for a full explanation. See also David Armstrong, *Original Signs* (Washington, D.C.: Gallaudet University Press, 1999), for an integration of these findings with the possible progression of gesture to language to speech.

14. For a discussion of grey parrots' speech see Irene Pepperberg, "Acquisition of the Same/Different Concept by an African Grey Parrot *Psittacus erithacus,*" *Animal Learning and Behavior* 15 (1987): 423–32.

15. Herbert Clark, "Space, Time, Semantics, and the Child," in *Cognitive Development and the Acquisition of Language,* ed. T. Moore, (San Diego: Academic Press, 1973), 28.

16. Ibid., 28, 33.
17. Ibid., 30.
18. Here the application of the term *nonverbal* becomes questionable. Once messages are being exchanged and understood, those exchanging them may not be using spoken words; but if there is any structure at all in the expression of the messages, whether the expression is in vocal sounds, manual gestures, or simply understanding looks, the parties to the exchange have experienced something much more like the use of language than the negative term *nonverbal* implies. The common usage of *verbal* and *nonverbal* is doubtless too deeply ingrained to be changed by an appeal to logic and evidence, but those who continue to use the terms with their popular meanings would do well to consider the damage this practice has done and is doing to deaf children.
19. Clark, "Space, Time, Semantics, and the Child," 35.
20. Ibid., 54f.
21. Ibid., 60.
22. See also Volterra and Iverson, "Modality Factors."
23. See Beaken, *Making of Language,* and Kingdon, *Self-Made Man.*

Chapter 7

1. Beaken, *Making of Language.*
2. Kingdon, *Self-Made Man.*
3. J. J. Gibson, *The Senses Considered as Perceptual Systems* (Boston: Houghton Mifflin, 1966).
4. Wilson, *The Hand.*
5. Barbara King, *The Information Continuum: Evolution of Social Information Transfer in Monkeys, Apes, and Hominids* (Santa Fe: SAR Press, 1994).
6. Clark, "Where Brain, Body, and World Collide," 267.
7. Kinsbourne, "Unity and Diversity in the Human Brain," 243, 246.
8. Keith Allan, "Classifiers," *Language* 53, no. 2 (1977): 285–311; Rebecca Kantor, "The Acquisition of Classifiers in American Sign Language," *Sign Language Studies* 28 (1980): 193–208.
9. See Gilbert Eastman, with Martin Noretsky and Sharon Censoplano, *From Mime to Sign* (Silver Spring, Md.: T. J. Publishers, 1989).
10. See *Daedalus* 127, no. 2 (Spring 1998).
11. Stokoe, *Sign Language Structure.*
12. Leslie White, "The Locus of Mathematical Reality: An Anthropological Footnote," in *The World of Mathematics,* ed. James R. Newman (New York: Simon and Schuster, 1956), 2348–49.

13. Pinker, *Language Instinct.*
14. Darwin, *Expression of Emotion;* King, *Information Continuum.*
15. Edward Klima, et al., *The Signs of Language* (Cambridge, Mass.: Harvard University Press, 1979); Baker-Shenk, "A Microanalysis of the Non-manual Components of Questions."
16. Doreen Kimura, *Neuromotor Mechanisms in Human Communication* (New York: Oxford University Press, 1993).

Chapter 8

1. For an eloquent statement of this, see Gregory Bateson, *Mind and Nature: A Necessary Unity* (San Francisco: Chandler, 1972).
2. See, for example, Farnell, *Do You See What I Mean?* 251–61.
3. Deborah Tannen, *Gender and Discourse* (New York: Oxford University Press, 1994).
4. King, *Information Continuum.*
5. See Armstrong, Stokoe, Wilcox, *Gesture and the Nature of Language.*
6. Farnell, *Do You See What I Mean?* 251–78.
7. Ibid.
8. Cairns-Smith, *Evolving the Mind,* 1.
9. Mitchell Cotter, *The Role Communication Plays in Human Development* (Raleigh, N.C.: Institute for Communication Research, 1995).
10. McNeill, *Hand and Mind.*
11. Farnell, *Do You See What I Mean?* 34f.
12. Ibid., 59.
13. Supalla and Newport, "How Many Seats in a Chair?"
14. For example, Bloomfield and Sapir appear to have gotten information about sign languages from those educators of the deaf committed to oral methodology and dedicated, like Alexander Graham Bell, to preventing the growth of a "deaf community" by stamping out sign languages; see Richard Winefield, *Never the Twain Shall Meet: Bell, Gallaudet, and the Communications Debate* (Washington, D.C.: Gallaudet University Press, 1987).

Chapter 9

1. Wilson, *The Hand,* chapter 1.
2. Michael Corballis, *The Lopsided Ape: Evolution of the Generative Mind* (New York: Oxford University Press, 1991); William Calvin, *How Brains Think: Evolving Intelligence, Then and Now* (New York: Basic Books, 1996).

3. King, *Information Continuum.*

4. Kimura, *Neuromotor Mechanisms.*

5. Catherine P. Browman and Louis Goldstein, "Gestural Specification Using Dynamically-Defined Articulatory Structures," *Journal of Phonetics* 18 (1990): 299–320.

6. Birgitta Söderfeldt, Jerker Rönnberg, and Jarl Risberg, "Regional Cerebral Blood Flow during Sign Language Perception," *Sign Language Studies* 84 (1994): 199–208.

7. Sebeok, *Signs,* 114.

8. Bateson, *Mind and Nature,* 180–93.

9. New York State's Erie Canal system carried 125,000 pleasure boats in 1995; Rochester *Democrat & Chronicle.*

10. J. J. Gibson, *The Senses Considered.*

11. Carl Sandburg, lecture at Cornell University, ca. 1940.

12. Volterra and Iverson, "Modality Factors."

13. Dwight Bolinger, *Intonation and Its Parts: Melody in Spoken English* (Stanford: Stanford University Press, 1986).

14. Stokoe, *Sign Language Structure;* Stokoe, Casterline, and Croneberg, *Dictionary of American Sign Language.*

15. Darwin, *Expression of Emotion.*

16. A striking example of this is the chimpanzee Jane Goodall observed and filmed; smaller than other males, his "schtick" of kicking and throwing an empty oilcan in front of him earned him the role of alpha male.

17. Sign languages can work without light—consider the great usefulness of sign language (and fingerspelling) to those both deaf and blind. Deaf families similarly use the tactile sense for "listening" to siblings, parents, children, or spouses in the dark. And blind persons who learned a sign language before their sight was totally lost can still sign and understand sign language by light hand contact on the signer's hand.

Chapter 10

1. James Woodward, "Lexical Evidence for the Existence of South Asian and East Asian Sign Language Families," *Journal of Asian Pacific Communication* 4, no. 2 (1996): 91–106.

2. Kingdon, *Self-Made Man,* 36.

3. These include monastic signing and fingerspelling to substitute for speech in times of enforced silence, signals used by baseball coaches and football umpires, bookmakers' semaphore at the track, and the gestures used by stock market traders.

4. Charles Hockett, "In Search of Jove's Brow," *American Speech* 53 (1978): 299.

5. Ibid., 300.

6. The disagreement may simply be in etymology: *language* derives from Latin *lingua,* meaning "tongue," and sign languages make only infrequent use of the tongue (as one of the nonmanual modifiers of signs or propositions manually expressed). As a good classicist, Hockett may have refrained from violating the literal meaning of *lingua.*

7. Morris Swadesh, *The Origin and Diversification of Language,* ed. Joel Sherzer (Chicago: Aldine, 1971), xii.

8. Quoted by Hymes in Swadesh, *Origin and Diversification,* vii.

9. James Woodward, "Historical Bases of American Sign Language," in *Understanding Language through Sign Language Research,* ed. Patricia Siple (New York: Academic Press, 1978).

10. Wescott, Hewes, and Stokoe, *Language Origins,* 5.

11. John Vickrey Van Cleve and Barry A. Crouch, *A Place of Their Own: Creating the Deaf Community in America* (Washington, D.C.: Gallaudet University Press: 1989), 34, 37–45.

12. Edward T. Hall Jr., "Deaf Culture, Tacit Culture, and Ethnic Relations," in *The Deaf Way: Perspectives from the International Conference on Deaf Culture,* ed. Carol J. Erting, Robert C. Johnson, Dorothy L. Smith, and Bruce D. Snider (Washington, D.C.: Gallaudet University Press, 1995), 31-39.

13. Robbin Battison, *Lexical Borrowing in American Sign Language* (Silver Spring, Md.: Linstok Press, 1978).

14. Sherman Wilcox, *The Phonetics of Fingerspelling* (Philadelphia: Benjamins, 1992); Armstrong, Stokoe, Wilcox, *Gesture and the Nature of Language.*

15. Kimura, *Neuromotor Mechanisms.*

16. Woodward, "Lexical Evidence."

17. Klima et al., *Signs of Language,* chapter 7.

18. Kingdon, *Self-Made Man,* 216.

Chapter 11

1. Kendon, *Sign Languages of Aboriginal Australia,* 4.

2. It is well worth noting that when such a system, called Signed Swedish, was put to use in Swedish schools for the deaf, the pupils were found to have gained no competence in Swedish or in Swedish Sign Language (SSL), and so the educational authorities promptly ruled that SSL, as

the first language of deaf people, would be the language of instruction, with literacy in Swedish to follow (Britta Bergman, "Verbs and Adjectives: Morphological Processes in Swedish Sign Language," in *Language in Sign: An International Perspective on Sign Language,* ed. James G. Kyle and Bencie Woll [London: Croom Helm, 1983]).

3. Although they vary in methods, each of these systems is designed to assist deaf students in learning English by use of a coded form of signing that corresponds to some characteristics of English. See Ronnie Wilbur, *American Sign Language and Sign Systems* (Baltimore: University Park Press, 1979).

4. Farnell, *Do You See What I Mean?* 143f.

5. Ibid., 144.

6. Mallery did, however, write of signing as "one language—the gesture speech of mankind—of which each system is a dialect" ("Sign Language among North American Indians, Compared with That among Other Peoples and Deaf-Mutes," in *First Annual Report of the Bureau of Ethnology to the Secretary of the Smithsonian Institution, 1879–1880,* [Washington, D.C.: Smithsonian Institution, Bureau of American Ethnology, 1881], 323). Because so many signed languages from around the world have been studied, I will continue the present practice here of talking about the systems as signed languages, not as dialects.

7. One of these used the first two fingers of the pronated hand drawn across in front of the signer—an icon of the travois; another put these fingers astride the radial edge of the other hand, equally horse or horse and rider; a third drew the edgewise hand with thumb up across in front of the eyes, which surely suggested the side view of the horses in a wild herd rushing by.

8. Robbin Battison and I. King Jordan, "Cross-Cultural Communication with Foreign Signers," *Sign Language Studies* 10 (1976): 69–80.

Chapter 12

1. DeLancey, "Lexical Prefixes."

2. Allan, "Classifiers."

3. Robbin Battison, Harry Markowicz, and James Woodward, "A Good Rule of Thumb: Variable Phonology in ASL," in *Analyzing Variation in Language,* ed. Ralph W. Fasold and Roger Shuy (Washington, D.C.:

Georgetown University Press, 1975); Klima et al., *Signs of Language,* chapter 2.

4. Supalla and Newport, "How Many Seats in a Chair?"
5. Allan, "Classifiers," 285.
6. Ibid., 287.
7. DeLancey, in his discussion of Klamath verbs, calls the stem "the lexical prefix" (DeLancey, "Lexical Prefixes").
8. This I called "semantic phonology" ("Semantic Phonology," *Sign Language Studies* 71 [1991]: 107–14) to suggest that unlike the structure of morphemes, which convention must link with meaning and which are arbitrary assemblies of arbitrary sounds, the parts of a sign language sign may contain more or less transparent hints to its meaning. The sign's "phonology" or sublexical structure, is thus semantic. Presently, however, I prefer to leave the term *phonology* to the linguistics of spoken languages and to describe sign language phenomena instead of trying to force sign languages into definitions that have been derived from spoken language phenomena.
9. Allan, "Classifiers," 297.
10. Ibid.
11. Brent Berlin and Paul Kay, *Basic Color Terms: Their Universality and Evolution* (Berkeley: University of California Press, 1969).
12. Terrence Deacon, *The Symbolic Species: The Co-Evolution of Language and the Brain* (New York: Norton, 1997), 116–20.
13. See Kuschel, "Silent Inventor."
14. Allan, "Classifiers," 301.
15. Ibid., 307.
16. Only a human hand is able to hold a club with the three ulnar fingers pressing it against the palm of the hand and the thumb and forefinger providing control. This extension of the natural reach from shoulder outward must have been immensely effective in allowing creatures with human characteristics to survive among creatures with far greater size and strength—but less developed hands and brains. See Wilson, *The Hand.*
17. Allan, "Classifiers," 298.

Chapter 13

1. Lane, *When the Mind Hears,* 100.

2. See Peggy Spear, "Look Who's Signing: UC Davis Leads Way as Toddlers Learn to Communicate with Gestures," *San Francisco Chronicle,* April 30, 1999.

3. Jeff Grabmeier, "Infants Use Sign Language to Communicate at Ohio State School," *Ohio State University Research News,* Jan. 25, 1999. Available at *http://www.osu.edu/units/research/archive/signlang.htm.*

4. Clark, "Where Brain, Body, and World Collide," 262.

5. See Betty Hart and Todd Risley, *Meaningful Differences in the Everyday Experience of Young American Children* (Baltimore: Brookes, 1995).

6. Ibid.

Bibliography

Aitchison, Jean. 1996. *The Seeds of Speech: Language Origin and Evolution.* New York and Cambridge: Cambridge University Press.

Allan, Keith. 1977. Classifiers. *Language* 53, no. 2:285–311.

Armstrong, David. 1999. *Original Signs.* Washington, D.C.: Gallaudet University Press.

Armstrong, David, William Stokoe, and Sherman Wilcox. 1995. *Gesture and the Nature of Language.* New York and London: Cambridge University Press.

Baker-Shenk, Charlotte. 1983. A Microanalysis of the Nonmanual Components of Questions in American Sign Language. Ph.D. diss., University of California, Berkeley.

Bateson, Gregory. 1972. *Steps to an Ecology of Mind: Collected Essays in Anthropology, Psychiatry, Evolution, and Epistemology.* San Francisco: Chandler.

———. 1979. *Mind and Nature: A Necessary Unity.* New York: Dutton.

Battison, Robbin. 1978. *Lexical Borrowing in American Sign Language.* Silver Spring, Md.: Linstok Press.

Battison, Robbin, and I. King Jordan. 1976. Cross-cultural Communication with Foreign Signers. *Sign Language Studies* 10:53–68.

Battison, Robbin, Harry Markowicz, and James Woodward. 1975. A Good Rule of Thumb: Variable Phonology in ASL. In *Analyzing Variation in Language,* ed. Ralph W. Fasold and Roger Shuy. Washington, D.C.: Georgetown University Press.

Baynton, Douglas. 1996. *Forbidden Signs: American Culture and the Campaign Against Sign Language.* Chicago: University of Chicago Press.

Beaken, Mike. 1996. *The Making of Language.* Edinburgh: Edinburgh University Press.

Bergman, Britta. 1983. Verbs and Adjectives: Morphological Processes in Swedish Sign Language. In *Language in Sign: An International Perspective on Sign Language,* ed. James G. Kyle and Bencie Woll, 3–9. London: Croom Helm.

Berlin, Brent, and Paul Kay. 1969. *Basic Color Terms: Their Universality and Evolution.* Berkeley: University of California Press.

Bickerton, Derek. 1995. *Language and Human Behavior.* Seattle: University of Washington Press.

Bolinger, Dwight. 1986. *Intonation and Its Parts: Melody in Spoken English.* Stanford: Stanford University Press.

Bonvillian, John D., et al. 1985. Language, Cognitive, and Cherological Development. In *SLR '83: Proceedings of the Third International Symposium on Sign Language Research,* ed. William Stokoe and Virginia Volterra, 19–22. Silver Spring, Md.: Linstok Press.

Braine, Martin D. S. 1963. Grammatical Structure in the Speech of Two-year-olds. *Proceedings of the Washington Linguistics Club* 1, no. 1:11–16.

Browman, Catherine P., and Louis Goldstein. 1990. Gestural Specification Using Dynamically-Defined Articulatory Structures. *Journal of Phonetics* 18:299–320.

Bullowa, Margaret. 1977. From Performative Act to Performative Utterance: An Ethological Perspective. *Sign Language Studies* 16:193–218.

Cairns-Smith, Graham. 1996. *Evolving the Mind: On the Nature of Matter and the Origin of Consciousness.* Cambridge: Cambridge University Press.

Calvin, William. 1996. *How Brains Think: Evolving Intelligence, Then and Now.* New York: Basic Books.

Calvin, William, and George Ojemann. 1995. *Conversations with Neil's Brain: The Neural Nature of Thought and Language.* Reading, Mass.: Addison-Wesley.

Chaves, Teresa, and Jorge Soler. 1974. Pedro Ponce de León, First Teacher of the Deaf. *Sign Language Studies* 5:48–63.

———. 1975. Manuel Ramirez de Carrión, (1579–1652?) and His Secret Method of Teaching the Deaf. *Sign Language Studies* 8:235–48.

Cheney, Dorothy L., and Robert M. Seyfarth. 1990. *How Monkeys See the World: Inside the Mind of Another Species.* Chicago: University of Chicago Press.

Chomsky, Noam. 1957. *Syntactic Structures.* The Hague: Mouton.

Clark, Andy. 1998. Where Brain, Body, and World Collide. *Daedalus* 127, no. 2:257–81.

Clark, Herbert. 1973. Space, Time, Semantics, and the Child. In *Cognitive Development and the Acquisition of Language,* ed. T. Moore, 27–63. San Diego: Academic Press.

Corballis, Michael. 1991. *The Lopsided Ape: Evolution of the Generative Mind.* New York: Oxford University Press.

Cotter, Mitchell. 1995. *The Role Communication Plays in Human Development.* Raleigh, N.C.: Institute for Communication Research.

Darwin, Charles. [1872] 1983. *The Expression of Emotion in Man and Animals.* Reprint, New York: Appleton.

Deacon, Terrence. 1997. *The Symbolic Species: The Co-Evolution of Language and the Brain.* New York: Norton.

DeLancey, Scott. 1999. Lexical Prefixes and the Bipartite Stem Construction in Klamath. *International Journal of American Linguistics* 65, no. 1:56–83.

Dennett, Daniel C. 1995. *Darwin's Dangerous Idea: Evolution and the Meanings of Life.* New York: Simon and Schuster.

Donald, Merlin. 1991. *Origins of the Modern Mind: Three Stages in the Evolution of Culture and Cognition.* Cambridge, Mass.: Harvard University Press.

Eastman, Gilbert, with Martin Noretsky and Sharon Censoplano. 1989. *From Mime to Sign.* Silver Spring, Md.: T. J. Publishers.

Eco, Umberto. 1979. *A Theory of Semiotics.* Bloomington: Indiana University Press.

Edelman, Gerald. 1987. *Neural Darwinism: The Theory of Neuronal Group Selection.* New York: Basic Books.

———. 1989. *The Remembered Present: A Biological Theory of Consciousness.* New York: Basic Books.

———. 1992. *Bright Air, Brilliant Fire: On the Matter of the Mind.* New York: Basic Books.

Ekman, Paul, and Wallace Friesen. 1975. *Unmasking the Face: A Guide to Recognizing Emotions from Facial Clues.* Englewood Cliffs, N.J.: Prentice-Hall.

———. 1978. *The Facial Action Coding System.* Palo Alto: Consulting Psychologists Press.

Farnell, Brenda. 1995. *Do You See What I Mean? Plains Indian Sign Talk and the Embodiment of Action.* Austin: University of Texas Press.

Fouts, Roger, with Stephen Tukel Mills. 1997. *Next of Kin: What Chimpanzees Have Taught Me about Who We Are.* New York: William Morrow.

Furth, Hans. 1966. *Thinking without Language: Psychological Implications of Deafness.* New York: Free Press.

Gardner, R. Allen, Beatrix. T. Gardner, and Thomas E. Van Cantfort, eds. 1989. *Teaching Sign Language to Chimpanzees.* Albany: State University of New York Press.

Garnett, Christopher. 1968. *The Exchange of Letters between Samuel Heinicke and Abbé Charles Michel de L'Epée: A Monograph on the Oralist and Manualist Methods of Instructing the Deaf in the Eighteenth Century.* New York: Vantage Press.

Gibson, James J. 1966. *The Senses Considered as Perceptual Systems.* Boston: Houghton Mifflin.

Givens, David. 1986. The Big and the Small: Toward a Paleontology of Gesture. *Sign Language Studies* 51:145–70.

Goldin-Meadow, Susan, and Heidi Feldman. 1975. The Creation of a Communication System. *Sign Language Studies* 8:225–34.

Goldin-Meadow, Susan, and Carolyn Mylander. 1998. Spontaneous Sign Systems Created by Deaf Children in Two Cultures. *Nature* 391:279–81.

Gould, Stephen J. 1982. Darwinism and the Expansion of Evolutionary Theory. *Science* 216, no. 3:380–87.

Grabmeier, Jeff. 1999. Infants Use Sign Language to Communicate at Ohio State School. *Ohio State University Research News,* Jan. 25. Available at *http://www.osu.edu/units/research/archive/signlang.htm.*

Groce, Nora. 1985. *Everyone Here Spoke Sign Language: Hereditary Deafness on Martha's Vineyard.* Cambridge, Mass.: Harvard University Press.

Hall, Edward T., Jr. 1994. Deaf Culture, Tacit Culture, and Ethnic Relations. In *The Deaf Way: Perspectives from the International Conference on Deaf Culture,* ed. Carol J. Erting, Robert C. Johnson, Dorothy L. Smith, and Bruce D. Snider, 31–39. Washington, D.C.: Gallaudet University Press.

Harnad, Stevan R., Horst D. Steklis, and Jane Lancaster, eds. 1976. *Origins and Evolution of Language and Speech.* New York: New York Academy of Sciences.

Hart, Betty, and Todd Risley. 1995. *Meaningful Differences in the Everyday Experience of Young American Children.* Baltimore: Brookes.

Hewes, Gordon. 1973. Gesture Languages in Cultural Contact. *Sign Language Studies* 4:1–34.

Hockett, Charles. 1978. In Search of Jove's Brow. *American Speech* 53:243–313.

Jordan, I. King, and Robbin Battison. 1987. A Referential Communication Experiment with Foreign Sign Languages. *Sign Language Studies* 56:275–87.

Kantor, Rebecca. 1980. The Acquisition of Classifiers in American Sign Language. *Sign Language Studies* 28:193–208.

Kendon, Adam. 1988. *Sign Languages of Aboriginal Australia: Cultural, Semiotic, and Communicative Perspectives.* Cambridge: Cambridge University Press.

Kimura, Doreen. 1993. *Neuromotor Mechanisms in Human Communication.* New York: Oxford University Press.

King, Barbara. 1994. *The Information Continuum: Evolution of Social Information Transfer in Monkeys, Apes, and Hominids.* Santa Fe: SAR Press.

Kingdon, Jonathan. 1993. *Self-Made Man: Human Evolution from Eden to Extinction?* New York: Wiley.

Kinsbourne, Marcel. 1998. Unity and Diversity in the Human Brain: Evidence from Injury. *Daedalus* 127, no. 2:233–56.

Klima, Edward, et al. 1979. *The Signs of Language.* Cambridge, Mass.: Harvard University Press.

Kuschel, Rolf. 1973. The Silent Inventor. *Sign Language Studies* 3:1–27.

Lane, Harlan. 1976. *The Wild Boy of Aveyron.* Cambridge, Mass.: Harvard Unversity Press.

———. 1984. *When the Mind Hears.* New York: Random House.

Lieberman, Philip. 1991. *Uniquely Human: The Evolution of Speech, Thought, and Selfless Behavior.* Cambridge, Mass.: Harvard University Press.

Mallery, Garrick. 1881. Sign Language among North American Indians, Compared with That among Other Peoples and Deaf-Mutes. In *First Annual Report of the Bureau of Ethnology to the Secretary of the Smithsonian Institution, 1879–1880,* 263–552. Washington, D.C.: Smithsonian Institution, Bureau of American Ethnology.

McNeill, David. 1992. *Hand and Mind: What Gestures Reveal about Thought.* Chicago: University of Chicago Press.

Mirzoeff, Nicholas. 1995. *Silent Poetry: Deafness, Sign, and Visual Culture in Modern France.* Princeton: Princeton University Press.

Montgomery, George, and Arthur Dimmock. 1998. *Venerable Legacy: Saint Bede and the Anglo-Celtic Contribution to Literary, Numerical, and Manual Language.* Edinburgh: Scottish Workshop Publications.

Moore, Timothy, ed. 1973. *Cognitive Development and the Acquisition of Language.* New York: Academic Press.

Pepperberg, Irene. 1987. Acquisition of the Same/Different Concept by an African Grey Parrot *Psittacus erithacus. Animal Learning and Behavior* 15:423–32.

Pinker, Steven. 1994. *The Language Instinct: How the Mind Creates Language.* New York: William Morrow.

Plann, Susan. 1997. *A Silent Minority: Deaf Education in Spain, 1550–1835.* Berkeley: University of California Press.

Plotkin, Henry. 1994. *Darwin Machines and the Nature of Knowlege.* Cambridge, Mass.: Harvard University Press.

Quine, Willard van Orman. 1972. Methodological Reflections on Current Linguistic Theory. In *Semantics of Natural Language,* ed. Donald Davidson and Gilbert Harman, 442–54. Dordrecht: Reidel.

Rée, Jonathan. 1999. *I See a Voice.* New York: Metropolitan Books.

Rose, Steven. 1993. *The Making of Memory: From Molecules to Mind.* New York: Anchor Books.

Sapir, Edward. 1921. *Language.* New York: Harcourt, Brace, and World.

Sebeok, Thomas A. 1994. *Signs: An Introduction to Semiotics.* Toronto: University of Toronto Press.

Söderfeldt, Birgitta, Jerker Rönnberg, and Jarl Risberg. 1994. Regional Cerebral Blood Flow during Sign Language Perception. *Sign Language Studies* 84:199–208.

Stokoe, William. 1980. Sign Language Structure. *Annual Review of Anthropology* 9:365–90.

———. 1991. Semantic Phonology. *Sign Language Studies* 71:107–14

———. 1993. *Sign Language Structure: An Outline of the Visual Communication Systems of the American Deaf.* Studies in Linguistics, Occasional Papers 8. Buffalo: University of Buffalo Department of Anthropology and Linguistics, 1960. Reprint, Burtonsville, Md.: Linstok Press.

Stokoe, William, Dorothy Casterline, and Carl Croneberg. 1976. *A Dictionary of American Sign Language on Linguistic Principles.* Washington, D.C.: Gallaudet College Press, 1965. Reprint, Burtonsville, Md.: Linstok Press.

Supalla, Ted, and Elissa Newport. 1978. How Many Seats in a Chair? The Derivation of Nouns and Verbs in American Sign Language. In *Understanding Language through Sign Language Research,* ed. Patricia Siple, 91–159. New York: Academic Press.

Swadesh, Morris. 1971. *The Origin and Diversification of Language.* Edited by Joel Sherzer. Chicago: Aldine.

Tannen, Deborah. 1994. *Gender and Discourse.* New York: Oxford University Press.

Trager, George L., and Henry Lee Smith. 1957. *An Outline of English Structure.* Studies in Linguistics, Occasional Papers 3. Norman, Okla.: Battenburg Press, 1951. Reprint, Washington, D.C.: American Council of Learned Societies.

Van Cleve, John Vickrey, and Barry A. Crouch. 1989. *A Place of Their Own: Creating the Deaf Community in America.* Washington, D.C.: Gallaudet University Press.

Volterra, Virginia, and Jana Iverson. 1995. When Do Modality Factors Affect the Course of Language Acquisition? In *Language, Gesture and Space,* ed. Karen Emmorey and Judy S. Reilly, 371–90. Hillsdale, N.J.: Erlbaum.

Wescott, Roger W., Gordon Hewes, and William Stokoe, eds. 1974. *Language Origins.* Silver Spring, Md.: Linstok Press.

White, Leslie. 1956. The Locus of Mathematical Reality: An Anthropological Footnote. In *The World of Mathematics,* ed. James R. Newman, 2348–64. New York: Simon and Schuster.

Whorf, Benjamin. 1941. Languages and Logic. *Technological Review* 43:250–72.

Wilbur, Ronnie. 1979. *American Sign Language and Sign Systems.* Baltimore: University Park Press.

———. 1987. *American Sign Language: Linguistics and Applied Dimensions.* 2d. ed. Boston: Little, Brown.

Wilcox, Sherman. 1992. *The Phonetics of Fingerspelling.* Philadelphia: Benjamins.

Williams, Judy. 1976. Bilingual Experiences of a Deaf Child. *Sign Language Studies* 10:37–41.

Wilson, Frank R. 1998. *The Hand: How Its Use Shapes the Brain, Language, and Human Culture.* New York: Pantheon.

Winefield, Richard. 1987. *Never the Twain Shall Meet: Bell, Gallaudet, and the Communications Debate.* Washington, D.C.: Gallaudet University Press.

Woodward, James. 1978. Historical Bases of American Sign Language. In *Understanding Language through Sign Language Research,* ed. Patricia Siple, 333–48. New York: Academic Press.

———. 1993. Lexical Evidence for the Existence of South Asian and East Asian Sign Language Families. *Journal of Asian Pacific Communication* 4, no. 2:91–106.

———. 1996. Modern Standard Thai Sign Language, Influence from American Sign Language, and Its Relationship to Original Thai Sign Varieties. *Sign Language Studies* 92:227–52.

Zeki, Semir. 1993. *A Vision of the Brain.* Boston: Blackwell Scientific Publications.

Index

Allan, Keith, 180, 181, 182, 188, 189

alternate sign languages, 14, 29, 164–68, 175, 178. *See also* Assiniboine people

American School for the Deaf, 155

American Sign Language, 12–13, 51, 61, 128; classifiers in, 180–84; dictionary of, 6, 59–60; facial expression in, 72, 73–74; head movements in, 72–73; as influence on other sign languages, 154; lexical borrowing in, 157–58, 159–61; morphemes in, 180–81; noun–verb distinctions in, 65–66; translation of, 111; verb structure in, 182–84

Amman, Johann Conrad, 53, 194–95, 199

Armstrong, David, 25

Assiniboine people, 14, 30, 62, 127, 129, 168–70

Australia, sign language in, 14–15, 164, 166–68

autism, and language acquisition, 88–92, 199–200

Baden–Powell, Robert, 170

Bateson, Gregory, 136–37, 139

Battison, Robbin, 158, 160, 172–73, 174

Beaken, Mike, 100–1, 104

Bede, Saint, 55–56

Boas, Franz, 28–29, 58, 64

body language, 61–62

Brace, C. Loring, 25

Braille, Louis, 38

Cairns–Smith, Graham, 62

Calvin, William, 50

Carroll, Lewis, 18

Cartesian philosophy. *See* Descartes, René

Casterline, Dorothy Sueoka, 6, 59

Center for Applied Linguistics, 8

chimpanzees, gestural communication among, 13, 81, 85

Chomsky, Noam, 28, 33–34, 58, 76, 79–80, 84, 111

Clark, Andy, 111–12, 197

Clark, Herbert H., 96–100

classifiers, 109, 180–85; categories of, 184–85; indicating color, 185–88; defined, 180; for nouns, 188–91; for verb structure, 182–84

Clerc, Laurent, 154, 155, 159, 194–95

cognition and language, 78–81, 200–1

color, 185–88

Croneberg, Carl, 6, 59

Darwin, Charles, 22, 54–55, 62, 113, 114

day care, 199
Deaf culture, 157
deaf people: differing views of, 4, 53, 56–57; education of, 2–4, 52–53, 56–57, 155–57, 194–201
DeLancey, Scott, 15
Descartes, René, 18, 24, 62, 78, 87–88, 127, 129
Detmold, George, 6
A Dictionary of American Sign Lanuage on Linguistic Principles (Stokoe, Casterline, and Croneberg), 59–60

education, deaf, 2–4, 52–53, 56–57, 155–57; and gestural theory of language, 194–201
Epée, Abbé Charles Michel de l', 52, 56, 57, 155, 165, 195

Farnell, Brenda, 14, 30, 62, 122, 127, 128, 168–70, 172
Feldman, Heidi, 33
fingerspelling, 158–59
form-meaning pairs, 18, 19
Fouts, Roger, 88–92, 200
French Sign Lanaguage, 154
Furth, Hans, 52

Gallaudet, Edward Miner, 170
Gallaudet, Thomas Hopkins, 53, 155
Gallaudet University, 3–4, 53
gender and language, 120–22
gesture: in infants, 31–32, 35–36; as language signs, 84–85; meaning attached to, 84, 96, 110–14, 131–32, 176–80, 199;

as origin of language, 20–22, 23–28, 85–88, 100–2, 193–201; as precursor of speech, 16, 116–17, 124, 125–26, 129–30, 135–36, 140–41, 168–70, 179, 198; and social organization, 81–82, 107–8; and spoken language, 40, 55, 62–63, 130, 126–27, 137–41, 174–75. *See also* signing
glottochronology, 148
Goldin–Meadow, Susan, 32–33, 34, 35
grammar, generative–transformational, 79–80, 111

Hall, Edward T., 157
Hall, Percival, 40
Hall, Robert A., 7
hand–arm movement, human, 104–5; as representation, 105–7, 108–9, 123
hands: human as distinguished from chimpanees, 86; as means of communication, 34, 36, 38, 44–45. *See also* gesture; manualism
Harnad, Stevan, 25
Heinicke, Samuel, 53, 57
Hertz, Heinrich, 78
Hewes, Gordon W., 24–25, 154–55
Hippocrates, 67
Hockett, Charles, 25, 151, 152
Holt, John, 197
Hymes, Dell, 153

iconicity, 66
icons, 10, 67, 68, 72, 74

indexes, 10, 68, 71, 72, 74
infants: gestural communication among, 31–32, 35–36; language growth in, 47, 50–51, 93, 96, 100
Iverson, Jana, 16, 91, 198

Jordan, I. King, 172–73, 174

Kangobai, 70–71, 188
Kendon, Adam, 14, 29, 126–27, 164, 166, 172, 175, 179
King, Barbara, 121, 133
Kingdon, Jonathan, 100–1, 104, 149
Kinsbourne, Marcel, 80–81, 106–7, 111–12
Klamath language, 15, 179–80
Kuschel, Rolf, 70–71, 188

Lancaster, Jane, 25
Lane, Harlan, 194
language: acquired by autistic children, 88–92; the body's role in, 37–39; and cognition, 78–81, 200–1; and culture, 59, 199; definitions of, 59, 61–62, 69–70; among early humans, 12, 43–44, 46–47, 81–85, 91, 100–101, 102, 105–6, 135, 136–37, 149, 151, 201; and gender, 120–22; history of, 147–50; and imagination, 123; in infants, 47, 50–51, 93, 96, 100; and instinct, 74–77, 149; logic applied to, 109–10, 124; metamorphosis of, 26–28; and the natural world, 128–30; origins of, 24–28, 41–42, 58, 124–25; and perceptual space, 96–100; and society, 44–45. *See also* signed languages; speech; written language
language signs, 17–18, 67–71, 74, 77; development of, 103–18, 119–20; gesture as, 84–85; meaning attached to, 18–23
Lewis, Meriwether, 170
linguistics, standard theory of, 25–26
Linguistic Society of America, 58–59
Lyons, John, 61

Mallery, Garrick, 170–71
manual alphabets, 48, 49
manualism, 57–58
Marx, Harpo, 188
mathematics, 113
Maxwell, James Clerk, 78
McNeill, David, 30, 127, 179
Mirzoeff, Nicholas, 56, 57
Modoc language, 179–80
Momberg, 188
monastic codes, 55–56
morphemes, 15, 42–43, 64, 70, 190; in signed languages, 180–81
Mylander, Carolyn, 32–33

Nakota language. *See* Assiniboine people
names, 68, 69, 74
Native American sign languages, 15, 30, 167–68, 170–72, 179–80. *See also* Assiniboine people
Newport, Elissa, 12, 51, 65, 181
noun classifiers, 188–91

noun-verb pairs, 51, 123, 128; in American Sign Language, 65–66, 128

oralism, 53; versus manualism, 57–58

Padden, Agnes, 3
Padden, Bobby, 3
Padden, Don, 3
Paget, Richard, 167
Paget-Gorman sign language, 165
Pāṇini, 11
Peirce, Charles Sanders, 8, 67, 68
Phillips, Richard, 3
philology, 58, 147–48
phonemes, 72
Pinker, Steven, 32, 74
Plains Indians. *See* Native American sign languages
Ponce de Léon, Pedro, 56
preliterate cultures, 163–64
Prieur de la Marne, 56–57
primates, nonhuman: language adaptability of, 92–93
proprioception, 38

Ramirez de Carrión, Manuel, 56

Sandburg, Carl, 141
Sapir, Edward, 153
Saussure, Ferdinand de, 18
Sebeok, Thomas A., 8, 67, 68, 69, 74, 76, 136, 137
semantic phonology, 82, 83
semiosis, 8
semiotics, 67–71, 74, 77. *See also* signs

sentences, 141–42; in signed languages, 142
Sicard, Abbé Roch-Ambroise, 52, 56, 57, 155, 167
signals, 67, 68
signed languages: classifiers in, 180–91; color in, 185–88; differences among, 150–52, 172–73; evolution of, 114–15; families of, 29–30, 147–55; misunderstandings about, 53–54; morphemes in, 180–81; and the surrounding culture, 157–61, 191–92; word order in, 189–90. *See also* alternate sign languages; American Sign Language; Native American sign languages
signes méthodiques, 56, 165
signing: and deaf education, 196–97; as distinguished from speaking, 6–8, 10–11; as language, 1–2, 4–6, 9, 40–43, 52–54, 59–61, 63–64, 75, 76–77. *See also* gesture; signs
Sign Language Structure (Stokoe), 59, 60
Sign Language Studies (*SLS*), 8, 9, 60
signs: defined, 9; function of, 8, 10; gestural, 72–73; iconicity of, 66; and instinct, 74–75; interpretation of, 10–11, 19–22, 65–66; phonology of, 83; species of, 67–69; survival value of, 81. *See also* language signs
Smith, Henry Lee, Jr., 8, 59, 111

Smithdas, Robert, 45–46
sound–response pairs, 132–33
speech: advantages of, 145–46;
and alternate sign language,
166–68; anatomical requirements of, 93–95, 149; decoding of, 133–34; evolution of,
116–17, 134–37, 144–45;
gestural codes for, 165–66; and
gesture, 40, 55, 62–63, 130,
126–27, 137–41, 174–75; as
language, 39–40, 71–72, 75–
76; as "superior" to signing,
53, 126; visual aspects of, 162–
63
Steklis, Horst, 25
Stokoe, Ruth, 8
Supalla, Ted, 12, 51, 65, 181
Suplee, Curt, 32, 35
Swadesh, Morris, 29, 148, 150, 151
symbols, 9, 10, 68, 69, 74–75; in
early languages, 20; and language,
69–70; processing of, 38–39
symptoms, 67, 72
syntax, 82; in gesture, 85–88,
142–44

Tannen, Deborah, 120
Total Communication, 156
touch, as language channel, 22
Trager, George L., 8, 59, 69, 71,
111

Usher syndrome, 46

verbs. *See* noun–verb pairs
Volterra, Virginia, 16, 91, 198

Warlpiri people, 14, 29
Washington Linguistics Club
(WLC), 8
Wescott, Roger, 25
White, Leslie, 113
Whorf, Benjamin Lee, 128, 129
Wilson, Frank R., 34
Woodward, James, 29, 154, 155,
159
word, defined, 64–65. *See also*
language
written language, 152, 162–63;
limitations of, 165

"zero language input," 32–33, 35